Principles of

Element Design

Principles of
Element
Design

Third edition

Peter Rich and Yvonne Dean

OXFORD   AUCKLAND   BOSTON   JOHANNESBURG   MELBOURNE   NEW DELHI

Butterworth-Heinemann
Linacre House, Jordan Hill, Oxford OX2 8DP
225 Wildwood Avenue, Woburn, MA 01801-2041
A division of Reed Educational and Professional Publishing Ltd

℞ A member of the Reed Elsevier plc group

First published in *Building* between 17 May 1974 and 31 December 1976.
Revised and published in book form by George Godwin, 1977
Second edition 1982
Third edition published by Butterworth-Heinemann 1999

© Peter Rich and Yvonne Dean 1999

British Library Cataloguing in Publication Data
A catalogue record for this book is available from the British Library

ISBN 07506 31139

Library of Congress Cataloguing in Publication Data
A catalogue record for this book is available from the Library of Congress

Composition by Scribe Design, Gillingham, Kent, UK
Printed and bound in Great Britain

Contents

Introduction

Although some construction textbooks recognize the need to state principles rather than merely describe solutions, they often jump from over-generalized principles to specific solutions. Because of the increasing variety of materials, components and aesthetic aims, textbook solutions tend to be short-lived. In addition, fluctuating cost ratios between materials and labour as well as deteriorating levels of site craftsmanship mean that textbook solutions can rarely be used by the designer without some degree of adaptation.

Not all the building failures of recent years can be blamed on designers, but too many, certainly, can be traced back to a point in the design stage at which an outdated textbook or well-tried solution was falsely adapted to meet a new set of circumstances. To help overcome the hazards of adaptation from textbook to drawing board or from job to job, these reference sheets are conceived as a simple checklist of principles. Thus for each building element the sheets systematically list the range of factors likely to require consideration. Most of the elements dealt with include at least one example in order to demonstrate a typical current solution to the problems discussed. An additional aim has been to inform the designer of the wealth of reference material applicable to each element. References have been separated into textbooks, Statutory Regulations, British Standards, Building Research Establishment Digests and Current Papers as well as good practice guides issued by the various trade and research organizations. No textbook or checklist can possibly keep pace with the ever increasing body of recommendations and mandatory regulations; however, it is hoped that the initial listing of sources in this format will make it easier for designers to update their references as and when they are required.

Peter Rich

Building Regulations
The documents referred to in this book relate to the Building Regulations 1991, Amd 1994, Documents A–N, apart from Document L (1995 edition).
See also Building (Scotland) Act (1959), revised 1977.

British Standards and Codes of Practice
Many standards and codes of practice have been amended since their first issue. Up-to-date amendment slips are supplied automatically when documents are purchased. Amendment slips may also be obtained separately. However, users should check which amendment is referred to in the Building Regulations.

To confirm the latest amendment for any particular BSI document, consult 'Update' published monthly by BSI.

BSI Standards
389 Chiswick High Road
London W4 4AL
Tel. 0181-996 9000
Fax 0181-996 7400
Customer Services – Tel. 0181-996 7000

Building Research Establishment publications
A full list of current BRE publications including Digests, Current Papers, Information Papers and Reports is given in the annual Construction Publications catalogue obtainable from:
Building Research Establishment: Construction Research Communications Ltd
Bucknalls Lane
Garston
Watford WD2 7JR
Tel. 01923-894040
Fax 01923-664010

Foreword

Older architects sometimes lament what they see as a decline in technical skill among their younger colleagues. What they often neglect to mention are the big developments in product design, building processes, environmental awareness, not to mention CAD, that have transformed architectural practice in the last two or three decades.

Comparing this edition of *Principles of Element Design* with its excellent predecessors (the common factor, of course, is Peter Rich) I am totally confident that the tradition of intelligent, scientifically based but practical teaching of constructional skills in British architectural schools has not been broken. This tradition in its thorough, unemphatic, open-ended, systemic way dates back to the founding of the Building Research Station (near BRE) over sixty years ago. It is a wonderful tradition. Quite evidently from the pages of this new edition, the spirit of enquiring, non-dogmatic, practical empiricism lives on.

And so does another tradition, equally precious. This is the ongoing habit in British architectural publishing of meticulously assembling references, technical data and sources of information, not just in dry lists, but with direct reference to design tasks that have to be addressed today. The amount of information, directly related to design invention, that Yvonne Dean has brought together in this new edition is astonishing, both in scope and in conciseness.

Architectural design is more than the mindless repetition of standard details. Nor is it mindless invention. It is the continuing programme, shared by all architects of development, in the context of action, of a body of experience intended to achieve the greatest benefits for clients and users with the most elegant and intelligent use of limited resources.

Principles of Element Design is a most useful source of technical information. It is also an outstanding manifestation of continuing professionalism.

Francis Duffy
Formerly President of the RIBA

Preface to the Third Edition

Since this book was originally published as *Principles of Element Design*, there have been a number of changes in how building is organized and how the very nature of building is perceived. Although the material was published as a series of information sheets in the *Architect's Journal* between 1974 and 1976, the contents reflected the period of the 1960s. There were very real difficulties facing practitioners who had to cope with a sudden expansion of new building techniques and products and this was comparable to the change in building culture that took place in the 1930s. A reassessment of buildings was carried out in this period and greater guidance given to the building industry. Publications such as *A Qualitative Study of Some Buildings in the London Area* published by the HMSO in 1963 reviewed some well-known buildings between 20 and 30 years old and recognized that the techniques and materials used were often experimental. The overriding conclusion in this review showed that original specifications had not been followed and was often a cause of failure.

Similarly the period of the 1960s and 1970s developed yet another quite different building culture of materials, assembly and knowledge of production techniques that often superseded this interwar period as well as traditional methods. However, new perceptions with regard to likely failure had highlighted areas where newly defined principles on building movement and weathertightness were now followed and these became incorporated into revised Codes of Practice and the Building Regulations. To their credit, George Godwin published, in book form, the series of articles that Peter Rich had compiled. These broke domestic architecture down into manageable elements with the overriding principles that should inform their construction. Checklists of the main factors that affected each element were published with key diagrams.

By its very nature adopting a principle-based approach implies a certain timeless application of ideology to building, and yet principles do change and certainly the priorities in the application of principles

shift. For example, the first volume of *Principles of Modern Building*, published in 1938 by the HMSO and then revised in 1959 with the publication of the second volume, stayed in print until the late 1960s. These books, written by experts at the Building Research Station, took the first step away from traditional textbooks by their clear application of building science to construction and the functional aspects of different elements. They also considered the building as a whole dealing with principles that impinged on every element including:

Strength and stability
Dimensional stability
Exclusion of water
Heat insulation
Ventilation
Sound insulation
Daylighting
Fire protection
Durability, composition and maintenance
Building economics
Principles of use of materials

Dealing with architecture in an elemental way is also not new. Viollet-le-Duc categorized elements of architecture in the first volume (1854) of his *Encyclopédie Médiéval* and these included individual structural elements such as arches, spatial elements such as types of rooms, and elemental types of architecture, ranging from houses to colombier (house for pigeons), and individual parts such as balustrades. However, the second volume was entitled *Architecture* and included *mobilier* – meaning literally movable possessions. Although the meaning today generally refers to furniture, the word then had a far wider meaning and included all movable artefacts including clothing. It is a reflection of how specialized we have become that the area of interest in building has become so narrow. True comfort does include clothing; the ability to live does necessitate storage of possessions (whether 'mobile' or fixed) and storage in buildings is an issue, but the totality of designing and building for living is now shared between different industries and as a result their integration is poor. Current research is re-evaluating comfort conditions in buildings and this cannot be done without allowing for clothing.

Principles of Element Design by Peter Rich applied different checklists to each element, listing the main factors that would impinge on any element. Although the fundamental preoccupations in building, for comfort and shelter, have not changed, sometimes the main aims for building can become lost in the plethora of discrete checklists. As specialisms develop, many elements which should be designed as a totally integrated building system become too abstracted.

This third edition categorizes the elements in such a way that their interdependence is considered.

What are the additional or rediscovered principles that impinge on how we might build today? Priorities certainly change and become major criteria in determining the performance of elements. Overriding concerns deal with a concept of efficiency that relates not just to the execution of a manufacturing process or arrangement of the building process, but to the minimization of the use of energy. In fact, the building itself must demonstrate increasingly not merely a compliance with current regulations with regard to thermal performance but an optimization of the use of energy given current knowledge.

The industry is also more client-led. There are increasing concerns with maintenance and quality and the growth of facilities management, a recognition of the need for looking after buildings in the long-term and being able to maintain them with the minimum of physical labour or disruption.

The dissatisfaction with modern architecture that experimented and failed in the application of many new materials and components has also led to a shift in responsibility. As the expectation of failure increases and insurance becomes a key component in the successful financing of buildings, a claims-conscious industry starts to set its own standards. As ownership and funding changes, the basic quality and equity of a building is increasingly led by mortgage societies who apply their own standards to their own assets. This factor alone has changed standards in building. As large commercial organizations, they can respond swiftly to changing conditions. Guidelines from mortgage and insurance companies to the use of NHBC standards now give additional demands and

sometimes a restrictive framework around the practice of building. The response to climatic change and identification of high risk areas where ground conditions are poor, is reflected in demands on home owners to pay additional insurance and improve the foundation structure of buildings where failure is likely or has occurred.

The changes in the responsibilities for health and safety have also delegated the mechanics for compliance back to professionals. This is no bad thing as self-certification should be inherent in a professional qualification instead of reliance on inspectors to regulate compliance. However, the burden of extra administration and the time involved in managing the building process does detract from the main rationale for building and consequently advances become incremental in the application of new ideas. As the information base becomes further fragmented, there are few overall guides to a holistic view of building. Even the BRE now deal with more self-contained aspects of construction and this fragmentation of knowledge is reflected in highly specific areas of research. Criticism of this approach is by no means new. In Barry Russell's introduction to *Building Systems, Industrialisation and Architecture*, published by Wiley in 1981, he quoted Stafford Beer on the analytic method of scientific enquiry.

We are not trained to think in systemic terms because our scientific approach has been analytic to the ultimate degree. We took things apart historically, and described the atomic bits. We did an experiment, historically on these bits deliberately holding invariant the behaviour of other bits with which in fact they were systematically interacting real life.

Peter Rich added that Bill Allen (of Bickerdicke Allen and Partners) also concluded that most building failures were the result of the 'unknown interactions between the known elements'.

This phenomena is by no means confined to research. It is prevalent in higher education with the division of subject areas into smaller pieces of packaged information. Although a broader approach can be found in textbooks, these have a long timescale in their production. Shelf life for books can be limited unless the book itself can be proactive in determining issues that will be relevant in the future as well as reviewing and reminding people of the basic issues that will always impinge on construction. For this reason the approach in the third edition has been to speculate on events that are likely to influence methods of building.

There are some events that can be reasonably predicted. The climatic variations experienced in the last 20 years led to a rationale to build for worst case scenarios, instead of compliance with legislation that sets minimum standards. Although there is still disagreement in the scientific community as to the reasons for climatic change and whether global warming is happening as predicted, there is evidence that change is occurring and the steady increase of CO_2 emissions is harmful and must be controlled.

As the demand for materials becomes more acute this is reflected in more limited choices. For example, the demand for softwood has resulted in the use of faster growing and inherently weaker timber that sets lower limits of performance.

As the building stock has increased, the application of building technology is inevitably concerned with the renewal of existing housing stock. Buildings also have to respond to shifts in use that are more profound and can allow for change: the easy stripping out of services and renewal of the fabric generally at the same time as minimizing waste. To build for specific use is no longer reasonable. Currently the conversion of 1960s and 1970s office buildings to housing is a major example of this change.

The prediction of trends in the long-term now takes on greater significance. The demographic changes of an ageing population flattening out to a steady state, the increase of an older and yet more fragile population brings its own constraints. Urban conglomerates are also increasing but the services for these become more cumbersome and there is a definite shift towards sustainability which will affect the storage of water, and other inbuilt facilities for sorting household waste to reduce the collection of rubbish. All of these issues relate even more to the conversion of existing housing stock where the workload will be greater rather than with or in new buildings. The sorting of building materials is also important as a valuable recycling resource, and to some extent eco-labelling deals with the life cycle of building products as well as their origin and processing.

Health issues also impinge on the construction of buildings. The removal of chimneys has resulted in poor ventilation and alternative methods of introducing fresh air to buildings. These have had to be rethought with filtration mechanisms to counteract high levels of pollution, especially in cities. The indoor surface environment is also poor and some current research implies that the removal of carpets to minimize infestation by house mites is important to relieve asthmatic conditions. This directly affects one major element of construction which may not be able to rely on simple slab systems that are not easily covered with more natural floorings. The concern with energy efficient construction will also combat condensation problems by evening out thermal differentials in the building shell.

The world economic climate can affect attitudes towards building. In the period of fast growth in the 1980s, fast turnovers in the property field were not conducive to building for long-term returns. A flatter growth curve encourages longer-term investment and a more careful review of building quality.

Today's list of principles varies somewhat from the 1959 list in *Principles of Modern Building* by stating the function of the principle more clearly and the reflection of current concerns, especially in response to energy usage and climatic change. A new list would include:

Structural stability
Weatherproofing
Construction for zero energy demand
Design for healthy air infiltration and high internal air quality
Use of external features, buildings, landscape for shading
Comfort levels to be achieved all year round
Daylighting for solar energy gain and health
Sustainable aspects of design, recyclable
Fire prevention/incombustible elements/protection-controlled fire spread/fire loading
Fire prevention and warning systems
Fully accessible buildings
Secure buildings
Materials and construction choice to minimize energy usage in production and delivery

Principles of Modern Building 1959	*Principles applied to building 1997*
Strength and stability	Structural stability
Dimensional stability	Weatherproofing
Exclusion of water	Construction for zero energy demand
Heat insulation	Design for healthy air infiltration and high internal air quality
Ventilation	
Sound insulation	Use of external features, buildings, landscape for shading
Daylighting	Comfort levels to be achieved all year round
Fire protection	Daylighting for solar energy gain and health
Durability, composition and maintenance	Sustainable aspects of design, recyclable
Building economics	Fire prevention/incombustible elements/protection-controlled fire spread/fire loading
Principles of use of materials	
	Fire prevention and warning systems
	Fully accessible buildings
	Secure buildings
	Materials and construction choice to minimize energy usage in production and delivery

Principles, by their nature, should be applied to existing as well as new buildings and, because additional principles and new priorities have been so significant, the conversion of existing housing stock has to be radical to meet the above demands. The inheritance of a fast-built Victorian housing stock also means a necessary review of the real inadequacies of those buildings.

The elements explored in this book and their related principles still apply in housing renewal. Even in new buildings the examination of these same elements is still relevant given the great changes in materials and techniques in the twentieth century, as 'at the same time many ways of building types of houses are structurally unchanged since the end of the last century' (Brian Montgomery in the Introduction to *Interbuild*, 1995, Montgomery Exhibitions Ltd).

> *This country of ours is fast becoming one great waste of badly formed, poorly designed and unhealthy houses simply because the architect has no force of mind, no feeling for his position, no self respect, no belief in his great purpose and no powers of public control.*
>
> *Raymond McGrath 1935*

One of the biggest problems in learning about and practising construction is information retrieval. It is a common problem for every profession that information used has to be current. National and European standards mean that part of the work in construction is making

sure that the specification of materials and organization of the construction process complies with various legislation. Most legislation is a means by which the best ways of gaining knowledge, gathered through experience and research, are available to everybody. For the student or practitioner the knowledge base is continually changing and has also become a commodity. The most useful access to a distillation of knowledge available is still through textbooks and compendia and also direct information on products from manufacturers. However, even after some familiarity is gained information needs to be checked to make sure it is still relevant. A simple way of doing this is to obtain the latest BRE catalogue for their publications on all aspects of building, and trade associations also have their own guidance sheets and books. The British Standards Institute publishes a catalogue every year which lists British and European Standards and Codes of Practice. A valuable commercial tool available for offices is the Barbour Microfile, now on CD-ROM, which contains the largest library of information, ranging from all Standards, Codes of Practice, BRE Digests and other relevant publications as well as product information. In this book relevant and up-to-date information and Standards (to October 1997) is given fairly extensively for each element.

In retrieving information it is rare to find parts of a building catalogued as elements apart from slabs, doors, windows or foundations. Generally, a decision would have to be made as to what an individual element would be made of, for example whether constructed in steel, timber or masonry, and then in the Code of Practice for that material you would find design advice for columns or beams or walling systems. *Co-ordinated project information* is a system that categorizes drawn and specification information sometimes referred to as part of a *common arrangement*. This system, which does list the elements and materials in building, is also used by British Standards to cross-reference back to relevant materials. It is used in the measurement of building works, called the Standard Method of Measurement which is abbreviated to SMM7. Conceptually the SMM7 system and the common arrangement is activity-based and then arranged in a sequence that mirrors the process of building. This does have differences in how the total building can be visualized by designers, where it is important that the whole is realized or understood first. The SMM7 categorization is listed at the beginning of each section and will be useful to quantity surveyors linking their knowledge of categorization to building principles for each element. SMM7 relates directly to the system of classification for the National Building Speci-fication (NBS).

The original book also ensured that all advice given was set within the framework of the Building Regulations and this edition is in the same spirit. The different documents of the Regulations also present a set of areas of interest that are generally relevant to all elements. All parts of a building, whether controlling structural stabil-ity, fire safety, ventilation, conservation of fuel and power or resistance to sound, moisture or full accessi-bility, must fulfil these basic criteria to be successful. There is still a danger that the categorization by any system into a checklist of concerns, whether in terms of elements or principles, can make the original purpose of a building elusive. A building has to provide comfortable shelter, without hazard and provide an alternative environment to the outside which is health-promoting and enables a range of activities to take place. On top of these basic needs it must be robust and low in its energy needs. Almost inevitably most of these basic concerns will be compromised by cost and location and for any designer wanting to implement a thoughtful agenda the going will be tough.

Ultimately breaking a building into identifiable elements is useful because it reveals the simple hierar-chy of parts that go to make a building and so demys-tifies the complexity of the whole. This book is useful for all professions and trades in the building industry.

Foundations: General Section 1

SMM7 D Groundwork, E In situ concrete, J Waterproofing

(See Section 2 for foundations in detail)

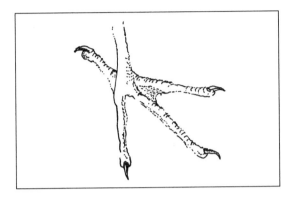

Heron's foot
A number of animals and insects have to spread the load of their body over fragile surfaces. Birds in watery habitats have large feet, snow hares and polar bears spread their body weight over large soft pads.

Japanese temple-posts on stone bases (Rich).

Notes and references

Numbered sections are cross-referenced from the diagrams and include comments followed, where appropriate, by technical references and relevant Building Regulations. Addresses of relevant trade and research organizations are listed at the end of the section. British Standards and BRE Digests should always be checked for current amendments. This section contains sub-sections 1 to 8, general factors. Greater detail is contained in **Foundations in Detail Section 2.**

General references

Mitchell's Building Series: Structure and Fabric, Part 1, Chapter 4, Jack Stroud Foster, *Structure and Fabric*, Part 2, Chapter 3, Jack Stroud Foster. Longman, 1994.
Specification 1995: Building Methods & Products, Architectural Press. Available on CD-ROM.
Foundation Design and Construction, M. J. Tomlinson. Pitman, 1995.
Lost Rivers of London, N. J. Barton. Phoenix House, 1962.
Dampness in Buildings: The Professional's and Homeowner's guide. T. A. Oxley and E. G. Gobert. Butterworth-Heinemann, 1994.

1 Foundation categories

At an early design stage of a building, consideration must be given to the interrelationship between the building form (plan, shape, loads, disposition and method of transmitting forces), the characteristics of the supporting ground under the building and its allowable bearing pressure. Subsoils should be considered as reacting dynamically to load and seasonal changes with the ability not only to compress under load but also able to heave and swell. The focus of this interrelationship is in the foundations of the building and this section covers the general design principles of the four main categories:

1 Strip and deep strip foundations for transmitting the loads of continuous walls to the ground;
2 Pad or slab foundations for transmitting the point loads from columns and piers to the ground;
3 Raft foundations for transmitting the combined loads of the whole building to the ground;
4 Piled foundations under beams for continuous walls or under piers or columns in order to transmit their loads to a greater depth than would be feasible with other forms of foundations.

Key Factors	Action	Counteraction
Gravity	Downward pull	Support
Wind	Motive force (eccentric loading)	Design accommodation, reduction
Water	Causes erosion, frost heave	Design accommodation, elimination
Sun	Ground shrinkage and decomposition	Design accommodation, protection
Chemicals	Erosion	Design accommodation, reduction, elimination
Vibration	Settlement	Design accommodation, reduction, elimination

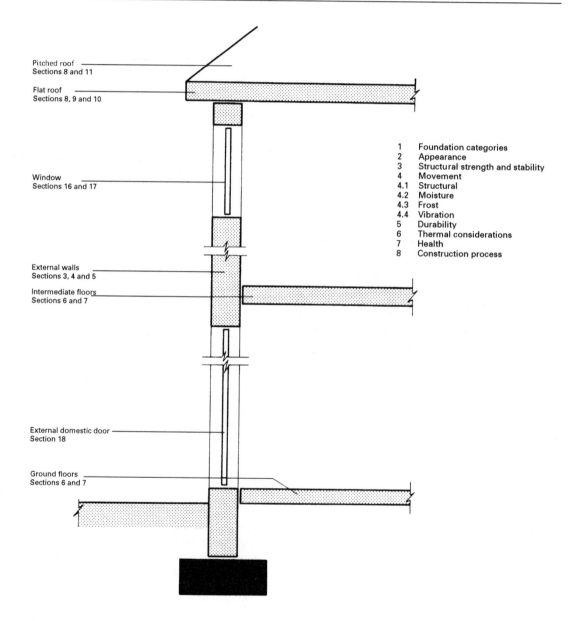

Pitched roof
Sections 8 and 11

Flat roof
Sections 8, 9 and 10

Window
Sections 16 and 17

External walls
Sections 3, 4 and 5

Intermediate floors
Sections 6 and 7

External domestic door
Section 18

Ground floors
Sections 6 and 7

1	Foundation categories
2	Appearance
3	Structural strength and stability
4	Movement
4.1	Structural
4.2	Moisture
4.3	Frost
4.4	Vibration
5	Durability
6	Thermal considerations
7	Health
8	Construction process

2 Appearance

Appearance is not normally a deciding factor in the choice of foundation type although care should be taken where they are exposed to view, e.g. certain raft edge details – see example in **Section 2**.

3 Structural strength and stability

The function of a foundation is to spread the total loads acting on a building being chiefly dead or self loads, live loads, and wind loads (see **Floors: General, Section 6**, item 3 for definitions) as well as the weight of the foundation itself to the supporting ground. This must be achieved economically, safely and not cause excessive or unequal consolidation of the soil particles which could result in settlement, cracking, or even complete building collapse. The strength or resistance of the ground to the downward force of the building load is dependent upon the type, condition and likely behaviour under load of the soil particles on which the foundation rests.

Soil engineering is beyond the scope of this section but underneath the top layer of soil, which consists of decaying vegetable matter and has little strength, are bearing soils of varying strengths according to their particle size and other factors such as moisture content and consistency. Typical bearing capacities for various soils are given in BS 8004:1986 (Foundations and substructures for non-industrial buildings of not more than four storey) and range from 600 kN/m^2 for certain gravels to less than 300 kN/m^2 for soft clays and 75 kN/m^2 for silts. See also BS 8103:1986 and BS 1377 Part 2:1990, Classification tests (for soils).

Detailed analysis of the soil is necessary as part of the first steps in the design process of the building structure since this will have a profound effect on the feasibility of a particular building form and the subsequent foundation type (see Foundation categories above). Soil investigations can be carried out with the assistance of some or all of the following methods:

1 Reference to geological, hydrogeological and topographical maps at the Institute of Geological Sciences, Exhibition Road, South Kensington, London SW7. These should be supplemented by information on climate from the Meteorological Office and, when building near coastal areas, by using Admiralty charts and publications which indicate high and low water marks or the levels of river beds. Contact the British Geological Survey, Kingsley Dunham Centre, Keyworth, Nottingham, NG12 5GG (tel. 0115-936 3241, fax 0115-936 3488) for a catalogue of all maps, specialist and technical reports on geology, hydrogeology and mineral resources. Most local libraries usually carry copies of detailed geological maps for the area and often hydrology maps too.

2 Empirical knowledge from local builders and officials, such as a local council's building inspectors.

3 Trial holes and excavations. These are potentially dangerous areas unless well strutted and protected. They should be formed in accordance with BS 8000 Part 1:1989, Code of practice for excavation and filling, and the CIRIA (Construction Information and Research) publication on *Trenching Practice* (R 97). See also the Health and Safety Executive booklet, *A Guide for Small Contractors* (HS(G)46). Depending on the layout and form of building, trial holes should not be formed further apart than 30 m and not less than one per 930 m^2 of site (*Mitchell, Structure and Fabric*, Part 1). Relative to soil type they are considered to be economical up to a depth of about 2 to 3 m and allow the exposed soil to be identified by simple visual, tactile or physical field tests.

4 Unlined hand-bored holes 100–150 mm diameter and lined hand-bored holes up to 200 mm diameter which are considered economical in softer soils up to a depth of 9 m and 24 m respectively (using a tackle and winch).

5 Mechanically-bored holes using mobile borers. These speed the investigation process and reduce costs when a large number of holes is required or where the soil is harder.

6 Geophysical methods of exploration which although rarely used for building purposes can be considered where deep investigation is needed. These consist of measuring the resistance of the soil strata by seismic, electrical or magnetic methods and involve using specialists.

The depth of soil investigation must go beyond the assumed depth of the foundation because it is the soil below the foundation which is subject to the full effect of the forces acting on the building. Generally, the required depth for soil investigation depends upon the 'bulb of pressure' exerted beneath the foundation. This is the volume of soil affected by the building load beneath the foundation and extends downwards for 1.5 to 3 times the assumed width of foundation depending on its form – (see item 1 Foundation categories above and *Mitchell, Structure and Fabric*, Part 2. Modification of this rule needs to be made when considering foundations which rely partly or wholly on friction between their sides and the soil for strength and stability, e.g. certain piling systems – see **Foundations in Detail Section 2**.

Once the soil type and consistency has been obtained and its characteristics ascertained (see items 4 and 5) the information can be analysed to arrive at a safe bearing capacity. For buildings up to four storeys (except those used for storage or factory purposes) reference can be made to the Building Regulations 1991. Table 12 in Regulation A1/2 gives simple strip foundation sizes for given wall loads up to 70 kN/linear metre on predictable soils.

Structural calculations for those buildings defined as applicable to the Table described in the above Regulation are not normally required where the soil is clearly identifiable and consistent. For more complicated structures and/or heavier buildings, foundation design must be subject to detailed calculations. In these cases even more rigorous attention must be paid to assessing site conditions, determining structural loadings and estimating foundation form and sizes relative to permitted ground stresses as well as making allowances for possible movement or other structural effects of the chosen foundation.

In dense urban areas it is essential to make exhaustive searches (documentary and physical) to establish the location of underground watercourses, sewers and service runs. For the scope of site investigation and fuller details of site exploration see BS 5930:1981, Code of practice for site investigations. See also BS 1377 Part 2:1990, Methods of test for soil for civil engineering purposes.

An important consideration in good foundation design is the materials which are to be used in their construction. Today foundations are normally of concrete either unreinforced or reinforced with steel bars. The Building Regulations 1991 require that the concrete mix used for strip foundations is composed of cement to BS12:1989 and fine and coarse aggregate conforming to BS 882:1983 in the proportion of 50 kg of cement to not more than 0.1 m³ of fine aggregate and 0.2 m³ of coarse aggregate (1:3:6). For chemically aggressive soils refer to BS 5328, Part 2:1991, Methods for specifying concrete mixes.

When deciding on a particular foundation form, the process of building is an important criteria for selection. Not only can foundation design and execution be affected by the plant available and access to the site,

but the way the foundations are loaded as the building progresses can be a factor. Loading may have to be evenly distributed across the site as the building mass increases, especially with soils of a low bearing capacity. Eccentric loading in construction must be avoided or allowed for.

BS 6399 Loading for Buildings. Part 1: 1984, Code of practice for dead and imposed loads

BS 6399 Part 2: 1997, Code of practice for wind loads (CP 3 Chapter V, Loading. Part 2: 1972 – Wind loads, can still be referred to)

BS 8004:1986, Code of practice for foundations

BS 8110 Structural use of concrete. Part 1: 1985, Code of practice for design and construction

BS 5930:1981, Code of practice for site investigations

BS 6031:1981, Code of practice for earthworks

BS 8002:1994, Code of practice for earth retaining structures

BS 2004:1986, Code of practice for foundations

BS 648:1964, Schedule of weights of building materials

BS 1377: Part 2: 1990, Methods of test for soils for civil engineering purposes

BRE Digest 63, Soils and Foundations: Part 1

BRE Digest 64, Soils and Foundations: Part 2

BRE Digest 67, Soils and Foundations: Part 3

BRE Digest 313, Mini piling for low rise buildings

BRE Digest 315, Choosing piles for new construction

BRE Digest 325, Concrete: Part 1 Materials

BRE Digest 326, Concrete: Part 2 Specification, design and quality control

BRE Digests 240, 241, 242. Low-rise buildings on shrinkable clay soils: Parts 1, 2 and 3

BRE Digest 251, Assessment of damage in low-rise buildings with particular reference to progressive foundation movement

BRE Digest 298, The influence of trees on house foundations in clay soils

National House Building Council 4.1 Foundations: Finding the hazards

The Building Regulations 1991 Document A, Sections A1–A4 and Document C, Sections C1–C4.

4 Movement

Movement of foundations is mostly caused by a preceding soil movement which is the result of one or a combination of the categories listed in 4.1. Movement can also occur due to inadequacies in construction materials through:

incorrect ratios for concrete mixes;

poor construction techniques such as incorrectly positioned reinforcement;

formation of voids;

chemical attack (see 5 Durability)

BRE Digests 240 (1993), 241 (1990) and 242 (1980), Low-rise buildings on shrinkable clay soils: Part 1, 2 and 3

BRE Digest 251: rev. 1993, Assessment of damage in low-rise buildings with particular reference to progressive foundation movement

BRE Digest 276: rev. 1993, Hardcore

BRE Digest 363: 1991, Sulphate and acid resistance of concrete in the ground

BRE Digest 383: 1993, Site investigation for low-rise buildings: soil description

BRE BR 69: 1994, Structural vibration and damage

4.1 Structural

Within broad classifications, soils behave similarly and loads from a building transferring to a foundation always cause slight settlement. Anticipating the magnitude and uniformity of this settlement depends on precise soil analysis and good design procedures which, as well as those already outlined, should consider the following:

(a) Initial overloading of the soil by too concentrated a load as a result of poor distribution of the building loads. This could also be caused by eccentric loading on a foundation from wind forces acting on a building resulting in unequal stresses in the soil.

(b) Additional loads on existing foundations by increasing the weight of the building (either uniformly or eccentrically) or by extending the building upwards or outwards.

(c) Forming new foundations near an existing foundation when the soil could then be overstressed from the combined loads of the two buildings.

(d) Forming trenches for services, or other excavations near foundations, reducing the bearing zone and causing overstressing of the remaining soil (see Building Regulations 1991).

(e) Forming foundations at different levels (e.g. basements adjoining ground-level areas or high-rise structures adjoining low-rise structures) causing differential settlement as a result of the varying loads from the two parts of the building.

(f) Forming foundations near or within unstable areas such as back-filled excavated sites (such as old chalk or clay quarries, filled basements or sites with

a different history of use), pits or wells, basements, drains and mining shafts. The materials used for back-filling low-lying sites in preparation for building must be carefully selected. They must be capable of thorough compaction in graded layers and free from harmful chemicals or material likely to decompose and form voids, such as metal containers or plastic bottles. Hard rock waste, gravels, coarse sand, chalk or even household and industrial wastes are used: all have differing characteristics of compaction and settlement – see BRE Digest 274, Fill, Part 1: Classification and load carrying characteristics, and BRE Digest 275, Part 2: Site Investigation, ground improvement and foundation design. Specialist advice should be sought when building on these sites and generally, except for the lightest of buildings, they are either best avoided altogether or the foundations must be sunk down through the fill to the natural ground, or consolidation techniques employed.

(g) The upward surge of some soils caused by formation techniques (pile driving) or positive pressure from water tables (see item 4.2.1) which could result in the lifting or tilting of nearby existing foundations.

(h) Forming foundations on sites subject to geological factors such as landslides and slips, swallow holes, slip planes, creep, internal combustion, etc.

BRE BR 230: 1993, Building on Fill: Geotechnical Aspects

4.2 Moisture

Climatic variations can result in variations in the moisture content of the soil, causing shrinkage and swelling. Seasonal changes can affect clay soils up to 5 m from the ground surface for basements and foundations. Fine particle soils such as clays are prone to this action as increased moisture results in a thickening of the water film surrounding each particle causing volumetric (horizontal and vertical) swelling and subsequent loss of strength. Conversely when the moisture content is reduced soil particles move closer together resulting in a reduction of volume. In addition, because of their 'sticky' or cohesive nature, clay soils tend to entrap large volumes of water and to a lesser extent air, which is gradually displaced as the load of a building is increased during its construction. This settlement could continue for up to 10 years after completion of the construction process (see BRE Digest 63: 1965, still current 1998).

4.2.1 Water table or groundwater level

The moisture content of soil is profoundly affected by the water table and any fluctuations, quite apart from seasonal variations in rainfall. When designing foundations, careful account must be taken of the predictable action of the water table and its effect on the bearing pressure of the soil – particularly if it exerts a positive upward pressure. According to section 2.4.1 of BS 8004 'All cellular construction below groundwater level to be checked for flotation'. This remark applies to basements and also to swimming pools that may have to use more substantial foundations to weight the construction and prevent uplift. Any excavation below the water table has to allow for seepage forces and hydraulic uplift. Refer to BS 5930 for notes on site investigations that must establish the groundwater hydrology on a site and the pattern of groundwater flow.

4.2.2 Services

Leaking water mains, or sewers, rainwater pipes discharging onto the ground or even heating installations which could cause localized drying of the soil beneath a foundation are some of the extraneous factors that can affect the delicate balance between foundation and subsoil.

4.2.3 Trees and vegetation

Vegetation can cause substantial movement in clay soils. In drought conditions grass can remove moisture to a depth of 2 m and trees to a depth of 5 m (Lombardy Poplar species). Except where special precautions are taken, it used to be recommended that buildings with foundations of not more than 1 m deep should be kept at a distance of at least the mature height of the trees. If there is a row of trees, this dimension should be at least 1.5 to 2 times the mature height of the trees. This rule should also be observed for trees planted after the building is completed. BS 8004:1986, Code of practice for foundations, now recommends that 'adequate space' is to be given between new buildings and existing trees.

When building on a clay subsoil where trees and large shrubs have been recently removed, the ground is likely to swell as the moisture content of the soil increases and water is no longer removed to sustain growth. For a detailed account of the effects of trees on buildings see BRE Digest 298: 1985, The influence of trees on house foundations in clay soils.

4.2.4 Drought

Foundation movements occurring as a result of extreme drought conditions (1976, 1995, 1996) have shown the necessity for a greater understanding of phenomena caused by the moisture content of clay soils. In London, seasonal drying in hot summers affects soils between 1.5 to 2.0 m below the ground; on undrained pasture the soil would revert to its original condition with water replenishment in summer.

The volume of coarse grained soils such as gravels is not affected by moisture content as much as the fine grained soils. However, consideration must be given when designing foundations on the coarser grained soils to the possibility of erosion caused by groundwater movement and penetrating roots. Details of methods adopted to counteract some of the problems associated with foundations in particular soils are given in **Foundations in Detail Section 2**.

BS 5837 Code of practice for trees in relation to construction
BRE DAS 96: 1987, Foundations on shrinkable clay: avoiding damage due to trees (BRE Defect Action Sheet)
BRE Digests 240, 241 and 242, Low-rise buildings on shrinkable clay soils: Parts 1, 2 and 3

4.3 Frost

Soils such as silts, chalk, fine sands and some clays are subject to expansion when frozen owing to the formation of ice lenses between their particles. This could cause heave of the soil resulting in the lifting or tilting of parts of the foundation and the structure above. The conditions most likely to lead to this are severe and prolonged frost. BS 8004 notes that for most places in the UK the frost line occurs at a depth of 450 mm below ground level. Recently we have been having particularly mild winters, but the winter of 1981/2 was a salutary reminder of the severity which can be expected from time to time. Freezing of certain subsoils in the UK has been recorded at 1 m depth where the groundwater level is close to the surface.

Consideration must be given to insulation around refrigeration plant in buildings if the effects of frost heave on nearby foundations or ground-floor slabs are to be avoided.

4.4 Vibration

Vibration from machinery, plant or vehicles represents a dynamic loading that can induce a vibratory response in a building and far greater stresses which are then transferred to the subsoil. Certain clays can disintegrate under cyclic loading. Specialist advice will need to be taken where foundations are adjacent to sources of vibration such as over or underground railways, heavy motor traffic, plant installations and aircraft activities.

BS 7385 Part 1: 1990, Guide for the measurement of vibrations and evaluation of their effects on building

BRE Digest 353: 1990, Damage to structures from ground borne vibration

BRE BR 69: 1994, Structural vibration and damage

5 Durability

Some characteristics of certain soils are potentially injurious to the concrete used to form foundations, for example, stiff-fissured clays and some peats containing soluble sulphates which, when in contact with groundwater, react with the cement causing expansion and disintegration of the exposed concrete surfaces. Concrete foundations protected against contact with water are virtually safe from such attack. However, where sulphates are present and are continually activated by groundwater, considerable erosion of the shape of the foundation will occur with resulting settlement of the building. Although not as serious, a similar form of attack on concrete can occur in acidic soil conditions such as are found in certain peats.

Where it is necessary to form foundations on backfilled sites, particular care should be taken to fully investigate its degree of compaction (see item 4.1(f)) and its chemical content. Artificial deposits, such as colliery shale, pulverized fuel ash or even building rubble, can contain high sulphate concentrations. Consequently the sulphate content in groundwaters or hardcore should be checked; if exceeding 0.5%, ordinary Portland cement cannot be used and sulphate-resisting cements will need to be specified. See BRE Digest 363 for guidance. The special cements that may be specified for the concrete foundation mix which will resist attack include sulphate-resisting cement, super-sulphated cement, high alumina cement (not to be used if high ground temperatures are likely to occur). Ordinary Portland cement could still be specified, but the resulting concrete foundation must be protected by an impervious membrane such as polythene or asphalt.

Concrete foundations below the ground are subject to continual wetting and drying as well as possibly frost attack and/or chemical action. For this reason, it is essential to ensure that any reinforcing bars in the foundation are given a minimum cover of 50 mm or preferably 75 mm. Failure to provide adequate protection will result in gradual exposure of the reinforcement owing to surface disruption of the concrete, and corrosion will occur resulting in possible structural failure.

See items 3 and 4 for references.

6 Thermal considerations

To minimize heat loss through the ground floors of buildings, the foundation and adjoining slab details have to be constructed to avoid thermal bridges which can also be a source of condensation due to temperature differences.

There can be considerable heat loss through the ground floors of buildings and construction details should limit the heat loss by providing sufficient isolation and insulation to maintain comfort and minimize energy wastage. Although a U-value of 0.35 W/m^2 is preferred for an exposed ground floor element, the whole building has to demonstrate overall compliance by using either an elemental method, a target U value method or an energy rating method, all three of which are set out in the Building Regulations 1991 (1995 edition) through Document L, Conservation of fuel and power. Appendix A of this document sets out how values can be calculated for ground floors and the minimum thickness of insulation needed given the thermal conductivity of the insulant used. The ratio of floor perimeter length to floor area has to be calculated first, and insulant thickness can then vary from 24 mm to 155 mm dependent on this ratio and insulant type.

7 Health

In some areas of the UK there are now well-documented health risks from building in areas which have a particularly high radon content. In other areas, change of land use means that sites are used for homes or offices that were previously subjected to heavy pollution from industrial workings or from gas processing which leaves heavy hydrocarbons. Building on landfill sites means dealing with the release of methane and carbon dioxide gases. In these cases ground investigation may reveal problems that affect foundation design by requiring ventilated areas below slabs or complete sealing of the ground with slabs or chemical neutralization of the ground.

BRE BR 211: 1991, Radon: a guide on protective measures for new dwellings

BRE BR 212: 1991, Construction of new buildings on gas contaminated land

BRE BR 227: 1992, Surveying dwellings with high indoor radon levels: a BRE guide to radon remedial measures in existing dwellings

BRE EP 18: 1993, The measurement of methane and other gases from the ground

8 Construction process

When deciding on a particular foundation type, other important selection criteria, apart from those already discussed, affect directly the construction process chosen. Below is a short list of some likely critical factors which must not be regarded as exhaustive since each building site will vary in its degree of complexity. Whenever possible, consult with the contractor to arrive at the quickest and most economic methods of construction relative to the availability of building resources.

(a) Site access. Check that road widths, surfaces and strengths are adequate and that there are no physical restrictions on the height for contractor's plant.

(b) Site layout. The plan shape, disposition and number of structural repetitive units in a building will have a profound effect on the choice of foundation type. Except for very small buildings, excavation today is mostly carried out by mechanical means using various kinds of machine. Their 'cost-in-use' advantages rely almost entirely on accessible repetitive bays and/or long straight runs of excavation. The economic advantages claimed for deep strip (trench) foundations over the conventional strip foundations are that the former method reduces the time, excavation and material handling factors by the use of mechanical diggers.

(c) Disturbance. Care should be taken when forming foundations to avoid nuisance to adjoining owners and their properties as a result of noise, dust or the depositing of soil. Many proprietary piling systems are now available which carry out the excavation process by 'silent' methods. Adjoining owners have the Right of Support to their building and land and it is sometimes necessary to use quite costly forms of foundations to avoid this problem on new sites where other buildings are close to the boundary.

Trade and research organizations

British Cement Association (BCA), Century House, Telford Avenue, Crowthorne, Berks RG11 6YS (tel. 01344-762676, fax 01344-761214).

Building Research Establishment (BRE), Bucknalls Lane, Garston, Watford, Herts WD2 7JR (tel. 01923-894040, fax 01923-664010).

Federation of Piling Specialists, 39 Upper Elmers End, Beckenham, Kent (tel. 0181-663 0947).

Health & Safety Executive, Broad Lane, Sheffield S3 7HQ (tel. 0114-2892345, fax 0144-289333).

Institution of Civil Engineers, Great George Street, London SW1P 3AA (tel. 0171-222 7722).

Foundations in Detail Section 2

SMM7 D Groundwork, E In situ concrete, J Waterproofing

(See Section 1 Foundations: General)

Notes and references

Items are cross-referenced from the diagrams. This section should be read in conjunction with **Foundations Generally Section 1,** which contains general factors 1 to 8, technical references and Building Regulations, and comments relating to foundation materials and their durability.

1 Strip and deep strip foundations

1.1 Building load and soil reaction

As outlined in **Foundations Generally Section 1**, the function of a foundation is to spread the total loads acting on a building to a safe supporting soil and avoid excessive and/or differential settlement. For general information on these building loads, which includes the weight of the foundation itself, reference should be made to item 3 of **Floors: General Section 6**.

The loads to be supported by strip and deep strip foundations generally result from buildings of continuous masonry construction, either stone, brick or concrete walls. In addition, timber-framed walls could also be supported by this category of foundation (see **External Walls: Basic Types Section 4**).

As loads from these walls are collected by strip foundations and distributed to the soil laterally and continuously, the volume of soil beneath the foundation which is affected by the load or bulb of pressure (see **Foundations Generally Section 1**) is more than would normally be expected for point loads on pad foundations. There is a cumulative effect which increases the depth of the bulb of pressure to three times the width of foundation.

Where the width of the foundation's horizontal bearing area is reduced to a minimum (as with deep strip foundations), support can be obtained by frictional forces between the vertical faces of the foundation and the adjoining soil – particularly when the soil is of a cohesive nature.

1.2 Ground level

Before commencing the design and construction of the foundation, the existing ground surface around the

proposed building needs attention. Existing debris and the topsoil (ranging upwards from 150 mm) is highly compressible and will have to be removed from the building area or may have to be removed or compacted along general access routes for builder's plant. Surface water from the site may also have to be extracted using mechanical pumps connected via hoses to an adequate drainage system (see 1.6 Construction process, below).

Once the building has been completed, some topsoil may have to be reinstated up to the perimeter of the building to form garden areas. Space will have to be allocated for a selected proportion of the removed topsoil and it should be stored carefully to a maximum height of 1 m to allow for sufficient aeration.

If the foundations are formed in soils of high moisture content due to an initial or fluctuating water table, then the condition should not be aggravated by allowing rainwater pipes, or temporary pumping to discharge locally. A continuous area of perimeter paving or concrete around the building about 3 m wide and laid to a slight fall can moderate the effects of rainfall on soils below foundations. In severe situations consideration should be given to the provision of land drains laid adjoining the foundation at its lowest level with a connection to the drainage system and covered with graded backfill. Conversely, the active collection of rainwater and redistribution of water to clay soils that suffer from excessive loss of water in drought conditions should also be considered. However, all of these methods are dependent on correct analysis of the soil conditions and the design of a suitable foundation system which is capable of being stable across seasonal and cyclic extremes.

1.3 Connection of wall to foundation

Because strip foundations are generally used to support masonry walls consisting of small bonded units of brick, block or stone, their top surfaces must be finished level. This avoids the necessity of providing mortar packing of varying depth beneath each first course of brick, block or stone, and the erection process of the walling will be faster and so more economical. This is vital when the ground slopes and vertical steps have to be

Each foundation type is discussed under the following headings:

1   Building load
2   Ground level
3   Connection of wall or column to foundation
4   Foundation shape
4.1 Width
4.2 Thickness
4.3 Stepping

5   Holes for services
6   Construction process
7   Depth below ground level

1 Strip and deep strip

2 Pad or slab

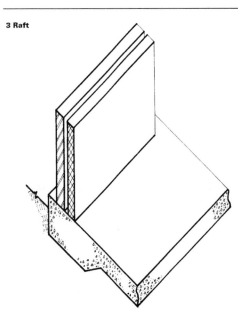

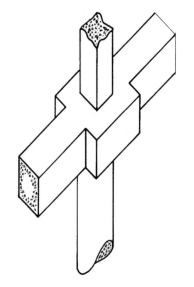

3 Raft

4 Pile

formed along strip foundation. The height of each step should comply with structural requirements (see item 1.4.3) and be determined by multiples of coursed dimensions of the brick, block or stone wall.

Where strip foundations are used to carry timber-framed buildings, they must be designed so that there is no ground contact with the timber. The timber wall should be supported at least 150 mm clear of the ground either on a brick, block or stone wall built off a normal strip foundation, or by continuing the concrete up above the ground (necessitating edge shuttering) in the case of deep strip foundations. With both forms of support, adequate fixings should be built into the projecting wall which will enable the light-weight timber wall to resist the horizontal force of the wind and also ensure that the dpc is not pierced. Shot-fired pins or cast-in bolts are common methods of securing the sole plate of a frame to the edge detail of the foundation (see *Timber Frame Construction* published by TRADA, 1994).

1.4 Foundation shape

The shape of a foundation results primarily from the need to avoid excessive and differential settlement as it transfers load to the supporting soil using the design analysis already discussed. The final shape is also influenced by the method of formation used in construction (involving consistency of soil, access and excavation technique), working tolerances and 'external' factors such as site obstructions, services and adjoining walls; with the requirement to use both materials and labour economically.

1.4.1 Width

The minimum width of normal unreinforced concrete strip foundations is determined by dividing the calculated load of the building (including assumed weight of foundation) in kN per metre run, by the permissible bearing pressure of the soil in kN per m². The building loads (dead, live and wind) can be calculated by reference to BS 6399 Part 1:1984, Code of practice for dead and applied loads, and BS 648:1964, Schedule of weights of building materials. A range of permissible bearing pressures for various predictable soils is given in BS 8004.

The Table to Regulation A1/2 of the Building Regulations 1991 lists 'deemed-to-satisfy' widths for normal strip concrete foundations to buildings having not more than four storeys (other than a factory or storage building). This Table deals with wall loads up to 70 kN/m run

(single-storey brick wall approx. 30 kN/m, two-storey house wall approx. 50 kN/m (party wall) and 40 kN/m (flank wall), on various types of subsoil ranging from rock (10 000 kN/m²) to silty clay (less than 75 kN/m²).

Structural calculations for those buildings defined as applicable to the Table to Regulation A1/2 are not normally required where the soil is clearly identifiable and consistent: for more complicated structures and/or heavier buildings on less predictable soils, foundation design must be subject to detailed calculations.

Where building loads are high or the supporting soil is weak, the use of normal unreinforced strip foundations will result in extensive width of concrete and also excessive thickness (see item 1.4.2). In order to reduce the amount of excavation and also the volume of concrete, steel reinforcing bars can be placed in the lower third of a smaller volume of concrete. This will counteract the stresses which would result because of the reduction in foundation size. Extra concrete cover to reinforcement should be provided to protect the steel reinforcement from the possibility of corrosion. BS 8004 recommends a minimum allowance to be added to the cover thicknesses recommended in BS 8110 (Tables 3.2 and 3.3) which relate to exposure. For mild exposure this would give a minimum cover of 60 mm and a maximum of 90 mm cover for extreme conditions.

The width (i.e. horizontal dimension) of the deep strip concrete foundation is usually also less than the normal unreinforced concrete strip foundation. In this case account can be taken of the increased frictional resistance between the longer vertical sides of the foundation and the adjoining soil as well as the higher resistance to overturning afforded by the greater vertical mass of concrete.

Another important factor concerning the width of strip foundations is the working tolerances required to ensure that the building wall is placed centrally on the foundation and avoids unequal stresses in the soil below. The process of excavation, whether by hand or mechanical means, makes it difficult to guarantee perfectly straight strip foundations but the wall above must be straight. Narrowly-designed foundations may not give sufficient working tolerance to avoid eccentric location of the wall above, so the minimum width of any strip foundation should be the thickness of the wall carried plus 150 mm.

Where the wall above a foundation incorporates a pier, buttress or chimney the strip foundation has to be increased in size at these points to spread the increased loads. Generally it is sufficient to ensure that the same projection from main wall to edge of foundation is carried around these features. If heavier loads are to be transferred to the soil below then wider localized foundations will be required.

1.4.2 Thickness

According to BS 8004 the minimum thickness of a strip foundation should equal the horizontal projection from base of wall to edge of foundation and never be less than 150 mm. This is also a 'deemed-to-satisfy' requirement for strip foundations under A1/2 Section 1E of the Building Regulations 1991.

For deep strip foundations the depth of concrete relates to the required depth of the foundation below ground level (see item 1.7). It should be remembered that the top of this form of foundation should be kept at least 150 mm below finished ground level to avoid its appearance at or above the ground.

1.4.3 Stepping

Where a building is to be erected on a sloping site and the required bearing strata more or less follow the ground slope, consideration should be given to forming strip foundations in a series of steps. In this way, excessive excavation and associated timbering can be avoided as can excessive amounts of walling below ground. BS 8004 recommends that at all changes of level in strip foundations, they should be lapped at the steps for a distance at least equal to the thickness of the foundation or twice the height of the step, whichever is the greater. However, where the step is greater than the thickness of the foundation, special precautions may need to be taken in order to avoid differential settlement which may be caused by the differing loads of the bulk of walling carried by individual lengths of foundation.

Regulation A1/2: Section 1E of the Building Regulations 1976 gives 'deemed-to-satisfy' requirements for stepped strip foundations and states that the amount of lap between higher and lower foundation should not be less than the thickness of the foundation and in no case less than 300 mm.

When stepped strip foundations are considered to be economically viable, an additional consideration is that the thickness of the foundation or height of step should be a multiple of the vertical dimension of the wall brick or block unit it supports (see item 1.3).

The foundations to internal walls are sometimes formed at a lesser depth than those to the external perimeter walls of a building and stepping at their intersection will be needed (see item 1.7).

1.5 Holes for services

Services entering a building below ground (water, electricity, gas, telephone, etc.) and those leaving a building (drainage, refuse systems, etc.) usually pass through, or in some cases under, the foundation.

In the case of normal strip foundations this presents few problems if certain precautions are taken. When services are to penetrate the wall below ground at known points or are already in position, holes can be left in the wall by using precast concrete lintels or brick arches depending on the size of hole required. Some contractors may prefer to build the wall normally, but bed the bricks where holes are required in sand instead of mortar to allow easy removal when positioning services.

With deep strip foundations the provision of holes is more difficult. Service routes need to be located before casting the foundation to avoid later and expensive drilling of set concrete. When the positions of holes are known, open-sided timber boxes of the correct size with a precast concrete lintel over can be cast into the foundation. These should be placed in the foundation as soon as possible after casting, by removing sufficient green concrete, placing box and lintel in position and then reinstating the concrete around and under the support area of the lintel up to the normal level of the foundation. Alternatively, sections of pipe or tube can be cast into the foundation. If a large number of services are to be run, the contractor may choose to use the normal strip foundation rather than using time and labour making provisions in deep strip foundations. Services in ducts or holes should be given 50 mm clearance in order to avoid later deflection or fracture of pipes if there is any settlement of the foundations.

It is best to avoid running services beneath foundations as precautions may have to be taken to ensure localized settlement does not occur below the foundation level.

1.6 Construction process

Site considerations will affect the form of foundation used for a particular building as well as design considerations. Detailed consideration of contract planning, site organization and continuous economical productivity is beyond the scope of this section. Whenever possible the contractor should be consulted in order to arrive at the quickest and cheapest methods of construction relative to the availability of building resources. Most excavations for foundations are executed with the aid of mechanical plant. If the plan shape of the building is too complex, then hand digging may be necessary and economies are less likely to be achieved because of the higher labour content. During the course of the work competent shoring of excavations to protect operatives, and the employment of competent personnel for their periodic inspection are vital. There are contractual responsibilities with respect to employers' liability insurance and indemnity insurance, as well as to health and safety now within the scope of the Construction Design and Management Regulations, that affect the whole building team and process of building. The extent and use of supporting timber work (scaffolding boards, wallings, struts, etc.) to retain the sides of excavation during the formation of the normal strip foundation and the wall below ground will depend upon the condition of the subsoil to be held back (for details see *Mitchell's Building Series: Structure and Fabric*, Part 1, chapter 2 and Part 2, chapter 2). If the soil is very loose even the foundation will have to be shuttered before casting the concrete.

The economic advantage claimed for deep strip foundations when compared with normal strip foundations is the reduction in the timescale by using concrete only below ground (except for the last 150 mm or so up to ground level) and the fact that building workers can avoid working in trenches. In addition, the foundation only needs to be set out once at ground level instead of having to set out the trench first, the concrete strip second and the walling below ground third.

The advantages of using deep strip foundations should be set against consistency of soil for unsupported excavations and the contractor's scope concerning availability, type and use of particular mechanical excavators and labour. See also the effect of the provision of services, item 1.5.

The depth of trench required to be excavated is usually determined by the use of levelled sight rails and boning rods; the thickness of concrete for the foundation by levelled pegs driven into the bottom of the trench at 1 000 to 1 200 m centres (see *Building Construction Handbook*, R. Chudley, Butterworth-Heinemann, 1995, which also gives typical trench timbering techniques).

The process of excavation, formation and subsequent loading of a foundation may affect the stability of adjoining buildings if close by. The foundation design will need to be undertaken accordingly.

Mandatory notices must be served on adjoining owners because of their inherent right of satisfactory support for their building(s). This is now governed by the Party Wall Act 1996 which applies to England and Wales. Briefly, notice must be given to adjoining owners of any work to be done and the adjoining owner has the right to appoint their own surveyor. In the event of a dispute, an independent third surveyor is appointed to review the situation and make 'a party wall award' which settles the dispute and apportions cost. For details on administering the process refer to: *Architect's Guide to Job Administration: The Party Wall Act 1996*, RIBA Publications, or *Party Walls and What to Do With Them*, RICS Books.

It is important that the bottom of exposed trenches should be protected from changes in moisture content before placing the concrete foundation. In cohesive soils the concrete could be affected by surface water lying in the bottom of the trench. Shrinkage or swelling caused by water at this lower level may affect the stability of the foundation. In clay soils these considerations are particularly important and it is recommended that either the last 100 mm or so of earth is retained unexcavated until just before casting the concrete or, alternatively, the excavation is completed and the exposed bottom protected by 50 mm blinding concrete (as recommended in BS 8004). In gravel soils there is the added danger that laitence from the concrete foundation mix will seep away through the soil before it has set and reduce its effective strength. This problem could be overcome by a stiff mix concrete blinding or by providing a layer of waterproof building paper or polythene at the base of the excavation to retain the full concrete mix. All trench excavation for foundations must be kept free of debris such as iron scrap, broken bottles, polythene containers, timber waste, etc. In some waterlogged soils both site and excavations may need surplus water to be pumped away to a drain.

1.7 Depth below ground level

Factors affecting the depth below ground level at which foundations should be formed have already been discussed in **Foundations Generally Section 1**.

The Building Regulations 1991 A1/2, Section 1E, gives design provisions regarding depth of strip foundations for buildings having not more than four storeys (other than factories or storage buildings). It states that there should be no made ground or wide variation in type of subsoil within the loaded area and no weaker type of soil on which the foundation rests as could impair the stability of the structure.

On some sites it will be found necessary to excavate to a great depth in order to find a satisfactory bearing soil for a strip foundation (4 or 5 m). In this case, the contractor may prefer to backfill the excavation with a relatively weak mix of concrete (1:10) up to the underside of the strip foundation rather than use alternative forms of foundation such as raft or piles. This decision relates to the contractor's need to ensure continuity of work and management of labour skills.

Strip foundations to internal walls of a building can be placed at a shallower depth than those used for the external walls because they are protected from seasonal variation in subsoil conditions (such as frost heave, swelling and shrinkage) by the building above. The safe bearing soil must still be reached for the load to be carried by the internal foundation. Rather than use a shallower wide strip foundation to compensate for weaker soils, it is better to use the normal width of strip (relative to load) at the same depth for the perimeter walls. Consistency in foundation details across a difficult site gives a more even site response.

Shallower internal wall foundations should step down as they approach the perimeter wall as otherwise subsoil protection will be reduced. The rules relating to the stepping of foundations in this way are mentioned in item 1.4.3.

Many of the comments made and references given relating to strip and deep strip foundations also apply in principle to the other three categories of foundations. Consequently further comments will be brief and relate to variations or peculiarities arising from the other categories.

2 Pad or slab foundations

2.1 Building load and soil reaction
The loads to be supported by pad or slab foundations usually result from framed buildings with columns of reinforced concrete, steel or timber. An exception to this is where pads are linked by ground beams which carry masonry walls of stone, brick, block or some form of prefabricated panel wall.

The point loads from these forms of structure are collected by individual pads or slabs which distribute the load to a safe bearing soil. The 'bulb of pressure' in these cases usually has a depth of 1.5 times the width of pad or slab.

Generally, individual point loads are carried on square pads of precast or in situ reinforced concrete which reduces the bulk of concrete that would otherwise be required if unreinforced. Where a column

support to a building has to be cast adjoining an existing structure it may be necessary to form eccentrically shaped bases to take the effects of the supported load away from the adjoining foundation to avoid overstressing the subsoil. Such column bases should be designed jointly with a structural engineer. It is essential for safety and stability that the centre of gravity of the loads supported always coincides with the centre of the column bases even if the assistance of adjoining column loads have to be used. (See *Mitchell's Building Series: Structure and Fabric*, Part 1, Chapter 3. Continuous column foundations, combined foundations, cantilever foundations and balanced base foundations.)

Steel column bases can also be formed of a grid of steel beams bolted together and encased in concrete for protection from corrosion, but this system is little used today (see *Mitchell's Building Series: Structure and Fabric*, Part 1).

2.2 Ground level
Normally the foundation pad is below ground level, the floor being formed as either an independently supported concrete slab, or as a reinforced concrete slab attached to the columns using ground beams. In both cases comments relating to ground level are similar to those under Raft foundations, item 3.3. For comments relating to concrete ground floors in general see **Floors: General Section 6** and in detail see **Section 7**.

2.3 Connection of column to foundation
The connection technique between a column and its foundation pad depends upon the materials of which the column is made.

2.3.1 In situ concrete columns
When the reinforcement bars to the foundation pad are positioned, starter bars are connected to them which are bent up at right angles so as to project above the finished foundation concrete on the line of the column reinforcement by approximately 30 times the diameter of one starter bar. The reinforcement cage of the column is then tied to them, the shuttering erected and the concrete column cast. To ease the erection and location of the shuttering for the concrete column, an upstand or 'kicker' is usually cast on top of the foundation pad. This consists of a 75 mm to 225 mm concrete projection at the centre of the pad of the same cross-sectional area as the proposed column. It may be cast integrally with the base if shuttering techniques permit

but usually it is added to the flat top of the base with the aid of a simple open box shutter. As timber/metal shuttering for the future column can be located and tightly clamped to the 'kicker' once it has cured, it also stops the laitance of the wet concrete for the column seeping away at this vital connection point. The top of the 'kicker' should be thoroughly cleaned before the formation process of the column is executed.

2.3.2 Precast concrete columns

One method is to weld a metal base plate to the exposed ends of the steel reinforcement bars projecting from the base of the precast concrete column. The metal plate is then fixed to the foundation by rag bolts or expanding bolts which have been positioned in the cast pad. To ensure that the column is plumb, the pad area where the plate is to be connected is provided with a bed of semi-dry mortar. The column, with a steel plate, is connected loosely to the foundation pad and steel wedges inserted at the four edges of the plate adjusted to give true vertical alignment of the column. Once the mortar has cured, the nuts on the bolts projecting through the base plate are finally tightened. All metal work below ground should be protected by 75 mm of concrete. Another method is to leave looped reinforcement bars protruding from the column. The column is then lowered into a pocket over starter bars projecting from the foundation base. After the column is made plumb with the aid of shims the connection is grouted with cement mortar.

2.3.3 Steel columns

A metal base plate sometimes incorporating spline pieces is welded to the base of the steel column and then column and plate are connected to the foundation pad in a similar method as described for precast concrete column connections (see *Mitchell's Building Series: Structure and Fabric*, Part 1, Chapter 6). Again all steel work below ground must be protected to standards given in BS 8004 and would be a minimum of 75 mm concrete.

2.3.4 Timber columns

Because of the presence of water at ground level, timber is liable to moisture attack when in contact with the ground. Preservative treatments may not overcome this problem entirely and do not have an indefinite life. For this reason, part of the concrete foundation to a timber column should project at least 150 mm above ground level. The timber column can then be connected to this projection by metal straps for holding in position and holding down purposes, or non-ferrous metal dowels concealed in the timber section can be used. A dpc should be placed on top of the concrete projection before the column is positioned. Alternatively, a metal bracket could be fixed to the foundation pad below ground to project and be connected to the timber column by a metal shoe or spline (see *Mitchell's Building Series: Structure and Fabric*, Part 1, Chapter 6). This bracket and shoe should be in galvanized steel or preferably stainless steel and incorporate drainage holes to prevent the accumulation of water.

2.4 Foundation shape

For comments on foundation shape see item 3.1 and refer for detail information to *Mitchell's Building Series: Structure and Fabric*, Part 1, Chapter 3.

2.5 Holes for services

General services as described under item 1.5 for strip foundations do not normally cause problems with isolated pad foundations except where their positioning affects a regular grid layout of the pads. It is essential that the extent of servicing is known at the early design stage of the foundation layout so that services can be grouped to avoid foundation pads or pad centres can be economically adjusted. Special foundation systems can be designed when conflict is unavoidable.

The idea of rainwater pipes, etc., passing through structural columns to emerge at their base above a foundation pad (or sometimes below!) should be considered as questionable practice. This approach to concealed services requires careful design consideration if the structural stability of both column and pad is not to be impaired and construction and maintenance problems are to be avoided.

2.6 Construction process

For general comments on construction process see item 1.6 for strip foundations.

If column foundation pads are closely spaced, the unexcavated soil left between them will have to be retained by timber shuttering to prevent them collapsing into the cleared foundation area. Timber shuttering could be expensive and obstruct free working conditions. In this case the contractor may well prefer to remove these areas of soil (also known as 'dumplings') completely and construct the foundation base on a clear unobstructed site.

When foundation pads are closely spaced there is also the danger that their bulbs of pressure will begin to merge, resulting in possible overstressing of the supporting soil. As a rough guide this is likely to occur if the bases are at closer centres than two or three times the maximum base width.

3 Raft foundations

3.1 Building load and soil reaction

A raft foundation consists of a large monolithic reinforced concrete slab which collects all the loads acting on the building and transfers them to the supporting soil. They are generally used where subsoils of only weak bearing capacity exist below ground for a considerable depth and then the maximum plan area of foundation is required in order to distribute the loads effectively. With a correctly designed raft foundation cracking of a building normally caused by differential settlement of a foundation should not occur as any movement of the subsoil will affect the whole building: the raft foundation can be compared to a boat resting on water.

Raft design involves a careful consideration of the disposition and distribution of the loads it transfers related to the problem that the resisting soil pressure is likely to fluctuate dramatically during the life of the foundation. Consequently raft design needs expert structural input. See BS 8004 for guidance with regard to foundation design and ground conditions. Where loading requirements dictate the use of a more rigid raft foundation thicker than 300 mm, then economies can be obtained in materials by the use of a beam and slab raft. This consists of a series of beams which collect the loads and transfer them to a flat slab of the normal 150 mm depth. The beams are either upstand above the raft slab when the soil is non-cohesive or downstand below the raft slab when advantages can be gained by using a cohesive soil to form the bottom and side 'shuttering'.

For even higher loads or greater rigidity a cellular raft can be employed. This consists of a two-way box beam at least 900 mm in depth. Where below-ground accommodation is required this form of construction (with the aid of external waterproofing techniques) can be several storeys deep. If the weight of the soil excavated for the cellular raft more or less corresponds with the load of both building and foundation, then little stressing of the soil will occur. However, if the weight of the soil relieved of its excavated load exceeds the building and raft loads, heave will occur and either friction piles or a weighty slab will have to be used as anchors.

3.2 Ground level

See comments under item 3.3.

3.3 Connection of wall to foundation

The edge details for raft foundations are vulnerable because of the possibility of soil deformation, damp penetration, cold bridge effect and poor appearance.

Simple slab raft foundations rest very near the surface of the ground and the soil under the perimeter edge is more vulnerable to the effects of seasonal variation in moisture content (frost heave, swelling and shrinkage). For this reason it is normal to have a downstand edge strip cast integrally with the raft at its perimeter. In cohesive soils this could be 1 m deep and in non-cohesive soils 500 mm deep. In this way the edges are protected from the effects of upward pressure resulting from swollen subsoil in winter and the effects of cantilevering caused by soil erosion or shrinkage in summer.

Raft foundations may form the exposed bottom edge of a building enclosure and unless precautionary measures are taken will form a direct path for damp and heat loss. See **Floors General Section 6,** item 7, for general comments and references relating to heat losses for solid ground floors where they extend to or beyond the external face. See **Floors in Detail Section 7,** item 24, for general comments and references relating to the protection of the floor slab where it extends to or beyond the face of an external wall.

See also **Floors in Detail Section 7**, items 50 and 51, for comments and references relating to the sub-floor and finishes for ground floor slabs which will also be applicable to simple slab raft foundations formed at or near ground level.

Consideration must also be given to the appearance of the exposed edges of raft foundations if they show at or above the finished ground level. There are various methods of finishing raft edges either by exposing them or concealing them by stepping the raft down to accommodate a brick wall.

3.4 Foundation shape

For comments on raft foundation shape see item 3.1 and refer to *Mitchell's Building Series: Structure and Fabric*, Part 2, Chapter 3.

3.5 Holes for services

The importance of the design process for raft foundations has already been stressed. Holes for services must be placed and sized in order not to reduce the structural effectiveness of the reinforced concrete slab. With upstand beam and slab rafts and cellular rafts the problem may be less acute, but services should always be carefully grouped and their routes discussed with the structural engineer. The contractor should also be consulted on the sequence, tolerances and method of installing services with raft foundations.

3.6 Construction process

Slab raft foundations can be conveniently formed at ground level with the aid of mechanical plant. The amount of trenching with its associated problems is minimal when compared with other forms of foundations and the contractor has clear access to the site for the fixing of steel and the casting of concrete. In addition, there is virtually no walling below ground.

Cellular raft construction, however, involves deep excavation and soil retention techniques as well as expensive waterproofing systems. For details of these see *Mitchell's Building Series: Structure and Fabric*, Part 2, Chapter 4: *Types of retaining walls*, Chapter 11: *Timber for excavations*.

3.7 Depth below ground level

For comments regarding depth of raft foundations below ground see item 3.1.

4 Pile foundations

4.1 Building load

Piles are a form of foundation where vertical supports are installed in the ground at intervals under walls, piers or columns in order to transfer the loads of the building onto soil at a depth far greater than would be economically feasible with strip or pad foundations. They work by either transferring the load directly to a better bearing capacity of subsoil or by frictional forces acting down the whole length of the pile. It is generally accepted that if it is necessary to excavate more than 2 m to reach a suitable bearing subsoil it will always be worth considering the use of piles. Piles are therefore suitable in the following conditions:

(a) where there is the presence of unsuitable material, such as shrinkable clay, near the surface which may

be capable of taking the required loads but is liable to movement due to change of moisture content (seasonal variations, fluctuating water table, extensive vegetation, etc.);

(b) if the soil has a low bearing capacity for a considerable depth, piles can be used to transfer the loads to a greater depth;

(c) when foundations have to be formed on a steeply sloping site.

The mechanism by which pile foundations transmit their loads to the lower strata of the subsoil depends on the interrelationship between the type of piles used, their method of formation in the ground and the consistency of the soil through which they pass. With this in mind, piles can be end-bearing (like columns with or without under-reamed bases to increase their load spreading capabilities rather like pad foundations), friction-bearing (relying on friction between the side of the pile and the surrounding soil) or, more usually, a combination of these two. They can be pre-formed (reinforced concrete, prestressed concrete, steel or timber), partly pre-formed (lining of reinforced concrete or steel tube for mass or reinforced concrete in fill) or formed in in situ reinforced concrete or by vibro-compaction of gravel into the ground (a form of soil stabilization).

These forms can be installed in the ground using a number of proprietary techniques employed by piling specialists which can be classed under two broad headings. These are *displacement techniques*, where the pile foundation is forced into the ground by driving, jacking, vibrating or screwing and *replacement techniques* where the soil is excavated by percussion, flush, grab or rotary borers and the pile foundation formed by inserting reinforcement and concrete into the resulting hole.

Detailed analysis of the types of pile foundation to be used for specific building problems and their method of installation involves specialists and is beyond the scope of this section. For more information see *Mitchell's Building Series: Structure and Fabric*, Part 2; *Specification*, Volume 1: Site works; BRE Digest 313: 1986, *Mini-piling for low-rise buildings*, BRE Digest 315: 1986, *Choosing piles for new construction*, and various specialist trade literature.

The notable exception to the need to involve highly specialized personnel is when considering the use of short-bored pile foundations. This form of foundation is primarily designed for use when relatively lightly loaded buildings are to be constructed on highly shrink-able clay subsoils. Depending on the subsoil conditions, short-bored concrete piles with or without a lining and up to 350 mm diameter are formed about 3.6 m long at about 3 m centres by a hand or mechanically operated auger. After the pile is cast a shallow reinforced concrete ground beam is then cast on a bed of sand blinding to connect with steel reinforcement projecting from the top of the pile. This beam links the piles together and provides a base for the wall of the building which is independent of the clay soil immediately below. Care should be taken to ensure that the ground floor slab is not connected to the ground beam unless it is a properly constructed suspended reinforced concrete slab. This is because of the possibility of differential settlement between the two elements (floor/wall) causing localized cracking and fracture of the damp-proof membrane in the floor. Buildings on short-bored piles are less likely to suffer the effects of differential settlement resulting from excessive drought conditions or the drainage of the subsoil by vegetation (see **Foundations Generally Section 1**, item 4.2).

The building contractor may have or can hire the required plant for short-bored pile foundations and their use will give an economical solution to the particular problems associated with firm shrinkable clays.

For further details on short-bored pile foundations see *Mitchell's Building Series: Structure and Fabric*, Part 1, Chapter 4.

4.2 Ground level
See item 4.3: Connection of wall/column to foundation.

4.3 Connection of wall/column to foundation
In order to transfer the loads of a building efficiently pile caps are formed at the top of each pile or group of piles (similar to a capital on a column) and these are linked by ground beams to give lateral support. A suspended reinforced concrete slab is also supported by the ground beams and is usually cast integrally with it.

The problems of the connection of walls to slabs or beams of foundation systems are similar to those associated with raft foundations: see item 3.3.

4.4 Foundation shape
Comments covered by item 4.1.

4.5 Holes for services
The problems associated with the provision of holes for services in connection with suspended reinforced concrete floor slabs, ground beams and pile foundations are similar to those discussed for raft foundations: see item 3.5.

4.6 Construction process
See item 4.1 and **Foundations Generally Section 1**, item 8: Construction process.

Probably the most important site considerations regarding the formation of pile foundations are site access, noise disturbance and heave effects on adjoining properties.

Certain piling rigs may be precluded from use by being unable to pass under low bridges or even buildings and also because their physical dimension and weight are difficult to manoeuvre about a confined site. There are frequently restrictions on the access into sites involving traffic hazards such as turning circles or rights of way as well as noise and dirt which may be carried from the site onto adjacent roads.

Many proprietary piling systems are available which carry out the excavation process by 'silent' methods. Generally these consist of jacking, rotary boring or vibro-compaction techniques: methods of flushing the spoil from the excavation are also adopted but great care must be taken to reduce the amount of free water on the site.

The process of driving piles into the ground can cause an upsurge of the surrounding soil and may affect the stability of nearby buildings. Driven piles are also noisy and these considerations may make it necessary to consider alternative methods for forming the pile foundation.

4.7 Depth below ground level
With the possible exception of short-bored piles, depth, like shape or diameter, are factors which invariably involve specialist design analysis.

External Walls: General Section 3
SMM7 F: Masonry

(See Section 4 for basic types and Section 5 for detailed sections)

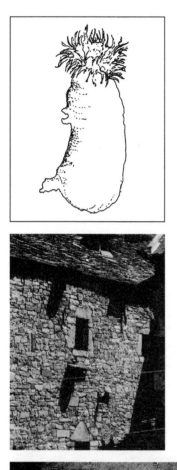

Tunicates
Soft walled sea animals like anemones have hydrostatic skeletons, flexible walls that protect the body cavity and organs from extreme wave shock and changes of temperature.

Stone wall in Broto, Spain (Dean)

Alhambra, Spain (Rich)

Notes and references

Numbered sections are cross-referenced from the diagrams and include comments followed, where appropriate, by technical references and relevant Building Regulations. Addresses for relevant trade and research organizations are given at the end of the section. British Standards and BRE Digests should always be checked for current amendments. This section contains general factors; **Section 4 External Walls: Basic Types** deals with basic wall types, and **Section 5 External Walls: Detailed Sections** shows typical detailed cross sections.

General references

Mitchell's Building Series: Structure and Fabric, Part 1, Jack Stroud Foster. Batsford 1994.
Masonry Walls: Specification & Design, Kenneth Thomas. Architectural Press, 1995.
BRE BR 1197: 1988, Rain penetration through masonry walls: diagnosis and remedial measures
BRE Digest 246: 1981, Strength of brickwork and blockwork walls: design for vertical load
The BDA Guide to Successful Brickwork, Brick Development Association

1 Wall categories

Wall systems are multifunctional and use a large range of materials and finishes, so the range of options given here is limited although found in general use. For simplicity this section will deal with the general factors relating to most external wall systems. Following sections will first cover the basic types used while others will list specific factors related to each basic type. Wall materials and finishes will be mentioned where appropriate under each item of information.

2 Appearance

Criteria for choosing a particular type of wall are outside the scope of this information sheet. Designers must choose a wall system that achieves a balance between their aesthetic aims and the quantifiable

Key Factors	Action	Counteraction
Gravity	Downward pull	Support
Wind	Motive force (suction), destructive, penetrative	Rigidity, resilience, sealing
Rain	Moisture saturation	Deflection, impervious skin, absorption and drainage, sealing
Snow	Moisture saturation, loading	Deflection, impervious skin, absorption and drainage, sealing
Sun	Temperature variation, movement, heat gain, chemical decomposition	Movement joints, insulation, shielding, invulnerable materials, reflection
Dirt and dust	Infiltration, deposition, surface pollution	Repulsion, exclusion, shielding, cleaning
Chemicals	Corrosion, disintegration, decomposition	Invulnerable materials, exclusion
Sound	Noise nuisance	Insulation
Capillary attraction	Moisture transfer	Impervious barrier, cavity

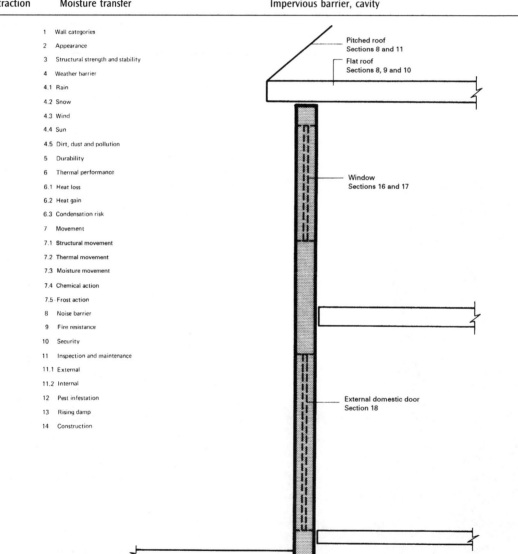

1   Wall categories

2   Appearance

3   Structural strength and stability

4   Weather barrier

4.1   Rain

4.2   Snow

4.3   Wind

4.4   Sun

4.5   Dirt, dust and pollution

5   Durability

6   Thermal performance

6.1   Heat loss

6.2   Heat gain

6.3   Condensation risk

7   Movement

7.1   Structural movement

7.2   Thermal movement

7.3   Moisture movement

7.4   Chemical action

7.5   Frost action

8   Noise barrier

9   Fire resistance

10   Security

11   Inspection and maintenance

11.1 External

11.2 Internal

12   Pest infestation

13   Rising damp

14   Construction

Pitched roof
Sections 8 and 11

Flat roof
Sections 8, 9 and 10

Window
Sections 16 and 17

External domestic door
Section 18

Foundations
Sections 1 and 2

criteria associated with cost, structural stability and environmental comfort.

The reasons why great importance is attached to the appearance of external walls are obvious. However, there is no consensus of opinion about what constitutes a good-looking contemporary wall or facade. This does not release the designer from the responsibility of anticipating and controlling how a building will 'weather' and what it will look like after a period of time. A conscious effort should be made to control the passage of rainwater and water-borne pollutants which can stain and erode the building fabric.

We seem to have lost the ability to detail external walls to accommodate time as an inevitable, positive and even enhancing feature. This common failure is in part due to the increased availability of new materials and fashions, often imported with only superficial understanding from other cultures, climates and technologies. Another cause is the difficulty of forecasting the interactions between various components of a wall. To control these requires a clear understanding of the roles (often duplicated or part overlapping) played by or required of the various parts. An external wall must therefore be considered as a single system of interrelated compatible components.

Brickwork Durability, Harding and Smith, Brickwork Development Association, publication DN7, 1983.

Efficient Masonry House Building – Detailing Approach, A. K. Tovey and J. J. Roberts, British Cement Association, 1990.

Textured and Profiled Concrete Finishes, W. Monks, British Cement Association, 1986.

Exposed Aggregate Concrete Finishes, W. Monks, British Cement Association, 1985.

BRE Digest 45 Part 1: 1964, Design and Appearance

BRE Digest 46 Part 2: 1964, Design and Appearance

Appearance Matters – 6: The Weathering of Concrete Buildings, F. Hawes. British Cement Association, 1986.

3 Structural strength and stability

The structural roles performed by external walls can be classified as follows:

1 Walls that play a positive part in a structural system by carrying dead and/or live loads, and/or by acting as stabilizing walls to resist wind, earthquake, etc., and/or by providing positive bracing to other walls or structural framework. Walls in this category may be required to resist some or all of the vertical, horizontal or oblique forces being transmitted from and to other parts of the building's structural system.

2 Walls that have only to carry their own weight plus certain live loads such as those produced by wind, building occupancy, maintenance accidents, etc.

To perform these varying degrees of structural roles external walls can be made of a range of materials and take various forms such as (a) small blocks laid in mortar, (b) dry jointed units of various sizes, (c) homogeneous materials like clay, mud and concrete, (d) sandwich panels of various materials, (e) walls in category 2 above could also be made of single sheet materials such as glass, metal, wood and plastics, or flexible sheets supported in tension on a framework or by air pressure. **External Walls Section 5** covers specific forms of construction.

Building regulations control the requirements for structural walls and BS 5628 (Part 1, Structural use of unreinforced masonry, 1978, and Part 2, Structural use of reinforced and prestressed masonry, 1985) gives design requirements and sets out a clear sequence of calculation procedure taking into account strength of materials, wall shape, length, height/thickness (slenderness) ratios, etc.

AJ Handbook of Building Structure (includes example calculations for concrete, masonry, steel and timber)

Building Structures. A Conceptual Approach, Malcom Millais. Spon, 1996.

The Elements of Structure, W. Morgan. Longman, 1978.

BS 8110 Part 1: 1997, Code of practice for design and construction (concrete), Part 2: 1997, Code of practice for special circumstances, Part 3: 1997, Design charts for singly reinforced beams, doubly reinforced beams and rectangular columns

BS 5628 Part 1: 1978, Structural use of unreinforced masonry and Part 2: Structural use of reinforced and prestressed masonry

BS 5268 Part 2: 1984, Structural use of timber, Code of practice for permissible stress, design, materials and workmanship (see also partial replacement by BS EN 338:1995)

BS 5268 Part 3: 1984, Code of practice for trussed rafter roofs

BS 449 The use of structural steel in building. Part 2: 1969, Metric Units Addendum No 8859:1995

BRE Digest 246: 1981, Strength of brickwork and block work walls: design for vertical load

BDA Handbook to BS 5628 Part 2: Section 1, Background and Materials, Haseltine and Tutt, 1991

BDA Handbook to BS 5628, Structural use of masonry, Part 1 – Unreinforced Masonry, Haseltine and Moore, 1981

BDA Technical Information Paper TIP1: The principles of multi storey cladding

BDA Design Guide 12: 1984, Design of free-standing brick walls

BS 6399 Part 1: 1984, Code of practice for dead and imposed loads

Timber Frame Construction, TRADA, 1994

The Building Regulations, 1991, Part A: Structure

Section 1C Thicknesses of walls in certain small buildings

Section 4 Loading, Structural work of masonry

Section 1E Strip foundations of plain concrete

Section 1B Sizes of timber floor, ceiling and roof members in certain small buildings

Appendix A Tables of sizes of timber floor, ceiling and roof members in single family houses

BRE BR 233: 1993, Briefing guide for timber framed housing

4 Weather barrier

In order to maintain the desired internal conditions an external wall must act as a partial or complete barrier to external conditions. Knowledge is needed of the full range of possible local climate conditions. Check with the local meteorological office and the references given in 4.1 on climate.

4.1 Rain

Rainwater penetration is related more closely to rainfall intensity plus wind pressure than to either the quantity of rain falling or the duration of the rainfall alone. The three basic wall construction methods used to exclude rainwater are:

1 Walls of thick permeable materials which absorb water and then dry out slowly. This method is hardly ever used today in this country (wet walls suffer considerable heat loss, see item 6).

2 Walls of permeable but discontinuous construction such as cavity walls and those covered with small dry jointed units leaving an air gap behind them. This is perhaps the most common and successful form, being based on a sound defensive tactic, i.e. allow the major force to dissipate itself on an outer defence allowing a small proportion to get through

and then provide a simple mechanism (cavity or felt!) for collecting and disposing of any water penetration.

3 Walls having outer faces of impervious materials such as plastics, glass, metal or waterproof renderings or films. This form has been much abused in recent years mainly because both old and new forms of impervious materials often rely for the success or failure of the wall upon the joints between such materials. It has been difficult to devise new joints to accommodate conflicting demands of thermal and structural movement, manufacturing and assembly tolerances as well as overcoming site workmanship and supervision problems.

Tall buildings can receive more rainwater on walls (especially on elevations facing the wind) than on roofs, and special drainage systems might have to be incorporated in the facade. Rain is often driven vertically up the facades of tall buildings and this calls for careful protection on the underside as well as over all weep-holes and projections. BRE BR 117: 1988, Rain penetration through masonry walls: diagnosis and remedial details, shows how the most common causes of rain penetration into buildings can be prevented by careful design.

See item 5 Durability.

BRE 350 Climate and site development: Part 1 General climate of the UK

BRE 350 Climate and site development: Part 2 Influence of microclimate

As water penetration can be severe with accompanying high winds, notice should be taken of *The designer's guide to wind loading of building structures. Part 1: Background, damage survey, wind data and structural classification*. N. J. Cook. Butterworths, 1986.

BS 8104:1992, Code of practice for assessing exposure of walls to wind driven rain.

Building Regulations 1991, Part C: Site preparation and resistance to moisture. C4 Resistance to weather and ground moisture. Section 1 Floors next to the ground. Section 2 Walls.

BRE IP 2/88: Rain penetration of cavity walls: a report of a survey of properties in England and Wales

4.2 Snow

If relevant, consider protecting certain wall openings with snow guards placed at eaves level. Check that wall detailing does not allow snow (or water) retention which upon freezing can damage profiles, joints or jointing materials.

4.3 Wind

Loading depends on shape and height of building, geographical location and exposure. Check extremes of local wind velocity and direction, also on the effect of adjacent buildings. Large buildings or complexes can be modelled in wind tunnel tests to predict turbulence, especially at the base of tall blocks, internal courts and light wells, pedestrian malls, etc. Projections from facades, especially at corners, can cause noise from wind turbulence. In exposed windy locations take special precautions with wall flashings, joint details and surface fixings.

BS 6399 Part 2: 1997, Code of practice for wind loads
Windloading Handbook: Guide to the Use of BS 6399 Part 2, Tom Lawson, Architectural Press, 1996.
BSCP 3 Chapter V, Part 2: 1972, Wind loads
BRE Digest 346: 1989, The assessment of wind loads. Part 1: background and method. There are eight parts to this digest which deal subsequently with the classification of structures, wind climate in the UK, terrain and building factors and gust peak factors, assessment with regard to topography, loading coefficients for building, serviceability and fatigue and internal pressures.
BRE 248: 1993, The gales of January and February 1990: Damage to buildings and structures
CP 47/75 Cladding and the Wind
BRE 138: 1988, The October gale of 1987: Damage to buildings and structures in the south east of England
BDA Design Guide DG4, External walls, design for wind loads, Haseltine and Tutt, 1978 (Rev. 1984)
BRE Digest 141: 1972, Wind environment around tall buildings
Building Regulations 1991, Part Section 4 refers to BSCP 3, Chapter V, Part 2: 1972, Wind loads

4.4 Sun

See item 6.2 Heat gain and item 7.2 Thermal movement. Ultra-violet radiation can cause the breakdown of some mastics and sealants. It can also cause some plastic wall finishes to become brittle due to the evaporation of the plasticizers or degradation of the polymer. Any degradation that changes the surface quality of a material can cause loss of gloss and specifications should be checked with manufacturers. See *Mitchell's Building Series: Finishes*, Yvonne Dean, Longman, 1996, and BRE Digests 227, 228, 229: 1979, Estimation of thermal and moisture movements and stresses, Parts 1, 2 and 3.

If heat is unwanted, especially on flat roofs or facades where the materials used could distort or deteriorate, then surfaces should be chosen that reflect the sun's energy either being as light as possible or of polished metal. High coefficients would be as close to 0.8 or 0.9 as possible (1.0 being theoretical total reflectance) and likely to be white or stainless steel. Low coefficients would imply highly absorbent surfaces like asphalt at 0.09 and unless treated would be severely affected by heat. In some cases high absorbency is wanted, especially if walls are to act as solar collectors, and then dark surfaces are used to absorb and re-radiate heat, termed as *high emissivity* materials. *Low emissivity* materials would then be used to control heat loss, for example certain glasses or aluminium foil used to coat plasterboard to prevent heat loss, as well as resisting the passage of moisture. For whatever solar performance is required the actual material performance and its reflection coefficient or emissivity should be checked with the manufacturer.

BRE IP 26/81: Solar reflective paints

4.5 Dirt, dust and pollution

In a polluted atmosphere the particles deposited on walls become chemically active when combined with rainwater. Check local sources of pollution such as type of industry, heavy traffic and proximity to salt-laden sea air. Choose facade materials to withstand local conditions and detail facade to be 'self-washing' and not overtextured which provides places to collect particulates and corrosive solutions. See item 2 Appearance.

In areas that are heavily polluted, in addition to using special materials and detailing, there is the need to gain regular access for cleaning and maintenance. See item 11 Inspection and maintenance.

Mitchell's Building Series: Finishes, Yvonne Dean, Longman, 1996,
Materials Technology, Yvonne Dean, Longman, 1996.
BRE Digest 280: 1983, Cleaning external surfaces of buildings
Appraising Building Defects, Chapter 8 Instability of Building Materials, G. K. Cook and Dr A. J. Hinks. Longman, 1992.
Environmental Protection Act 1990
Data is available from Local Authorities who have their own monitoring stations for pollution levels.

5 Durability

While load-bearing walls are usually very durable structurally, problems often arise concerning the durability of external finishes and appearance (item 2). On the other hand, lightweight claddings often contain new and relatively untried materials. Matters are made worse because there are still tax incentives to utilize low capital costs and high maintenance costs. Designers should help their clients choose their policy by drawing up alternative initial capital and maintenance cost ratios. Check for compatibility between wall materials and finishes and likely usage by occupants or processes, i.e. school children and their games, vulnerability to damage by various forms of traffic, vandals, etc. Cladding and infill panels can be designed to have shorter life-spans than the structural framework to which they are attached and in this case access and replacement methods must be considered.

A major cause of failure in external wall design is incompatibility not only between but sometimes within the various sub-systems of the wall, the paint system, metal fixings (electrolytic action), mastic and sealant systems. Metals must be protected from corrosion. Some mortars when damp can cause metals – even zinc, lead and aluminium – to corrode. Timber can decay from fungal and insect attack, and brickwork can deteriorate from frost and chemical attack.

BS 7543:1992, Guide to durability of buildings and building elements, products and components
BS 8000 Part 12: 1989, Code of practice for decorative wallcoverings and painting of buildings
BRE 263, 264 and 265: The durability of steel in concrete, Parts 1, 2 and 3
Mitchell's Building Series: Finishes, Yvonne Dean, Longman, 1996
Materials Technology, Yvonne Dean, Longman, 1996.
BR 292: 1995, Cracking in buildings
BRE Digest 177: 1975, Decay and conservation of stone masonry
BS 5268 Part 5: 1989, Code of practice for the preservative treatment of structural timber
BDA Design Guide DG18, 1992, Brickwork Cladding to Steel Framed Buildings, Bradshaw, Buckton & Tonge
BRE Digest 354: 1990, Painting exterior wood
BRE Digest 73: 1985, Preventing decay in external joinery
BRE BR 222: 1992, Recognizing woodrot and insect damage in buildings
BRE Digest 246: 1981, Strength of brickwork and blockwork walls: design for vertical load

The Weathering of Concrete Buildings, F. Hawes. British Cement Association, 1986.
Visual Concrete: Design and Production, W. Monks. British Cement Association, 1988.
Textured and Profiled Concrete Finishes, W. Monks. British Cement Association, 1986.

6 Thermal performance

The required conditions for comfort inside a building are obtained by the passive performance and properties of the external enclosing elements, together with any active internal mechanical services. This relationship must be examined at an early design stage.

Check local weather conditions and orientation of various walls. Heat loss, heat gain and degree of rainwater saturation may vary on different walls of a building and be dependent on microclimate and occupancy.

External walls act as a partial or complete thermal barrier in three main ways:

1 Thermal resistance of the component materials. This is the rate at which heat will travel through a wall by conduction. This is known as thermal transmittance or the U-value of the wall; it is in fact the measure of its thermal insulation. This is defined as the quantity of heat that will pass through a unit area of the wall when the air temperatures on either side differ by one degree. Watts per m² per degree centigrade (W/m² deg C) are the units used for U-values. The lower the U-value the greater the insulating effect of the material. It is important to check mean U-values, i.e. over the complete wall including glazed areas, and to use one of the three methods shown in the Building Regulations for calculating the overall performance of a building. See general references below.

2 Thermal capacity. This is the quantity of heat necessary to raise a unit volume of the wall by unit temperature. Walls of high thermal capacity require a greater amount of heat to raise their temperature by a given amount than do walls of low capacity.

Upon cooling the stored heat is lost by radiation. The degree of loss will depend on the difference in temperature between the wall and its surroundings. The length of time it takes to lose its heat will depend on the amount of heat originally stored. So walls of high thermal capacity are slow to react to temperature changes, whereas walls of low thermal capacity are quick reactors. This implies that greater thermal advantages can be obtained if walls of high thermal capacity are used for buildings which are continuously heated and occupied whereas walls of low thermal capacity might be better used for intermittently heated buildings where quick reaction is required. Low thermal capacity internal linings can be fixed to high capacity walls (item 6.3 Condensation risk).

3 Air movement (*convection*). Air movement through doors, windows and the fabric of external walls has an important and quick-acting effect on heat losses and gains, but it must not be cut down too much – see item 6.3 Condensation risk. (See also **Windows Section 16** and **External Doors Section 18**).

Energy and Environment in Architecture, Nick Baker and Koen Steemers. Spon, 1997.
Energy Efficient Building – A Design Guide, Roaf and Hancock. 1992. Blackwell Scientific.
BS 3533:1981, Glossary of relating thermal insulation terms
BRE Digest 108: rev. 1991, Standard 'U' values
BRE Digest 190: 1976, Heat losses from dwellings
BRE Digest 191, Energy consumption and conservation in buildings
CIBSE Guide: Vol A, Design Data, Section A3, Thermal and other properties of building structures
CIBSE Guide: Vol A, Building Energy Code, Part 1 Guidance towards energy conserving design (1977) Part 2A Calculation of energy demands and targets for new buildings (1981)
The Building Regulations 1991, L Conservation of fuel and power

6.1 Heat loss

Factors that determine heat losses through external walls:

1 Site: geographical location, orientation, local climate, especially wind velocity and rain direction and quantity (walls of porous material lose insulation value when wet).
2 Building design: Building and wall configuration, amount of glazed area, thermal character of wall system as described in item 6.

Heat losses can be modified by the designer and/or the client making adjustments to some or all of the above factors. The usual methods are reducing glazed areas

and increasing the thermal resistance (lowering the 'U' value) of the wall. An acceptable balance must be obtained between the cost of lessening heat losses and taking advantage of passive solar gain. Although the Building Regulations set minimum standards for thermal performance in any building the designer should seek to optimize the energy efficiency of the building fabric and to minimize the use of auxiliary heating to achieve comfort. Some energy-efficient measures may need life-cycle costings checks to measure whether their choice is outweighed by prohibitive initial costs.

Heat loss through windows, see **Windows Section 16**, item 5.

Improving standards of insulation in cavity walls with an outer leaf in facing brickwork, Brick Development Association Publication DN11, 1990.

6.2 Heat gain

Factors that determine heat gain are:

1 Site: all as item 6.1.
2 Building design: amount of glazed area: building and wall configuration; thermal character of wall system; surface colour and texture; degree of heat absorption of the outer facade material.

Heat gain through walls can be modified by adjustment of some or all of these factors. The usual methods adopted are: shading or screening devices; increasing the thermal capacity; optimizing the insulation or adopting a reflective outer surface. A balance must be achieved between optimizing heat gains from solar radiation during the day with unacceptable loss at night.

Heat gain through windows, see **Windows Section 16**, item 5.

6.3 Condensation risk

Modern forms of construction and living patterns have greatly increased the risk of condensation, not only upon internal surfaces but also within wall, floor and roof systems. Traditional wall construction allowed moisture vapour to pass more easily through its fabric as well as through air gaps around doors and windows. In addition there was often less moisture vapour to be vented owing to lower domestic temperatures combined with much greater ventilation rates at moisture sources (through air bricks and chimney flues). With modern wall systems it is essential for designers to estimate by calculation the degree of condensation risk. This check list can only underline the importance of the subject and designers are advised to consult the references listed below.

Avoidance of condensation will rely on a combination of the following points depending on particular circumstances:

1 Keeping the internal surfaces at a temperature above the dew point (this is the temperature at which air becomes saturated and thus deposits moisture; warm air can carry more vapour than cool air). In general this can be achieved by balancing wall insulation, heating and adequate ventilation rates.
2 Reducing the moisture content of the air reaching the vulnerable parts of the wall system. In general this implies ventilation at source (kitchens, bathrooms, laundry rooms etc.) and in some cases, ventilation within the wall system.
3 Using a correctly positioned and efficient vapour barrier. This implies a vapour barrier located on the warm side of the insulation layer to prevent moisture vapour reaching a point within the construction where the lower temperature would cause the air to become saturated and deposit its moisture, i.e. to reach the dew point. Where this point is reached inside building materials it is called interstitial condensation and can cause severe damage to materials as well as saturating porous components (such as insulation), thus reducing insulation values still further and so setting up a worsening spiral of condensation.

In practice vapour barriers are often less efficient than in theory because they become discontinuous through gaps between boarded materials having integral vapour barriers, or because of holes for services and light switches, or by being badly fitted around ducts and corners etc. Unless very special precautions are taken vapour barriers should be regarded as vapour checks only.

BS 8207:1995, Code of practice for energy efficiency in buildings
BRE Digest 110: 1972, Condensation (deals with principles and methods of estimating risks)
BRE DAS 6 External walls: reducing the risk from interstitial condensation
BS 5250:1995, Code of practice for control of condensation in dwellings

7 Movement

Many building failures are the result of inadequate provision for movement in or between materials, elements and components. In certain cases such movement can be in opposite directions, i.e. **a brick infill** panel might expand after laying whereas a **surrounding** concrete frame might shrink upon drying. It is easy to forget that a building always moves by responding to changes in loading and environment. The movements may be small and due to seasonal changes as well as to changes in materials during construction.

Appraising Building Defects, G. Cook and Dr A. J. Hinks. Longman, 1992.
BRE BR 292: 1995, Cracking in buildings, R. B. and L. L. Bonshor
BRE Digest 353, Damage to structures from ground-borne vibration
BRE Digest 223, Wall cladding: designing to minimize defects due to inaccuracies and movement
BRE Digests 227, 228 and 229: 1979, Estimation of thermal and moisture movements and stress, Parts 1, 2 and 3

7.1 Structural movement

These may be caused by:

1 Foundation settlement. Check points of differential loading, i.e. new to old or tall to low buildings, etc.
2 Changing soil conditions, such as the expansion and contraction of clay soils due to wetting and drying, mining and subsidence, etc.
3 Deflection (initial or under load) of cantilevers and spanning members can cause damage to infill panels and cladding systems.

7.2 Thermal movement

Depending on orientation, surface colour and materials, the sun can heat up a facade in this country to between 60°C and 70°C. Under certain conditions this could result in an annual temperature range of around 80°C. Although daily temperature ranges are smaller they can be more damaging because larger temperature gradients may be set up giving stronger internal stresses. Check the linear coefficients of thermal expansion of the proposed wall materials and make adequate allowance (especially at joints between dissimilar materials). For example, an aluminium sheet 5 m long can expand by up to 10 mm and a PVC sheet of the same length by as much as 25 mm.

7.3 Moisture movement

Porous building materials shrink on drying and expand on wetting. Moisture movement (which in normal building conditions is less then thermal movement, except for timber) can nevertheless be quite serious if not allowed for. Cement products, concrete, sand lime bricks, plaster, external renderings, etc. will shrink upon drying and this initial shrinkage is irreversible. 'Controlled' shrinkage joints, cover beads, rebated surrounds etc. are methods usually adopted to accommodate or hide this movement. Clay products expand after firing up to 1% and sometimes even more. Half this initial expansion will have taken place after about one week; this is the reason why bricks should not be laid straight from the kiln (a 2-week delay is normally recommended).

Timber products, in addition to initial movements after fixing, are subject to seasonal movement. In some species radial movement is as little as half the tangential movement whilst movement in length can normally be disregarded. Hardwoods can vary from 'small' to 'large' movements, softwoods vary from 'small' to 'medium' – see *Materials Technology* below.

Materials Technology, Yvonne Dean. Longman, 1996.

7.4 Chemical action

Water must be present for movement to result from chemical action. Examples are: sulphate attack on brickwork which can cause expansion of mortar joints; corrosion of metals which can cause pressure on surrounding materials.

BRE DAS 128, Brickwork: prevention of sulphate attack (design)
BRE Digest 349, Stainless Steel as a building material
BRE IP 14/88: 1988, Corrosion protected and corrosion resistant reinforcement in concrete
BRE IP 13/90: Corrosion of steel wall ties: recognition and their replacement

7.5 Frost action

If water penetrates cracks in the facade and then expands upon freezing, considerable pressures can be exerted causing local movement. Damage can also occur if water used in the building process is allowed to freeze.

Mitchell's Building Series: Finishes, Section 4.5 Frost and freezing mechanisms, Yvonne Dean. Longman, 1996.

8 Noise barrier

Factors that determine sound transmittance through external walls are:

1 mass;
2 air tightness;
3 degree of stiffness.

Traditional walls provided adequate mass and stiffness for most noise reduction purposes (a 275 mm cavity brick wall can give approximately 50 dB reduction) but open windows reduce overall sound reduction. Site and building planning should be organized to reduce noise pollution.

Airborne noise will be a factor for most building types adjacent to airports, flight paths, railways, or existing or proposed trunk roads, or motorways. To check that an external wall will provide sufficient sound insulation, first calculate the amount of external noise, then establish acceptable internal noise levels for building type and occupancy. This will give the degree of sound insulation to be provided by the external wall including openings. Simplified methods of calculation together with tables of acceptance noise levels are contained in the references below.

BS 7445:1995, Description and measurement of environmental noise, Guide to quantities and procedures
BS 8233:1987, Code of practice for sound insulation and noise reduction for buildings
BRE Digests 333 and 334: Sound insulation of separating walls and floors, Part 1 Walls (1988), Part 2 Floors (1993)
BRE Digest 337: 1988, Sound Insulation: basic principles (outlines the physical principles used in other digests)
BRE Digest 338: 1988, Insulation against external noise
BRE BR 238: 1993, Sound control for homes
BRE IP 12/89: 1989, The insulation of dwellings against external noise
BRE IP/21/93: 1993, The noise climate around our homes
The Building Regulations 1991, Part E Resistance to the passage of sound
Mitchell's Building Series: Environment and Services, Chapter 6, Sound, Peter Burberry. Longman, 1997

9 Fire resistance
External walls must:

1 reduce the chance of fire spread to other buildings by containing the fire;
2 reduce the chance of fire spread into a building from outside;
3 avoid the collapse of a building as a result of fire;
4 allow for ease of firefighting;
5 allow for escape.

These objectives can be achieved by the use of suitable materials, correct design and suitable spacing of buildings. Actual fire behaviour can be affected by all the interrelated characteristics of the wall such as materials, openings, building and wall shape, etc.

At an early design stage check the appropriate Building Regulations for their requirements of fire resistance (given in hours) under the Designation of Purpose Groups table.

Roofs at an angle of more than 70° to the horizontal are regarded as walls for fire protection purposes by the Building Regulations.

BS 5588 Part 1: 1990, Code of practice for residential buildings (guide on structural fire precautions and means of escape)

10 Security
Control of illegal entry is an important function of external walls. Check that the degree of security provided is compatible with the degree of risk. The primary and often cheapest defence is the building fabric, its walls, roofs and especially the location and design of its windows and doors (including ironmongery). See **Windows Section 16**, item 11 – Security.

Watchmen and mechanical devices might be necessary for certain degrees of risk but they can rarely – without great expense – make up for high risk construction or high risk location of doors, windows and roof lights. Where security is of prime importance (banks, warehouses, etc.) specialist consultants should be brought in at an early stage.

Advice on security can be obtained from police officers for domestic security and from insurers for commercial and industrial security.

BRE DAS 87 Wood entrance doors: discouraging illegal entry
BRE IP/94: The role of windows in domestic burglary

11 Inspection and maintenance

11.1 External
Check the following:

1 Annual costs, include for regular inspection, cleaning, renewal of finishes, repairs to moving parts.
2 Provision for safe access routes for workmen, safety harness anchorage, provision of mechanical cradles or platforms.
3 Suitability of wall finishes for type of occupancy and usage, i.e. schoolchildren and their games, wheeled or foot traffic close to walls. Consider special protection over vulnerable wall areas.

Cladding of Buildings, Alan J. Brookes. Spon, 1997.
BRE Digest 280: 1983, Cleaning external surfaces of buildings
BRE Digest 297, Surface condensation and mould growth in traditionally built dwellings
BDA Practical Note 7, 1976: Repointing of brickwork
BS 6270 Code of practice for cleaning and surface repair of buildings. Part 1: 1982, Natural stone, cast stone and clay and calcium silicate brick masonry
Cleaning Historic Buildings: Vol 1 Substrates, Soiling and Investigation, Vol 2 Cleaning materials and processes. Nicola Ashurst, 1994. SPAB.
Removal of Stains and Growths from Concrete, D. D. Higgins. British Cement Association, 1982

11.2 Internal
Check the following:

1 If hygiene is important (hospitals, farm buildings, industrial and food processing and storage, etc.) design all edge details to inhibit or prevent the harbouring of dirt.
2 Access for cleaning and maintaining areas above normal height including access to electrical fittings.
3 Suitability of wall finishes as in 11.1.

12 Pest infestation
If relevant (from client or site information) check nature and degree of risk with local authority Environmental Health Department. Wall construction must not allow the entry or harbouring of pests. In some areas bird droppings can be very harmful to certain wall materials. Consider provision of insect and bird screens over openings, including vents to wall cavities.

BRE Digest 238, Reducing the risk of pest infestations, design recommendations and literature review

13 Rising damp

Ground dampness will be transmitted to walls by capillary attraction through permeable materials unless it is prevented by a correctly specified, detailed and installed impervious barrier. This 'damp-proof course' can be of metal; slates (two courses with lapped joints); hot asphalt or pitch; three courses of suitable engineering brick; proprietary materials made of various compositions of bitumen, hessian, felt, metals or polymers.

Points to watch:

1 Appearance. Stepped dpcs on sloping ground can be unsightly. Try to pre-plan the location of vertical links. Thick horizontal dpcs can be ugly. Check type of joint required.
2 Building Regulations call for a minimum height of 150 mm above ground level. Check all finished ground levels around building to make sure this is possible. This is essential when using cladding and industrialized systems of construction because only larger increments are available for adjustment.
3 Continuity of wall and floor damp-proof membrane.
4 Wall cavities must extend at least 150 mm below dpcs to avoid bridging by mortar droppings.
5 When specifying dpc materials consider loading, flexibility and methods of joining materials.
6 Faults often occur because too narrow a dpc is either specified or actually used, or because a dpc material which is quite satisfactory on a straight run cannot accommodate complex changes of level or direction.

BSCP 102:1973 and 1978, Protection of buildings against water from the ground
BRE Digest 245, Rising damp in walls: diagnosis and treatment
BRE Digest 380: 1993, Damp proof courses
BS 743:1970 and 1991, Specification for materials for damp proof courses
Building Regulations 1991, Part C Site Preparation and resistance to moisture

14 Construction

External walls, like other building elements, should not be designed without consideration of the site and construction processes. Site location, access, layout and storage facilities, together with the availability of local materials, craftsmen and production capacity must all be taken into account.

The specific implications of various wall types are mentioned under the headings of the basic wall types in **Walls Section 4**.

Trade and research organizations

Brick Development Association (BDA), Woodside House, Winkfield, Windsor, Berks SL4 2DX (tel. 01344-885651, fax 01344-890129).

British Cement Association (BCA), Century House, Telford Avenue, Crowthorne, Berks RG11 6YS (tel. 01344-762676, fax 01344-761214).

British Institute of Cleaning Science, Whitworth Chambers, George Row, Northampton NN1 1DF (tel. 01604-30124, fax 01604-231489).

Building Conservation Trust, Apartment 39, Hampton Court Palace, East Molesey, Surrey KT8 9BS (tel 0181-943 2277, fax 0181-943 9552).

Building Maintenance Information, 85–87 Clarence Street, Kingston upon Thames, Surrey KT1 1RB (tel. 0181-546 7555, fax 0181-547 1238).

Chartered Institution of Building Services` Engineers (CIBSE), Delta House, 222 Balham High Road, London SW12 9BS (tel. 0181-675 5211, fax 0181-673 5880).

Chartered Insurance Institute, 20 Aldermanbury, London EC2V 7HY (tel. 0171-606 3835).

Steel Construction Institute, Silwood Park, Ascot, Berks SL5 7QN (tel. 01344-6233454, fax 01344-22944) (for publications on structural steelwork, handbooks and design guides).

Structural Clay Products Ltd, Peck House, 95 Fore Street, Hereford TRADA Technology Ltd (Timber Research and Development Association), Stocking Lane, Hughenden Valley, High Wycombe, Bucks HP14 4ND (tel. 01494-563091, fax 01494-565487).

External Walls: Basic Types Section 4

SMM7 F Masonry

(See Section 3 for general factors; and Section 5 for detailed sections)

Notes and references

Items are cross-referenced from the diagrams. This section deals in general terms with basic forms of external wall construction. It should be read in conjunction with **External Walls Section 3** (which contains general references for external walls and general factors) and **External Walls Section 5** (which covers specific forms of construction). British Standards and BRE Digests should be checked for current amendments. Addresses of relevant trade and research organizations are listed at the end of the section.

Definitions

Although external walls have been classified by their degree of permeability they can also be described by the following structural roles they perform:

1 Walls that play a positive part in a structural system by carrying dead and/or live loads; and/or by acting as stabilizing walls to resist wind, earthquake, etc.; and/or by providing positive bracing to other walls or structural framework. Walls in this category may be required to resist some or all of the vertical, horizontal or eccentric forces being transmitted from and to other parts of the building's structural system.
2 Walls that have only to carry their own weight plus certain live loads such as those produced by wind, building occupancy, accidents, maintenance, etc.

To perform these varying degrees of structural role, external walls can be made of a wide range of materials and take many forms such as (a) small blocks laid in mortar; (b) dry jointed units; (c) homogeneous materials like clay, mud and concrete; (d) sandwich panels of various materials; (e) single sheet materials. Walls in category 2 above could be of rigid sheet materials such as glass, metal, plastics, or fibreboards bound with cement etc., or of flexible membranes supported in tension on a framework or by air pressure.

Depending on the circumstances, and with varying degrees of economy and performance, external walls in each of the above structural categories can also fall into any of the categories of permeability shown in diagrams 15 to 17.

Depending on the materials and insulation used, dew point calculations should be done to make sure there is no interstitial condensation in the wall.

15 Impermeable facing wall or skin

Impermeable walls depend upon an outer barrier impervious to air or moisture, their success or failure resting in turn upon a complex set of physical and human interactions. Like all elements made up from separate parts the aim is to achieve a single system of interrelated compatible components.

Water barriers can be made of relatively thin and rigid materials such as glass, ceramics, metal, plastics, cement-based fibreboards, etc., or of flexible materials such as bituminous felts and plastics sheet, or of coatings such as waterproof renderings, or of thin films such as paint and silicone systems.

General points to watch

(a) The joints and edges of the water barrier are more vulnerable than the barrier material itself, not only because of the care necessary in design, workmanship and site supervision but also because rainwater collection and run-off on impermeable surfaces can result in heavy rainwater penetration at joints and edges. These are also the details which have to accommodate movement.

BRE DAS 98 Windows: resisting rain penetration at perimeter joints (design)
BRE Digest 217: 1978, Wall cladding defects and their diagnosis
BRE 214: 1992, Understanding and improving the weathertightness of large panel system dwellings
BR 93: 1986, Overcladding external walls of large panel system dwellings
BS 6093:1993, Code of practice for design of joints and jointing in building construction
BRE Digest 223: 1978, Wall cladding: designing to minimize defects due to inaccuracies and movement

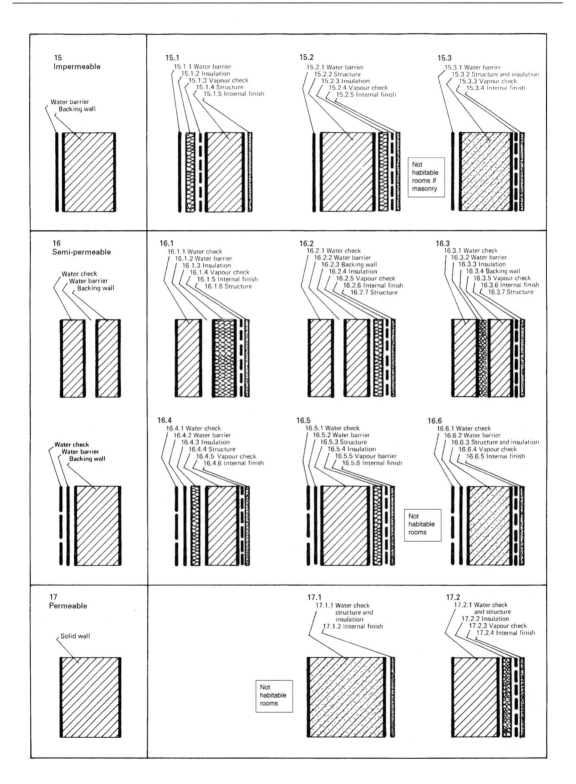

15
Impermeable

Water barrier
Backing wall

15.1
15.1.1 Water barrier
15.1.2 Insulation
15.1.3 Vapour check
15.1.4 Structure
15.1.5 Internal finish

15.2
15.2.1 Water barrier
15.2.2 Structure
15.2.3 Insulation
15.2.4 Vapour check
15.2.5 Internal finish

15.3
15.3.1 Water barrier
15.3.2 Structure and insulation
15.3.3 Vapour check
15.3.4 Internal finish

Not habitable rooms if masonry

16
Semi-permeable

Water check
Water barrier
Backing wall

16.1
16.1.1 Water check
16.1.2 Water barrier
16.1.3 Insulation
16.1.4 Vapour check
16.1.5 Internal finish
16.1.6 Structure

16.2
16.2.1 Water check
16.2.2 Water barrier
16.2.3 Backing wall
16.2.4 Insulation
16.2.5 Vapour check
16.2.6 Internal finish
16.2.7 Structure

16.3
16.3.1 Water check
16.3.2 Water barrier
16.3.3 Insulation
16.3.4 Backing wall
16.3.5 Vapour check
16.3.6 Internal finish
16.3.7 Structure

Water check
Water barrier
Backing wall

16.4
16.4.1 Water check
16.4.2 Water barrier
16.4.3 Insulation
16.4.4 Structure
16.4.5 Vapour check
16.4.6 Internal finish

16.5
16.5.1 Water check
16.5.2 Water barrier
16.5.3 Structure
16.5.4 Insulation
16.5.5 Vapour barrier
16.5.6 Internal finish

16.6
16.6.1 Water check
16.6.2 Water barrier
16.6.3 Structure and insulation
16.6.4 Vapour check
16.6.5 Internal finish

Not habitable rooms

17
Permeable

Solid wall

17.1
17.1.1 Water check structure and insulation
17.1.2 Internal finish

Not habitable rooms

17.2
17.2.1 Water check and structure
17.2.2 Insulation
17.2.3 Vapour check
17.2.4 Internal finish

BS 3712, Building and construction sealants, in four parts covering methods of test for all aspects of materials and application.
Cladding of Buildings, Alan J. Brookes. Spon, 1997.

(b) Differential movement between the components of the backing wall must be calculated and allowances made for this movement in the sizes and detailing of components. Movement can be caused by the different thermal and structural characteristics of the components (expansion, contraction, bending, deflection, warping, etc.). Another form of movement is caused by drying and wetting from initial drying out after construction, or seasonal cycles). See **External Walls Section 3**, item 7 Movement.

(c) Workmanship and site supervision must be of a high standard and both are related to cost. Even 'fail-safe' and rear drainage systems require careful installation. If the water barrier relies on joints being perfect, the contract documents must be clear regarding legal responsibilities and guarantees. This is often covered by writing a performance specification for the materials and construction. On large contracts, specialist supervision may be needed and sums allowed for the building and testing of typical construction details to simulate joint and edge performance.

(d) Mechanical fixings, bonding and backing materials using adhesives and beddings should be chosen with extreme care for they must accommodate differential movements between facing materials and backing wall, have to be fully compatible in terms of strength, chemical composition (consider corrosion and breakdown), thermal characteristics (consider cold bridges and pattern staining), as well as cost and durability. Advice should be sought from the relevant research organizations.

(e) Dimensional compatibility might be essential where the water barrier is formed of rigid sheets or panels which are required to be fixed back to forms of construction with very different rates of movement, such as onto a coursed masonry backing wall. Similarly, factory-made components fixed to site-made, or erected structural frames, may also have to accommodate quite different tolerances and rates of movement.

BRE Digest 199: 1977, Getting good fit
BS 5606:1990, Guide to accuracy in building

BS 6954, Tolerances for building. Part 1: 1988, Recommendations for basic principles for evaluation and specification

(f) Condensation risk must be estimated particularly for non-traditional wall systems. This is critical where a water barrier of an impermeable material is placed directly over an insulant as in diagram 15.10. See **External Walls Section 3**, item 6.3 Condensation risk.

(g) Sequence of erection and access for application of water barrier. Some wall systems require external access whereas others can be constructed off floor slabs. (Also consider access for maintenance and cleaning. See **External Walls Section 3**, item 11.)

(h) Vandalism could destroy the water barrier or its jointing system. Estimate degree of risk adjacent to walking/playing areas and external staircases and provide any necessary protection.

15.1 Impermeable wall with insulation external to structure

One of the merits of this form of wall is that the structure is maintained at room temperature and where it is of solid (as opposed to framed) construction lends itself to buildings with continuous heating. See **External Walls Section 3**, item 6 Thermal performance. This system can be made up from prefabricated parts or from site assembled materials. In both cases the aim must be to achieve continuity of water barrier, insulation and vapour check. Where the water barrier is placed directly in front of the insulation check that the barrier material can withstand the resulting thermal stresses. This will influence the colour and the reflective properties of the barrier.

15.1.1 Water barrier

In this case the water barrier can be metal, glass, asbestos, plastics, treated timber, various compositions and forms of bituminous products, etc. See standard references for comprehensive list of materials and their qualities.

Cladding of Buildings, Alan J. Brookes. Spon, 1997.
BS CP 143 Code of practice for sheet roof and wall coverings.
    Part 1: 1958, Aluminium, corrugated and troughed
    Part 5: 1954, Zinc
    Part 10: 1973, Galvanised corrugated steel
    Part 12: 1988, Copper

Part 15: 1986, Aluminium metric units

Part 16: 1974, Semi-rigid asbestos bitumen sheet

BS 8297:1995, Code of practice for design and installation of non-loadbearing precast concrete cladding

BS 8298:1994, Code of practice for design and installation of natural stone cladding and lining

BS 3830:1973 (1994), Specification for vitreous enamelled steel building components

BS 4868:1972, Specification for profiled aluminium sheet for building

'Cor-ten steel', British Steel Corporation

The Lead Sheet Manual, Lead Development Association

BRE Digest 161, Reinforced Plastics cladding panels

BRE Digest 407, Timber for joinery

BRE BR 299: 1992, Wood preservation in Europe: development of standards for preservatives and treated wood

15.1.2 Insulation

A wide range of insulating materials is possible in this location. They can be in the form of rigid or semi-rigid boards, quilts, expanded or foamed plastics, etc. Normally, the basic materials would be glass fibre, mineral wool, expanded plastics, wood/straw/cementitious compositions, shredded paper, natural wool etc. Check required ratings for spread of flame, combustibility, smoke emission and 'drip' quality. The thickness of insulation should be derived from thermal calculations. In this case check that the specified insulant can withstand the estimated temperatures behind the water barrier. There is considerable concern over the manufacture of insulation and as to whether the manufacturing process is CFC-free for the polymeric materials. The fibre length and diameter for the mineral wool/glass wool products is also of concern, where installers have to be particularly careful because of health risks in handling these materials. Specifiers should satisfy themselves that insulation products comply in their manufacture and installation with latest EC regulations and health and safety issues.

BS 3958 Thermal insulating materials. Part 5: 1986, Specification for bonded man-made mineral fibre slabs

BS 2972:1989, Methods of test for inorganic thermal insulating materials

BS 3533:1962, Glossary of thermal insulation terms

BS 3837 Expanded polystyrene boards. Part 1: 1986, Specification for boards manufactured from expandable beads. Part 2: 1990, Specification for extruded boards

BS 3869:1965, Rigid expanded polyvinyl chloride for thermal insulation purposes and building applications

BS 3927:1986, Specification for rigid p (PF) for thermal insulations in the form of slabs and profiled sections

BRE Digest 236: 1980, Cavity insulation

BRE GBG5 1990: Choosing between cavity, internal and external wall insulation

Manufacturers' literature for blockwork walls is usually very comprehensive with regard to their insulation values and detailing with integrated insulation.

Cavity Insulated Walls, Specifier's Guide. Brick Development Association, 1985.

15.1.3 Vapour check (see also 15.2.4)

If proposed as an integral part of a panel system make sure continuity is achieved across the jointing system, and that the insulant is fully protected around its edges. Materials normally used are bituminous felt, metal foil, plastic sheet, etc. All materials must be specified thick enough to reduce their water vapour permeability as much as possible. Overlapping and sealing at joints, around openings and at edges is essential and good site supervision important for once the vapour check is covered up it is difficult to detect faults. The reasons why vapour checks are located on the warm side of the insulation are given in **External Walls Section 3**, item 6.3.

BS 3012:1970, Low and intermediate density polythene sheet for general purposes

BS 4646:1970, High density polythene sheet for general purposes

BS 747:1977, Specification for roofing felts

15.1.4 Structure

In this case the support system may be of solid or framed construction. See item 15 for comments relating to compatibility and differential movements between backing wall and facing materials, and item 15.1 for the thermal merits of solid construction.

External Walls Section 3, item 3 Structural strength and stability contains general points listing both general and specific structural references.

15.1.5 Internal finish

If required at all, this can be any of the standard wet or dry finishes such as paint, plaster, plasterboard, plywood, plastics, etc. On solid backing walls foil-backed plasterboard on treated battens would reduce considerably the risk of condensation. Check the spread of flame properties relative to the building type.

Building Regulations 1991, Part B Fire Spread
Mitchell's Building Series: Finishes, Yvonne Dean. Longman, 1996.
BS 5492:1990, Code of practice for internal plastering
BS 1230:1994, Part 1 Specification for plasterboard excluding materials submitted to secondary operations
BS 1191 Specification for gypsum building plasters. Part 1: 1973 (1994), Excluding premixed lightweight plasters. Part 2: 1973 (1994), Premixed lightweight plasters.
BS 6160 Part 6: 1984, Section 6.6.2, Plaster glossary of building and civil engineering terms

15.2 Impermeable wall with insulation on the inside of the structure

One of the aspects of this form of construction is that internal air and surface temperatures can be raised quickly. It is therefore suited to buildings likely to receive intermittent heating inputs, and which can warm up quickly particularly if the structure is of solid construction. However, the range of temperatures across the wall can be extreme, making the building susceptible to frost attack in winter, and the structure should therefore be checked for condensation risks.

Whether or not this form of construction will use less or more energy than that shown in 15.1 will depend on the individual circumstances. Another advantage is that both the insulation and vapour check can be fixed from the inside under relatively sheltered conditions, and this is often the only way of installing insulation in existing solid wall constructions. The insulation is also less likely to be damaged by rain penetration. With some forms of framed or solid structures this form of construction has the disadvantage that as the structure is outside of the insulation it will be subjected to both seasonal and overnight temperature changes.

15.2.1 Water barrier

In addition to the methods and materials mentioned in item 15.1.1, this type of water barrier can be constructed of frost-resisting ceramic or mosaic facings suitably bonded to a solid backing wall. Alternatively, a panel system can be used supported by a framed or solid backing wall; with waterproof renderings, or coatings or thin films such as paint or silicone seals. Very great care is required in specifying, detailing, workmanship and supervision if a successful water

barrier is to be achieved. It is normal practice to work closely with a manufacturer, or to provide a performance specification that can be complied with. For large installations it is normal to construct and weather-test sample sections of construction.

Thin films and coatings are subject to cracking, after shrinkage from hardening, or to movement of the backing wall. Thin films also require regular maintenance if they are to remain efficient. See the general notes on compatibility and movement in item 15.

On rendered solid walls, cracks in the water barrier can result in severe frost and chemical (efflorescence and sulphate) damage to the water barrier and/or the backing wall. On framed walls, cracks in the water barrier can result in metal corrosion and rot and/or moisture movement in timber framework. (Similarly water vapour produced inside a building must not be allowed to penetrate the structure or insulation. This means that ventilated cavities and/or correctly designed and installed vapour checks are essential.)

BS 6477:1992, Specification for water repellants for masonry surfaces
BRE Digest 196: 1976, External rendered finishes
BRE Digest 197: 1982, Painting walls. Part 1: choice of paint
BRE Digest 198: 1977, Painting walls. Part 2: failures and remedies
BRE Current Papers: CP21/77 Porosity of building materials, a collection of published results; CP29/76 External rendering, Scottish experience
BS 5262:1991, Code of practice for external renderings
Mitchell's Building Series: Finishes, Chapter 5, section 5.3 Renders, Chapter 5, section 5.1 Internal and external tiling, Yvonne Dean. Longman, 1986.
BS 5385 Code of practice for wall tiling. Part 2: 1991, External ceramic wall tiling and mosaics
Recommended methods of fixing frost ceramic wall tiles; technical specification for ceramic wall tiles, British Ceramic Tile Council

15.2.2 Structure

Comments and references as for 15.1.4. In this case the structure will be subjected to overnight and seasonal external temperature changes. Check that adequate allowance has been made for thermal movement.

15.2.3 Insulation

Comments and references as for 15.1.2. Avoidance of cold bridges is more difficult when the insulation is on the inside of the wall as in this case, careful detailing being required at all horizontal and vertical structural junctions. See **Flat Roofs in Detail, Section 10**, eaves detail. Where the insulant has an integral vapour check, make sure continuity is achieved across joints.

In this case special care must be taken in respect of fire risk when choosing the insulation material. See references under item 15.1.2.

15.2.4 Vapour check
Comments and references as for 15.1.3. In this location, the vapour check is vulnerable to being punctured as services are installed and before it is protected by the internal finish, so is likely to need local sealing. It is therefore essential that site supervisors make special inspections before the vapour check is covered up.

15.2.5 Internal finish
This would normally be a dry-boarded system laid over the vapour check or it could be integral with the vapour check (foil-backed plasterboard) and/or the insulation (proprietary finishes are available). The latter are very useful for upgrading existing walls. See references 15.1.5.

15.3 Impermeable wall with combined insulation and structure
This form of construction could be assembled on site from prefabricated components or separate materials; or it could be prefabricated as a structural unit. The general points mentioned in item 15 apply, particularly those concerning joints, compatibility and differential movement. If made from masonry, this wall would only be suitable for enclosures not needing to have a good thermal performance and, because of the lack of insulation, could not be used for habitable rooms. If the structural form can incorporate insulation (see 15.3.2) it would have a wider application. Some more unusual building solutions could comply with current regulations. These may include straw bale structures that are rendered for weather protection and earth-built walling systems, for example the French 'Iso-chanvre' system of hemp and cement.

15.3.1 Water barrier
Comments and references as for 15.1.1 and 15.2.1. Some forms of structural panel or tray may have an integral water barrier.

15.3.2 Structure and insulation
This could be either a proprietary panel or pans of structural metal, concrete or plastics, prefabricated with an insulated core; or an in situ system of lightweight aggregate or aerated concrete slabs or blocks or 'poured in place' no-fines concrete.

15.3.3 Vapour checks
Comments as for 15.2.4.

15.3.4 Internal finish
Comments as for 15.2.5. References as for 15.1.5. Plastering on no-fines concrete and lightweight aggregate concrete requires special attention. Check with aggregate suppliers.

16 Semi-permeable facing wall or skin
This category covers all wall systems which allow rain or snow to penetrate beyond the overall external face before being stopped by a water barrier. This may be in the form of a cavity or a sheet material such as bituminous felt, plastics or a waterproof building paper. Included in this category are walls covered with small dry jointed units such as tiles, slates, shingles, etc. This is the most common domestic wall system now in use in this country as it is well suited to our climatic conditions and building traditions. It offers two levels of defence as well as allowing greater tolerances in materials and workmanship than those wall systems described in item 15. General points to watch:

(a) The water barrier (whether a cavity or a sheet material), being the final defence, must be carefully detailed and constructed. The most vulnerable parts of a semi-permeable wall occur in those positions where if water has penetrated the water check, it must be collected and then routed back to the outside before reaching the backing wall. These vulnerable locations will usually be around openings, at parapets and where floors or roofs interrupt the general line or plane of the barrier. The final responsibility in this wall system will rest upon damp-proof courses, cavity trays, unbridged cavities, flashings and/or sheet-water barriers. Once these details are built in and covered up, faults can be both difficult to locate and costly to remedy.

(b) The siting of individual component fixings which make up a wall system must comply with theoretical design requirements, e.g. correct centres for stability and resistance to wind forces, as well as accessibility for assembly allowing for sequence of trades, access for specialist fixers and their tools. To achieve this requires a full understanding of the functions of an external wall, including structural support, weather resistance, thermal and noise control, fire resistance, and moisture vapour control.

(c) Compatibility of the various components and fixings is essential. Check in terms of differential thermal, structural and moisture movement as well as for chemical compatibility, especially between fixings and components. Where new materials or methods are combined with traditional construction check for harmful interactions, which include chemical reactions or mechanical stress. If in any doubt consult the appropriate national research organization or manufacturers of components.

(d) Condensation risk must be calculated. See **External Walls Section 3**, item 6.3 for comments and references.

(e) Fixings, flashings and dpc systems require careful specification, design and installation in respect of chemical interaction (corrosion and breakdown), accessibility (renewal), durability and strength. If possible avoid complex profiles for dpcs and cavity trays. If unavoidable make sure the material is suitable and that craftsmen can construct the detail. Three-dimensional drawings are advisable for all dpc details, particularly around openings and at junctions etc. For complex details, it should not be left to site operatives to make up ad-hoc details at awkward or complex junctions and sample panels/junctions should be used together with good supervision.

(f) Vandalism can damage vulnerable facing materials, fixings and flashings. Once exposed, a sheet water barrier can easily be punctured. Estimate the risk to surfaces and details adjacent to walking/playing areas and external staircases, adding protection if necessary.

16.1 Semi-permeable wall with cavity water barrier and thermal-insulating backing wall

This is a common form of construction for domestic buildings. It provides an economic and practical arrangement of materials to achieve normal domestic standards of strength, weather protection, thermal and sound insulation as well as fire resistance. Brick veneer over a framed backing wall is considered under 16.4.

16.1.1 Water check

The outer leaf can be of concrete blocks or panels, bricks or other forms of masonry. Half-brick thick outer

leaves in stretcher bond are most common. Specifications for mortar are of great importance and must be related to the masonry, particularly in terms of strength. Both vertical (perpend) and horizontal (bed) joints must be well made to avoid gaps which will give direct rain penetration and frost damage.

The more impermeable the brick, the more critical the joint workmanship. Various ways of jointing and pointing brick and blockwork should be investigated as they seriously affect the appearance of the outer leaf.

In practically all locations it is to be assumed that at certain times in a cavity wall water will be present on the inside face of an absorbent outer leaf, and adequate precautions must be taken to ensure that it drains to the outside and does not reach the backing wall. See 16.1.2. For comments relating to dampness rising from the ground, see **External Walls Section 3**, item 13.

BS 5628 Code of practice for use of masonry. Part 1:1992, Structural use of unreinforced masonry

BRE Digest 246: 1981, Strength of brickwork and blockwork walls: design for vertical load

BRE Digest 157: 1992, Calcium silicate (sand lime, flint lime) brickwork (includes advice on mortars)

BRE Digest 362: 1991, Building mortar (gives advice on mixes and their suitability for various locations)

BRE BR 117: 1988, Rain penetration through masonry walls: diagnosis and remedial detail

BRE IP16/88: Ties for cavity walls, new developments

BS 3921:1995, Specification for clay bricks

BS 4729:1990, Specification for dimensions of bricks of special shapes and sizes

BS 187:1978, Specification for calcium silicate (sand lime and flint lime) bricks

BS 6073 Part 2: 1981, Method for specifying pre-cast concrete masonry units

BS 6073 Part 1: 1981, Specification for pre-cast concrete masonry units

BS 4315 Part 2: 1983, Permeable walling construction (water penetration)

16.1.2 Water barrier

Cavity water barriers must be continuous to function properly and not be bridged by anything that will allow moisture to be transferred from the outer to inner leaf. Site supervision is essential. Cavities should be free of all projections (including mortar from bed joints) in order to avoid the formation of accidental bridging by mortar droppings or other debris. Cavities should be wide enough to allow for cleaning as the work proceeds; 50 mm is considered the normal minimum width for masonry walls. See BS 5628 Code of practice for use of masonry, Part 3: 1985, Materials and components, design and workmanship. It is usual to recommend a maximum of 75 mm cavity where either of the leaves is less than 100 mm thick. For structural reasons 150 mm is considered a maximum width in order for wall ties to adequately tie two leaves together. See 16.1.6 for comments and references to wall ties.

Dpcs must be placed between inner and outer leaves wherever they are returned into each other such as around openings. Cavities should be continued down at least 150 mm below the lowest dpc and closed off at roof level to prevent damp air reaching the roof construction. Cavities should not be ventilated other than by the normal drainage weep-holes because the wall would lose much of its thermal and noise insulation value. In extremely wet conditions, such as exposed sites at high level or near the coast, drainage weep-holes may not be appropriate and a completely different system of external wall detailing may have to be devised. All cavities should be drained and in brick outer leaves it is normal practice to provide weep-holes at the bottoms of cavities in the form of open vertical joints at 900 mm c/c.

BS 5628 Part 1: 1992, Structural use of unreinforced masonry
Building Regulations 1991, Part C9 Site preparation and resistance to moisture
BRE Digest 380, Damp proof courses

16.1.3 Insulation and backing wall
This could be in the form of lightweight aggregate blocks; aerated autoclaved concrete blocks or panels; or a framed backing wall with insulation placed between framing members. (Metal and concrete frame components require protection from corrosion and insulation to prevent cold bridges; timber frames require protection from moisture originating either internally or externally.)

Lightweight concrete block inner leaves contribute to an improved thermal performance for external domestic walls and are cheaper to build than brick inner leaves. However, cavity insulation must be used to bring the wall up to standard for habitable rooms or premises.

Blocks 100 mm thick with a minimum strength of 2.8 N/mm^2 are normal for inner leaves of two storey domestic buildings. Type 'B' lightweight concrete blocks (BS 6073) may be used on inner leaves below dpc level (but check for presence of ground sulphates).

Concrete blocks are manufactured which contribute to the overall thermal performance and sound insulation properties of a wall. Specifiers and designers are advised to consider carefully the 'as built' moisture content of lightweight concrete blocks (high actual moisture content can seriously upset U-value calculations as well as causing movement problems – see also 16.1.4).

Design in Blockwork, M. Gage and T. Kirkbride. Architectural Press, third edition, 1980.
BRE Digest 108, Standard U-values
BRE Digest 190, Heat losses from dwellings
BS 6073 Part 2: 1981, Method for specifying pre-cast concrete masonry units
BS 6073 Part 1: 1981, Specification for pre-cast concrete masonry units

16.1.4 Vapour check
See 15.1.3 for general comments and references and 15.2.3 where insulation is placed between members of a framed backing wall. It is normal practice to incorporate a vapour check, which should be positioned on the inside of the construction, usually behind plasterboard on ceilings. The object is to prevent moisture-laden air from getting into the construction and then condensing on timber components causing rot, or on insulation making it become ineffective. For certain domestic rooms of high risk, foil-backed plasterboard on treated battens will provide an extra degree of safety. Designers should be guided by calculations derived from 'in-use' figures relating to intermittent heating and moisture content of wall components.

There is an alternative view which considers that the wall should act as a 'breathing' form of construction, allowing any moisture-laden air to permeate and evaporate without harming the construction; various experiments have been carried out, chiefly with timber framed construction. In timber houses the plywood sheathing acts as a moisture barrier in its own right (the Gimson/TRADA ecowall for example). Houses designed with a negative air pressure will only receive outdoor air and there is little risk of indoor air migrating back into the construction. The traditional airways in old fireplaces often ensured this one-way airflow.

Whatever systems are designed, the main point is to keep materials dry, to keep air circulating and not to allow the dew point to fall within the construction.

16.1.5 Internal finish
Comments and references as for 15.1.5.

16.1.6 Structure
The Building Regulations lay down limits of height and length of walls and thickness of leaves for cavity walls. See general comments and references for structure, **External Walls Section 3**, item 3.

If possible the roof loads should be distributed over both leaves but eccentric loading from roofs or floors is acceptable providing the two leaves are properly tied across the cavity and made to act together. In this way the two separate leaves can be stiffened and be thinner than if they had to act independently. Wall ties must be corrosion-resistant and strong enough to provide this extra stiffness in the separate leaves. They must also prevent water passing across the cavity as well as discouraging mortar droppings resting upon them during wall construction. BS 1243 (1982) specifies three types of metal wall tie which satisfy these requirements. Note the important Amendment to this BS which increases protection against corrosion required on ferrous wire wall ties – the result of recent failures. See BRE IP 12/90: Corrosion of wall ties: history of occurrence, background and treatment. Wall ties should not be bent up or down across cavities as this will impair their strength. BS 5628 gives guidance on the spacing of wall ties, but generally they are staggered at 900 mm horizontally and 450 mm vertically, and at 300 mm vertically at jambs of openings. (Only wall ties of the butterfly wire type should be used where sound reduction is important across cavity walls, particularly party walls.)

Below ground level the cavity is usually filled with weak concrete up to 150 mm below dpc level. This prevents the tendency of the two leaves to move towards each other due to pressure from the surrounding ground.

The weep-holes mentioned in 16.1.2 are placed above the concrete filling.

BRE Digest 246, Strength of brickwork and block work walls: design for vertical load
BS 1243:1982, Specification for metal ties for cavity wall construction and Amendment
BS 5628 Part 1: 1992, Structural use of unreinforced masonry
The Building Regulations 1991, Part A Structure

16.2 Semi-permeable wall with cavity water barrier and thermal insulation on the inside of backing wall
This form of construction is often used where the backing wall consists of brick or dense concrete block to accommodate high loading (e.g. for 'calculated' brickwork or where support is required for certain types of concrete floors or roofs).

Another use is where existing brick cavity walls of insufficient thermal insulation require to be upgraded and where cavity infill (see 16.3.3) is inappropriate.

Serious interstitial condensation can arise if the dew point is allowed to occur in the region of the interface between insulant and backing wall; see comments and references in **External Walls Section 3**, item 6.3 Condensation risk. An advantage of this form of construction is that internal air and surface temperatures can be raised quickly – see 15.2.

16.2.1 Water check
Comments as for 16.1.1

16.2.2 Water barrier
Comments as for 16.1.2.

16.2.3 Backing wall
For new work this might consist of brick or concrete block, or be a framed inner leaf. In the latter case it would be subjected to external temperature variations and allowance might have to be made for thermal movement.

16.2.4 Insulation
General comments and references as for 15.1.2.

Particular comments as for 15.2.3. Interstitial condensation must not be allowed to occur in the region of the interface between insulant and backing wall, especially if an adhesive is proposed as a method of fixing. Failures of this kind have occurred due to wrongly specified adhesives and faulty or non-existent vapour checks. Rigid insulation on treated battens is more advisable for upgrading existing buildings. See Guide 155, Energy efficient refurbishment of housing, published by BRECSU at the BRE for the Department of the Environment, 1995.

16.2.5 Vapour check
General comments and references as for 15.1.3.

Particular comments as for 15.2.4. Where vapour checks are being installed over insulation applied to existing walls, great care is required if continuity and insulant edge protection is to be achieved around openings, electric light switches, etc.

16.2.6 Internal finish
Comments as for 15.2.5.

16.2.7 Structure
Comments and references as for 16.1.6.

16.3 Semi-permeable wall with cavity water barrier containing thermal insulation
Two forms of cavity filling are covered by this type of wall construction; the first and most controversial is where the cavity width is completely filled with an insulant, whether of the foamed, loose fill, rigid slab or batt variety. The second is where rigid or semi-rigid boards are placed in, but do not fill, the cavity space. Depending on the insulant specified, an air gap may be needed, especially if joints between panels might provide a clear pathway for water seepage.

Comments relating to the various kinds of insulating materials are made under 16.3.3.

The subject of completely filled wall cavities may be summarized briefly as follows:

(a) An existing cavity brick wall (250 mm or 11") plastered on the inside and of 'normal' exposure, will only give a U-value of about 1.7 W/m^2 deg C. Cavity insulation must be used to achieve the minimum elemental value of exposed walls of 0.45 W/m^2 K.

(b) Cavity fill insulation (loose) must comply with the Building Regulations C4 2.13 and be installed in accordance with BS 8208 Guide to the assessment of suitability of external cavity walls for filling with thermal insulants. Part 1: 1985, Existing cavity construction.

(c) Cavity fill should be used only where it is covered by an Agrément Certificate or alternatively a BSI Certificate, when urea formaldehyde foam is used in accordance with BS 5618 and BS 5617 and certain notifications are given to the local authority. Paragraph 4.15 of Document C requires that the filling of cavity walls should follow BS 8208. Guide to assessment of suitability of external cavity walls for filling with thermal insulants, Part 1: 1985 Existing traditional cavity construction.

(d) In new buildings a cavity of 50 mm must be maintained if there is partial insulation fill in the cavity. Building Regulations, Section C.

(e) Cavity fill leaves the mass of the backing wall on the side to be heated; this implies that it is more suited to buildings receiving continuous heating as described in 15.1 (see also **External Walls Section 3** item 6 Thermal performance). As most housing receives intermittent heat inputs (which with increasing energy costs might become even more intermittent), careful calculations are required before deciding whether to upgrade existing buildings by internal lining or cavity filling. Although any solution should optimize performance it is useful to calculate the payback period. This compares initial costs with running costs (assuming intermittent heating) and will give the number of years 'paid for' by the savings made in heating costs.

(f) The possibility of frost damage to some types of brick outer leaves under certain conditions. In prolonged very cold winters, various types of brick and mortar are vulnerable to frost attack especially if the building is well insulated and little residual heat warms the outer fabric. Moisture vapour migrating from inside the building to the outside will also add to the moisture of the outer leaf. In other words cavity insulation will, under certain weather conditions, result in an outer leaf which is colder and damper for longer periods.

BS 5617:1985, Urea formaldehyde foam for thermal insulation of cavity walls

BS 5618:1992, Code of practice for thermal insulation of cavity walls by filling with urea formaldehyde foam

BRE Digest 236: 1980, Cavity insulation

BRE GBG5 1990: Choosing between cavity, internal and external wall insulation

Agrément Board Information Sheet 10, Method of assessing the exposure of buildings for cavity wall insulation

Agrément Board Information Sheet 11: 1978, Method of determining the U-values of cavity walls with and without cavity wall insulation

Agrément Board Information Sheet 36, BBA Certificates for external wall insulation

Improved standards of insulation in cavity walls with an outer leaf in facing brickwork. Brick Development Association Design Note 11

16.3.1 Water check
General comments and references as for 16.1.1, but see 16.3(f) for remarks relating to possible frost damage.

16.3.2 Water barrier

General comments and references as 16.1.2 and 16.3. The quality of an outer leaf may need to be improved because of poor construction or its degree of exposure (otherwise more water may reach the insulant than it can repel). External waterproof rendering is one way of overcoming this problem.

A cavity and its filling must still act as a water barrier; this means a cavity bridged only by the insulant (and wall ties) must still provide a complete water repellent barrier at its interface with the outer leaf. The insulation must in every respect be in accordance with its Agrément or BSI Certificate, which among other criteria gives recommendations relating to degrees of exposure to driving rain – see 16.3.3.

16.3.3 Insulation

See general introduction 16.3. Use only installers, materials and methods covered by an Agrément or BSI Certificate. The most common materials used for filling cavities are:

(a) urea formaldehyde foam;
(b) blown-in waterproofed mineral wool;
(c) blown-in polyurethane granules;
(d) glasswool or mineral wool batts which fill the cavity space. These are manufactured in various thicknesses but can only be incorporated in new walls (see Agrément Certificates issued). The batts are butt jointed and placed between wall ties fixed at standard spacings;
(e) rigid or semi-rigid boards or slabs of glass wool, mineral wool, phenolic foam, rigid urethane or polystyrene placed against the cavity face of the inner leaf and only partly filling the cavity and thus may not contravene C9(2). For new cavity walls only. The cavity should be widened to allow room to accommodate the insulant plus allowing adequate space for cleaning mortar droppings from brickwork, wall ties and the proprietary clips used to retain the insulant in position. Good workmanship and supervision is essential to ensure unbridged cavities. Wider than normal dpcs around openings might also be advisable. See references under 16.3.

16.3.4 Backing wall

For existing walls this would probably consist of brick but new walls might be of brick, concrete block or panel. See references under 16.1.6.

16.3.5 Vapour check

Not normally added when existing cavity walls are thermally upgraded by cavity fill, but see 16.3(9). If condensation risk is found to be high for new work, a combined vapour check and internal finish might be considered.

16.3.6 Internal finish

General comments and references as for 15.1.5.

Cavity fill offers the opportunity to gain required U-values where an applied finish is not wanted (i.e. an exposed brick finish). In this case the thickness and type of cavity fill should be derived from heat loss calculations.

16.3.7 Structure

Comments and references as for 16.1.6.

16.4 Semi-permeable wall with sheet water barrier

This category includes all walls covered externally with small dry jointed units which can allow wind-blown rain or snow to penetrate between the joints before being stopped by a sheet water barrier. It also includes framed walls covered with an absorbent brick veneer. Small unit wall claddings are often used for purely visual reasons but they can also offer good weather protection to an otherwise sound wall system of either solid or framed construction. They allow moisture vapour to escape through the joints to the outside, and accommodate considerable movement in the supporting structure.

For general points to watch see item 16 (a) to (f). Specific points to watch with dry unit cladding (excluding brick veneer) are:

(a) Ensure that fixings such as nails and clips are corrosion resistant and chemically unreactive with both the cladding and the supporting material.
(b) Design and make all edge details, projections and flashings waterproof against the heavy rainwater run-off from non- or semi-porous claddings.
(c) Pay special attention to junctions with other materials – or at ground level – to avoid rain penetration, movement damage or staining.
(d) Check availability and delivery dates of all required profiles and fittings where non-traditional claddings are used.
(e) Treat all fixing battens for slating and tiling to resist insect and fungus attack.

(f) Check vulnerability to vandalism or damage from hard wear adjacent to certain areas for small units of cladding. See comments 16(f).

(g) Check the Building Regulations with regard to materials and workmanship and their durability. Generally all materials specified must be either to a British Standard or Agrément Certificate. Also check the performance of materials with regard to fire resistance.

(h) Place a moisture barrier (see 16.4.2) behind the brick and in front of the framing. A cavity of approx 25 mm is normal and must be over 12 mm to avoid capillary action.

(i) Use flexible enough metal ties that hold the brick veneer back to the supporting structure to avoid damaging the brickwork should the frame undergo structural or thermal movement.

(j) Extend a flexible dpc from the bottom of the cavity, up the backing wall for a minimum of 200 mm and tuck under the moisture barrier.

(k) Provide weep-holes as described in 16.1.2 at the base of the brick veneer.

16.4.1 Water check
Impervious units such as clay or concrete tiles; natural or asbestos slates; timber shingles or various forms of vertical or horizontal boarding; plastics, asbestos cement or metal sidings can be used.

This classification also includes brick veneer on a framed backing wall as described in 16.4.

Timber Frame Construction, TRADA, 1994

Mitchell's Building Series: Structure and Fabric, Part 1 and Part 2. Longman, 1996.

BS 5534 Code of practice for slating and tiling. Part 1: 1990, Design

BS 690 Asbestos-cement sheets. Part 2: 1981 (1985)

BS EN 492:1994, Fibre cement slates and their fitting for roofing

BS 402 Part 1: 1990, Specification for plain tiles and fittings

BS 680, Roofing slates. Part 2: 1971, metric

16.4.2 Water barrier
This must stop moisture from outside reaching the backing wall, while at the same time allowing water vapour from inside to escape to the outside, and so is often referred to as being of the 'breather type'. The material is usually a building paper to BS 4016 when used over a framed backing wall. It may be an impervious felt when used over a brick or concrete block backing wall.

Tile hanging on a solid backing wall does not usually require a moisture barrier but one should be used if there is any danger of the backing wall being damaged by moisture, e.g. in the case of a lightweight concrete block wall.

Timber cladding of any description should be fixed over a water barrier whatever the nature of the backing wall.

Water barriers must be well lapped at joints and carried over flashings to facilitate correct drainage.

BS 4016:1972, Building papers (breathing type)
BS 747:1977, Specification for roofing felts

16.4.3 Insulation
Sheet or board insulation is not normally used in this location as it does not provide a good fixing for traditional cladding materials. Lightweight concrete blocks which combine structural and insulating qualities are covered in 16.6. If, however, insulation is required in this position, condensation risk calculations must be made and water barriers and vapour checks will be essential if the insulant is not to get wet.

16.4.4 Structure
This may be of framed or solid construction. **External Walls Section 3**, item 3 Structural strength and stability, contains general points and lists both general and specific structural references.

For timber framed structures consider which vulnerable parts (if not all) must be protected against insect and fungus attack.

Mitchell's Building Series: Structure and Fabric, Part 1, Jack Stroud Foster. Longman, 1996.

16.4.5 Vapour check
General comments and references as for 15.1.3 and 15.2.4. On a normal timber framed backing wall it is essential to obtain as good a vapour check as possible; all edges around openings and joints must be sealed. Some forms of timber framed wall might not require a vapour check if water vapour can easily escape through them to either the outside or to a ventilated cavity without damaging the insulation.

16.4.6 Internal finish
Comments and references as for 15.1.5.

16.5 Semi-permeable wall with sheet water barrier and thermal insulation on the inside wall or backing wall.

General comments and references relating to external claddings as for 16.4.

See item 15.2 for general comments relating to the merits of placing the insulation on the inside of the wall system.

16.5.1 Water check
Comments and references as for 16.4.1.

16.5.2 Water barrier
Comments as for 16.4.2.

16.5.3 Structure
Comments and references as for 16.4.4.

16.5.4 Insulation
Comments and references as for 15.1.2 and 15.2.3.

16.5.5 Vapour check
Comments and references as for 15.1.3 and 15.2.4.

16.5.6 Internal finish
Comments and references as for 15.1. 5 and 15.2.5.

16.6 Semi-permeable wall with sheet water barrier on combined structure and insulation

General comments and references relating to external claddings as for 16.4.

General comments and references relating to combined structure and insulation as for 16.1.3. If masonry is used, it will not comply with thermal requirements for habitable rooms.

16.6.1 Water check
Comments and references as for 16.4.1.

16.6.2 Water barrier
Comments and references as for 16.4.2

16.6.3 Structure and insulation
General comments and references as for 16.1.3 and 16.4.4.

16.6.4 Vapour check
Comments and references as for 15.1.3, 16.1.4 and 16.4.5.

16.6.5 Internal finish
General comments and references as for 15.1.5.

17 Permeable walls
This category includes all solid walls of permeable materials.

17.1 Thick permeable wall without additional insulation
In this country the walls of habitable buildings are rarely built in this form due to contemporary material/labour cost ratios as well as increased standards of thermal performance and internal comfort.

Mitchell's Building Series: Structure and Fabric, Part 1, Jack Stroud Foster. Longman, 1996.
BS 5628 Code of practice for use of masonry. Part 1: 1992, Structural use of unreinforced masonry
BS 5390:1976, Code of practice for stone masonry

17.1.1 Water check, structure and insulation
This form of construction relies on thickness and mass to provide combined functions of weather protection, structural support and insulation. For normal domestic purposes it is structurally uneconomic being far too strong, although if an abundant local resource it would be sensible to use. As a weather barrier it has strict limitations (unless excessively thick) because moisture from outside can, at certain times of the year, penetrate to the inner face. This occurs due to capillary attraction, mainly through hair cracks in the joints of masonry walls, or through hair or large cracks caused by shrinkage during drying out (or thermal or structural movement with concrete walls). A characteristic of this type of wall is that it has a large thermal capacity. This is discussed in **External Walls Section 3**, item 6, Thermal performance. When a permeable wall absorbs water its insulation value decreases and the building will require increasing amounts of heat to keep internal air temperatures at a comfortable level. If wall surface temperatures drop then there will almost certainly be areas of condensation during some periods of the year. See **External Walls Section 3**, item 6, Thermal performance. Water trapped within a wall can cause severe damage by expanding upon freezing during very cold weather. If built from traditional masonry it will not comply with current regulations for thermal performance and could not be used for enclosures for habitable rooms.

17.1.2 Internal finish

Comments and references as for 15.1.5. For remedial work to existing permeable walls various methods and materials are available which place a water barrier on the internal wall face and behind the finish. Although these methods may to varying degrees be successful in stopping dampness showing on internal surfaces, they cannot on their own eradicate the danger of frost damage or overcome the problem of decreasing thermal performance values as the wall becomes saturated.

17.2 Permeable wall with added insulation

This form of construction is often attempted for remedial work but the following remarks apply to both new and existing walls. A vapour check on the inside is essential, but is often incorrectly omitted in remedial work.

17.2.1 Water check and structure

Comments as for 17.1.1.

17.2.2 Insulation

General comments and references as for 15.1.2 and 15.2.3. Where the insulation is placed on the inside of a permeable wall there is a real danger of interstitial condensation occurring at the interface of the two materials if the temperature in this region falls below the dew point. See **External Walls Section 3**, item 6.3, Condensation risk. A good water barrier and vapour check is essential in this form of construction if the insulant is to remain dry. Fixing the insulation to the wall can raise new defects such as deterioration of adhesives from moisture or puncturing of the water barrier if attached by nails or screws. The risk of interstitial condensation can be reduced by using rigid insulation on treated battens fixed over a water barrier,

or a proprietary combined insulant, vapour barrier and integral finish on treated battens. Dense concrete walls are sometimes cast against wood wool (or similar) slabs to provide both permanent shuttering and some insulation. This method requires very careful consideration in respect of both moisture penetration from the outside and condensation as mentioned above. The insulation also tends to get very wet as well as damaged during construction.

17.2.3 Vapour check

General comments and references as for 15.1.3 and 15.2.4. See note above advocating a combined vapour check, insulant and internal finish for this form of wall construction. Check that continuity is achieved across joints in such a combined system.

17.2.4 Internal finish

Comments and references as for 15.1.5 and 15.2.5.

Trade and research organizations

Brick Development Association (BDA), Woodside House, Winkfield, Windsor, Berks SL4 2DX (tel. 01344-885651, fax 01344-890129).

British Board of Agrément, PO Box 195, Bucknalls Lane, Garston, Watford, Herts WD2 7NG (tel. 01923-670844, fax 01923-662133).

British Cement Association (BCA), Century House, Telford Avenue, Crowthorne, Berks RG11 6YS (tel. 01344-762676, fax 01334-761214).

British Ceramic Tile Council, Federation House, Station Road, Stoke-on-Trent, Staffs ST4 2RU (tel. 01782-747147, fax 01782-747161).

National Cavity Insulation Association, PO Box 12, Haslemere, Surrey GU 27 3AH (tel. 01428-654011, fax 01428-651401).

External Walls: Detailed Sections Section 5

SMM7 F Masonry

(See Section 3 for walls, general; and Section 4 for basic types)

Notes and references

Items are cross-referenced from the diagrams and divided into sections with a general comment followed by technical references and the Building Regulations in context. Addresses of relevant trade and research organizations are given at the end of the section. British Standards and BRE Digests should be checked for current amendments.

This section shows typical examples of the basic wall types covered in **External Walls Section 4**, and should also be read in conjunction with **External Walls Section 3**, (External Walls: general). Items are cross-referenced from the sketches as well as those in **External Walls Section 4**.

15 Impermeable facing wall or skin

15.1 Impermeable wall with insulation external to structure

See **External Walls Section 4** for general comments and references. Specifically, the example shown provides poor sound insulation. This may be remedied by using extra thick or double layers of plasterboard as an internal lining.

15.1.1, 2 and 3 Water barrier, insulation and vapour check

Metal panels containing insulation with an integral or additional vapour barrier. The vapour barrier may be fixed directly to the metal panel edges. Various colours and finishes (gloss, matt, semi-matt and eggshell) are available.

Points to watch with this form of cladding panel:

(a) Strict supervision is required when off-loading and storing panels. Crazed, scratched, chipped or non-matching panels should not be accepted.

(b) The panels will be subject to thermal movement. Colour will affect the amount of movement. Check that the jointing system (including sealants, if any) can accommodate the direction and calculated magnitude of the movement.

(c) Check with manufacturers the amount of thermal buckling or bowing expected for the particular panel size chosen. Areas of misshapen panels can ruin the appearance of an otherwise good-looking facade.

(d) Check rigidity of panels and if necessary consider stiffening with ribs or panel configurations.

(e) Check on how a damaged panel can be removed for repairs or renewal.

15.1.4 Structure

See **External Walls Section 3**, item 3 for general comments on structural strength and stability.

The timber stud frame should be protected by a layer of 'breather type' building paper. Timber frames should be protected against insect and fungal attack. In addition to structural requirements, the location and size of timber components must be compatible with the fixing requirements of the external cladding.

For comments and references in connection with fire resistance see **External Walls Section 3**, item 9.

BS 4016:1972, Building papers (breathing type)
Mitchell's Building Series: Structure and Fabric, Part 1. Jack Foster. Longman, 1994.

15.1.5 Internal finish

12.7 mm thick plasterboard fixed with 14 swg galvanized flat head nails 38 mm long at 200 mm centres and at 100 mm centres around edges. All edges of boards should be supported by timber studs or noggings. Boards are available with tapered and feathered edges which, when taped and scrimmed at joints only, are ready for final decoration.

15.1.6 Drained cavity

Cavity drainage systems must collect and drain to the outside any water penetrating through the joints as well as collecting moisture forming on the vapour check. On high or exposed buildings, baffles behind weep-holes will prevent wind, noise and water penetration by wind-blown rain being driven vertically up the building facade.

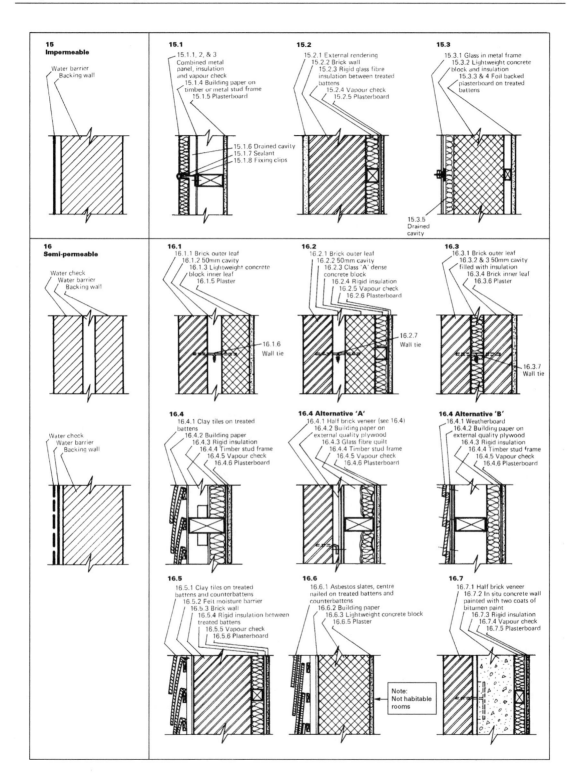

15 Impermeable

Water barrier
Backing wall

15.1
15.1.1, 2, & 3 Combined metal panel, insulation and vapour check
15.1.4 Building paper on timber or metal stud frame
15.1.5 Plasterboard
15.1.6 Drained cavity
15.1.7 Sealant
15.1.8 Fixing clips

15.2
15.2.1 External rendering
15.2.2 Brick wall
15.2.3 Rigid glass fibre insulation between treated battens
15.2.4 Vapour check
15.2.5 Plasterboard

15.3
15.3.1 Glass in metal frame
15.3.2 Lightweight concrete block and insulation
15.3.3 & 4 Foil backed plasterboard on treated battens
15.3.5 Drained cavity

16 Semi-permeable

Water check
Water barrier
Backing wall

Water check
Water barrier
Backing wall

16.1
16.1.1 Brick outer leaf
16.1.2 50mm cavity
16.1.3 Lightweight concrete block inner leaf
16.1.5 Plaster
16.1.6 Wall tie

16.2
16.2.1 Brick outer leaf
16.2.2 50mm cavity
16.2.3 Class 'A' dense concrete block
16.2.4 Rigid insulation
16.2.5 Vapour check
16.2.6 Plasterboard
16.2.7 Wall tie

16.3
16.3.1 Brick outer leaf
16.3.2 & 3 50mm cavity filled with insulation
16.3.4 Brick inner leaf
16.3.6 Plaster
16.3.7 Wall tie

16.4
16.4.1 Clay tiles on treated battens
16.4.2 Building paper
16.4.3 Rigid insulation
16.4.4 Timber stud frame
16.4.5 Vapour check
16.4.6 Plasterboard

16.4 Alternative 'A'
16.4.1 Half brick veneer (see 16.4)
16.4.2 Building paper on external quality plywood
16.4.3 Glass fibre quilt
16.4.4 Timber stud frame
16.4.5 Vapour check
16.4.6 Plasterboard

16.4 Alternative 'B'
16.4.1 Weatherboard
16.4.2 Building paper on external quality plywood
16.4.3 Rigid insulation
16.4.4 Timber stud frame
16.4.5 Vapour check
16.4.6 Plasterboard

16.5
16.5.1 Clay tiles on treated battens and counterbattens
16.5.2 Felt moisture barrier
16.5.3 Brick wall
16.5.4 Rigid insulation between treated battens
16.5.5 Vapour check
16.5.6 Plasterboard

16.6
16.6.1 Asbestos slates, centre nailed on treated battens and counterbattens
16.6.2 Building paper
16.6.3 Lightweight concrete block
16.6.5 Plaster

Note: Not habitable rooms

16.7
16.7.1 Half brick veneer
16.7.2 In situ concrete wall painted with two coats of bitumen paint
16.7.3 Rigid insulation
16.7.4 Vapour check
16.7.5 Plasterboard

15.1.7 Joint sealant

Sealants are elastic, whereas mastics are not. Oil based sealants require protection (by cover strips etc.), from sunlight, dust and polluted air. A chemically stable sealant is recommended for this detail.

BRE Digest 217: 1978, Wall cladding defects and their diagnosis

BRE Digest 223: 1979, Wall cladding: designing to minimize defects

15.1.8 Metal fixing clips

Corrosion resistant metal clips and brackets must be capable of adjustment in all directions to allow for site inaccuracies and manufacturing tolerances. Screws, bolts and washers must be compatible with clips and brackets to prevent electrolytic action. Fixings must be strong enough to transfer the live (wind) and dead loads back on to the structural supports whilst allowing for thermal and structural movements.

15.2 Impermeable wall with insulation on the inside of the structure

See **External Walls Section 4**, for general comments.

15.2.1 Water barrier

External rendering requires extremely careful specification, edge detailing and site supervision. British Standard recommendations should be followed. Rendering has been included here because its normal function is to exclude water from the backing wall. However, being porous it absorbs some moisture when it rains and dries out when the rain stops.

Points to watch:

(a The degree of exposure of the building, the particular facade, and the background onto which the rendering is to be fixed must be taken into consideration when specifying mixes.

(b) Precautions must be taken at the junctions of dissimilar backgrounds and at structural movement joints.

(c) Two-coat work is recommended for 'moderate' exposures and three-coat for 'severe' exposures.

(d) Cracking and crazing are common failures, often caused by mixes being too strong for their backing or where large areas of rendering have not been divided by movement joints.

(e) Edges must be protected by flashings, drips, cills etc. and detailed to throw rain clear of the facade. Dpcs are essential under copings and cills to protect the top edges of the rendering.

(f) Walls exposed to the elements on two sides should not be rendered both sides, e.g. on parapets and free standing walls (one side needs to be able to 'breathe' or dry out). The side not rendered must not allow moisture to penetrate the wall and damage the rear of the rendering. This can be prevented by using a vertical water barrier in the form of a cavity, sheet dpc or bitumen paint (which would require maintenance).

(g) Rendering must not be carried across dpcs in such a way as to provide a bypass for moisture. This is particularly important at ground level where rendering should be stopped above dpc level and finished with a 'bell mouth' and/or drip detail.

BS 5262:1991, Code of practice for external rendering
BS 1369:1987 (1991), Specification for expanded metal and ribbed
Mitchell's Building Series: Finishes, Yvonne Dean. Longman, 1996.

15.2.2 Structure

See **External Walls Section 3**, item 3, Structural strength and stability. Brickwork should have the joints well raked out to provide a good key. Alternatively keyed bricks, spatter dash or other bonding treatments can be used.

Bricks and mortars should be chosen to avoid a high sulphate content and a high risk of efflorescence.

15.2.3 Insulation

See **External Walls Section 4**, item 15.1.2 for references.

In this example rigid glass fibre boards are fixed between battens treated to resist decay.

15.2.4 Vapour check

See **External Walls Section 4**, item 15.1.3 for comments and references.

The polythene sheet (500 or 1000 gauge) should be well lapped at joints and stapled to the battens. It must also be fitted snugly around window and door openings, and around service junction boxes where it should be sealed by adhesive tape or sealing compound. The vapour check should be lapped around all exposed edges of the insulant.

15.2.5 Internal finish
As for 15.1.5.

15.3 Impermeable wall with combined insulation and structure
This example shows a typical form of construction consisting of a glass infill panel held in a metal frame which in turn is supported by a lightweight concrete block wall. Where the frame is supported or hung from structural members at floor or roof level it comes under the heading of 'curtain walling' and, as it is more normally associated with commercial buildings, is outside the scope of this book but the general points in the following sub-sections are still relevant.

15.3.1 Water barrier
In this example opaque coloured glass is held by metal glazing beads in a frame consisting of standard metal window sections. This is a complex form of construction and designers are advised to consult the references given below.

Points to watch:

(a) Thermal movement between infill panel and frame must be calculated and manufacturers' recommended edge clearances strictly followed on drawings and on site. Plastic, dense rubber, lead or hardwood setting blocks (two per infill panel) are used to obtain the correct bottom clearance. It is also essential to follow the recommended face clearances between glass and frame and glass and glazing head. Clearance dimensions are determined by such factors as the frame material and colour as well as the glass type; sheet size and colour; and degree of transparency. Heat build-up in the cavity can lead to excessive movement of the backing wall.

Ventilated cavities behind glass infill panels will cool the glass and backing wall, reduce expansion differentials and the risk of condensation on the inside face of the glass.
(b) Differential movement must be accommodated between the horizontal and vertical members of the framing system as well as between the frame and the supporting structure.
(c) The glass infill panel and metal frame will have to transmit wind loads back to the supporting structure. This will affect the size, thickness and proportion of the glass. Wind load calculations are important for all components.

(d) Fixings. Comments as for 15.1.8 above.

Mitchell's Building Series: Structure and Fabric, Part 2, Foster and Harrington. Longman, 1994.
Cladding of Buildings, Alan J. Brookes. Spon, 1997.

15.3.2 Structure and insulation
Lightweight concrete block backing wall. See **External Walls Section 4**, item 16.1.3 for comments and references.

15.3.3 and 4 Vapour check and internal finish
Foil backed plasterboard on battens treated to resist decay. See **External Walls Section 4**, item 15.1.5 for reference.

15.3.5 Drained cavity
See 15.1.6.

16 to 16.3.6 Semi-permeable facing wall or skin
See **External Walls Section 4**, for comments and references. The construction shown in 16.1 could not be used for habitable rooms unless insulation was incorporated in the cavity as in 16.3.

16.4 to 16.4.2 Semi-permeable wall with sheet water barrier
See **External Walls Section 4** for comments and references. The example shown provides poor sound insulation. This can be remedied by using thicker than normal or double layers of plasterboard.

16.4.3 Insulation
Rigid glass fibre boards or extruded polystyrene boards placed between the timber studs. If pre-cut boards are not available to the sizes required, it might be more economical to run larger boards over the studs as in 16.4 alternative B.

16.4.4 to 16.6.5 inclusive; 16.4 Alternatives A and B
See **External Walls Section 4**, for comments and references. Note that example 16.6 could not be used for habitable rooms as a form of construction as there is no provision for insulation as shown.

16.7 Semi-permeable wall with a bitumastic painted concrete wall water barrier (a variant of 16.5)
This example shows a brick veneer over a concrete wall but the principle is equally applicable over a concrete column.

16.7.1 Water check

The half-brick veneer is not structural, therefore it need not be bonded and straight joint patterns can be used. The weight of the brickwork is normally taken by projections from the structure at each floor level. As the brickwork will move differentially to the backing wall (or structure) compressible joints are required under the structural supports at the top of each brick panel. (See *Mitchell's Building Series: Structure and Fabric*, Part 2, for details of movement joints to brick panel walls, and for fixing details for briquettes over supporting structure.)

The veneer is anchored back to the concrete wall by corrosion resistant fishtailed cramps set in dovetailed metal slots cast in the concrete.

Windloading Handbook: Guide to the Use of BS 6399 Part 2. Tom Lawson. Architectural Press, 1996.

BS 6399 Part 2:1997, Code of practice for wind loads

BDA Design Guide DG18, 1992, *Brickwork Cladding to Steel Framed Buildings*, Bradshaw, Buckton & Tonge.

BDA Design Guide DG4: External walls, design for wind loads

BDA Technical Note 9, 1975: Further observations on the design of brickwork cladding to multi-storey frame structures

16.7.2 Structure

The in situ concrete wall (or column) is painted with two coats of emulsion type bitumen paint (this type allows moisture vapour to escape). In certain weather conditions water will penetrate to the inside face of the brick veneer and in the absence of a cavity barrier will find its way (via projecting mortar bed joints and debris) to the face of the concrete. The bitumen paint will prevent most moisture penetration as well as preventing salts within the concrete coming to the surface and staining the exterior face of the brickwork. In exposed conditions a full 50 mm unbridged (other than by wall ties or cramps) cavity is recommended.

16.7.3, 4 and 5 Insulation vapour check and internal finish

All as 15.2.3, 4 and 5.

Trade and research organizations

APA The Engineered Wood Association, 65 London Wall, London EC2M 5TU (tel. 0171-287 2765, fax 0171-408 8020).

Finnish Plywood International, PO Box 99, Welwyn Garden City, Herts AL6 0HS (tel. 01438-798746, fax 01438-798746).

Floors: General Section 6

SMM7 E In situ concrete, G Structural carcassing, M Surface finishes

(See Section 7 for floors in detail)

Bird's nest (Black Swan, Australia)
Most nests have to span between branches, providing a sheltered platform to carry 2 birds and their growing brood. This one floats.

Brighton West Pier (Dean)

Notes and references

Items are cross-referenced from the diagrams and divided into sections with a general comment followed by technical references and the Building Regulations in context. Addresses of relevant trade and research organizations are given at the end of the section. British Standards and BRE Digests should be checked for current amendments.

General references

Mitchell's Building Series: Structure and Fabric, Part 1, Jack Stroud Foster, Part 2, Floor structures, Jack Stroud Foster and Raymond Harrington. Longman, 1994.
Concrete Ground Floors: Their design, construction and finish. K. C. Deacon, British Cement Association, 1986.

1 Floor categories

This section covers general design principles of both ground and intermediate floors. It does not include floors below ground level or podium decks.

2 Appearance

Floor surfaces (see item 11, Finishes) make a major contribution to the overall internal effect of a building. Colour, scale, texture and pattern will give visual as well as psychological characteristics such as feelings of formality, luxury etc.

The degree of effect will depend on the total area exposed when occupied. Changes in appearance over time and the intensity of use should be considered when choosing quality and type of finish. In some cases appearance criteria can affect the type of sub-base and form of structural floor.

Ceilings are outside the scope of this check list but where relevant the appearance of exposed floor soffits should be considered

3 Structural strength and stability

Load and span are the main factors controlling structural floor design. These together with all the other criteria should be used to achieve the most economic weight/strength ratio. The total load is composed of dead loads, live (or imposed) loads, moving loads and wind loads. In addition, account must be taken of collapse loads and the effect of giving lateral bracing to supporting walls.

1 Dead loads are the weight of all the materials used in the permanent construction of the floor, and

Key Factors	Action	Counteraction
Gravity	Downward pull	Support
Wind	Motive force (suction), destructive, penetrative	Rigidity, resilience, sealing
Rain	Moisture deposition	Deflection, impervious skin, absorption and drainage, sealing
Snow	Moisture deposition, loading	Deflection, impervious skin, absorption and drainage, sealing
Sun	Temperature variation, movement, heat gain, chemical decomposition	Movement joints, insulation, shielding, invulnerable materials, reflection
Dirt and dust	Infiltration, deposition, surface pollution	Repulsion, exclusion, shielding, cleaning
Chemicals	Corrosion, disintegration, decomposition	Invulnerable materials, exclusion
Sound	Noise nuisance	Insulation
Capillary attraction	Moisture transfer	Impervious barrier, cavity

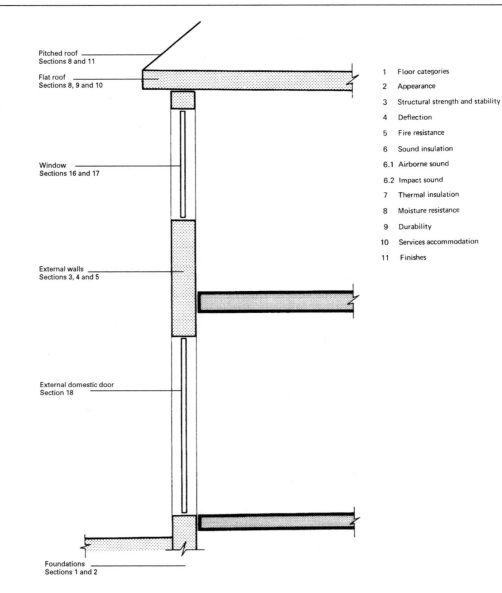

Pitched roof
Sections 8 and 11

Flat roof
Sections 8, 9 and 10

Window
Sections 16 and 17

External walls
Sections 3, 4 and 5

External domestic door
Section 18

Foundations
Sections 1 and 2

1   Floor categories

2   Appearance

3   Structural strength and stability

4   Deflection

5   Fire resistance

6   Sound insulation

6.1 Airborne sound

6.2 Impact sound

7   Thermal insulation

8   Moisture resistance

9   Durability

10   Services accommodation

11   Finishes

finishes including any services. Building Regulations (Section A Structure) state that all dead and imposed loads shall be calculated in accordance with BS 6399 Parts 1 and 3, and wind loads should be calculated in accordance with BS 6399 Part 2: 1997, Code of practice for wind loads. *Windloading Handbook: Guide to the Use of BS 6399 Part 2*, Tom Lawson. Architectural Press, 1996.

2 Live (or imposed) loads are the loads produced by the intended occupancy or use including distributed, concentrated, impact, inertia and snow loads but excluding wind loads. These too are calculated in accordance with BS 6399 Parts 1 and 3, which must be checked for latest amendments before use.

3 Moving loads are usually assumed to be slow-moving and so not exerting braking or impact loads. Vibrating machinery should be placed on anti-vibration mounts or pads.

4 Wind loads are loads due to the effect of wind pressure or suction, and the Building Regulations lay down that calculations shall be in accordance with the Code of practice for wind loads, now BS 6399 Part 2: 1997, which must also be checked for latest amendments before use. Generally floors can be affected by wind forces in two ways: (a) by acting as bracing to transfer wind loads across a structure, and (b) during construction floors may be exposed to wind pressure along their edges and frictional drag on their surfaces. BRE BR 173 1990 gives guidance on this point.

5 Collapse loads. The Disproportionate Collapse Requirement (Building Regulations Document A3 and A4) for buildings is designed to provide for alternative routes for loadings in the event of the removal or collapse of a single member, so that the whole building would not collapse, and is limited to 15% of the area of the storey or 70 m² whichever is greater.

BS 6399 Loading for buildings. Part 1: 1984, Code of practice for dead and imposed loads and Part 3:1988, Code of practice for imposed roof loads

BS 6399 Part 2: 1997, Code of practice for wind loads

Windloading Handbook: Guide to the Use of BS 6399 Part 2, Tom Lawson. Architectural Press, 1996.

BS 8110 Structural use of concrete. Part 1: 1985, Code of practice for design and construction, Part 2: 1985, Code of practice for special circumstances, Part 3: 1985, Design charts for singly reinforced beams, doubly reinforced beams and rectangular columns

BS 5268 Structural use of timber. Part 2: 1991, Code of practice for permissible stress design, materials and workmanship. Part 3: 1985, Materials and components, design and workmanship

BS 5950 Part 3: Design in composite construction. Section 3.1: 1990, Code of practice for design of simple and continuous composite beams. Part 1: 1990, Code of practice for simple and continuous construction: hot rolled sections

BS 648:1964, Schedule of weights of building materials

BRE Digest 346, The assessment of wind loads. Part 1: Background and methods.

The Building Regulations 1991, Section A.

4 Deflection

A floor may be of adequate structural strength yet, if it deflects excessively, can cause damage to materials and components that are dependent upon it. Deflection must then be calculated and kept within tolerances allowed by the relevant codes of practice. Designers should then check that allowable deflection can be tolerated by floor and ceiling finishes, partitions and service runs (particularly watch falls in waste pipes). Designers should note that the tables for timber joists contained in the Building Regulations, Appendix A of A1/2 do not distinguish spans at which certain joists will be subject to excessive deflection.

BS 5268 The structural use of timber Part 2: 1991 states that maximum deflection should be 0.003 of the span

BS 8110 The structural use of concrete, also relates permissible deflection to the span/depth ratio of the floor members and limits deflection to 0.0025 of the span.

BS 5950 Part 1: 1990. The use of structural steel in building gives maximum allowable deflection of 0.0036 of the span. Where the floor is used to transmit wind loads (see references under item 3) it must be stiff enough to avoid buckling.

5 Fire resistance

Designers should use Section B of the Building Regulations as a basic guide. The general principles and references are given below but the local fire prevention officer should be consulted about recent revisions to regulations, standards and interpretations. General principles:

1 Floors should be designed to contain a fire and prevent its spread to the compartments above. Fire resistance has three criteria:
   (a) Stability, it must continue to support loads.
   (b) Integrity, it must not crack or break-up and allow the passage of hot gases or smoke.
   (c) Insulation, the top surface must not get hot enough to ignite.

2 The degree to which a floor provides fire protection is given in terms of its resistance to fire measured by time in an international standard test (BS 476 Part 8).

3 The degree of fire resistance necessary for a floor depends on the height, volume and usage of the building in which the floor is located. The various categories are set out in Building Regulations.

4 A floor must resist fire long enough to allow occupants to escape and allow time for fire fighting services to arrive. Thus building usage categories are important as some (such as dwellings in multi-storey buildings) have a possible high human risk but low fire load (defined as the quantity of combustible material). Other building types (such as factories and warehouses) might have a low human risk (i.e. low occupancy) but a high fire load because of the types of materials stored or fabricated.

5 Generally high human risk, low fire load buildings require good means of escape and lower grades of fire resistance whilst low human risk but high fire load buildings will require higher grades of fire resistance together with adequate means of escape.

6 Fire resistance periods used by the Building Regulations are 30 min, 1 hr, 2 hrs, and 4 hrs (although BS 476 includes a 6-hr rating).

7 Fire insurers often have different standards to those embodied in mandatory controls and official recommendations. The Fire Offices Committee have their own rules for the guidance of insurers, clients and architects. For certain uses and building types the higher standards indicated in their rules will result in lower rates of insurance. This point should be discussed with clients for in some cases higher insurance premiums can be far more expensive than the initial incorporation of slightly better standards of fire protection. Fire engineering is now an established discipline with the likely fire load calculated and likely risk used as tools to optimize fire protection.

8 The complete floor construction must be considered when assessing its fire resistance. Regulations control the finishes on ceilings and soffits in terms of surface spread of flame. Smoke emission and the likelihood of molten material falling from ceiling finishes should also be checked.

Regulations do not control floor finishes. Suspended ceilings can count towards fire resistance if the building is below 15 m high. Above this height and for higher periods of resistance than 1 hour only jointless systems can be considered as contributing to fire resistance. Thickness of screeds can be included but not voids within floors.

9 The structure supporting a floor must have a fire resistance at least that of the floor itself.

10 Regulations and Standards (BS 4422 Part 2: 1990) require fire stops to prevent the spread of fire, smoke and hot gases in cavities within and between building elements and compartments. Particular attention must be paid to details around pipes and ducts, junctions between walls and floors and cavities above suspended ceilings.

BS 5588 Precautions against fire. Part 1: 1990, Code of practice for residential buildings, Part 2: 1985, Code of practice for shops, Part 3: 1983, Code of practice for office buildings

See item 3 for references to Codes of practice relating to timber, concrete and steel

BS 476 Part 4: 1970 (1984), Non-combustibility test for materials. Part 6: 1989, Method of test for fire propagation for products. Part 7: 1987 (1993), Methods for classification of the surface spread of flame of products. Part 20: 1987, Method for determination of the fire resistance of elements of construction (general principles)

BS 4422 Glossary of terms associated with fire. Part 1: 1987, General terms and the phenomenon of fire. Part 2: 1990, Structural fire protection. Part 6: 1988, Evacuation and means of escape. Part 4: 1994, Fire extinguishing equipment

BS EN 2 1992: Classification of fires

BS 5268 Code of practice for the structural use of timber. Part 4: 1978, section 4.1, Fire resistance of timber structures

BRE Digest 208: rev. 1988, Increasing the fire resistance of existing timber floors

Fire-CD: combines information on fire information from Home Office, Loss Prevention Council, Fire Protection Association and Fire Research Association. BRE, FPA, Home Office and Loss Prevention Council, January 1996 version. Obtainable from HMSO

Design Principles of Fire Safety, Bickerdicke Allen and Partners, DOE, 1996. Obtainable from HMSO

Fire and the Design of Educational Buildings. Building Bulletin No 7, HMSO, 1981.

The Building Regulations 1991, Part B Fire Safety, Section B1: Means of escape, Section B3: Internal fire spread (structure)

6 Sound insulation

The first and most economic step is to plan the separation of noisy and quiet areas. Special precautions will be required around lift motor, water tank and other plant rooms; access galleries or corridors over bedrooms; and mixed use occupancy. Similar use of areas can also give noise reduction problems where audial privacy is important or where noise could cause loss of concentration such as in classrooms.

While all sounds are airborne, their origins can be different and need different methods of reduction. Airborne sound refers to sounds made in the air in an adjoining compartment before being transmitted to the receiving compartment by way of the structure – in this case the floor. Impact sound is created by a direct blow on any part of the structure in the adjoining compartment.

It is essential to understand the difference between direct and indirect sound transmission as expensive precautions against direct transmission can be made redundant if the sound is still travelling by indirect transmission. Direct sound transmission is carried into a compartment by the separating element – in this case the floor. Indirect sound transmission reaches the compartment by other elements – such as adjoining columns or walls. This is called *flanking* sound. So the junction between wall and floor should be carefully detailed and have a similar sound reduction capacity as the floor itself. In critical cases flanking sound can be reduced by controlling the density and form of supporting walls, or practically eliminated by structural discontinuity. Sound is measured by a decibel scale (dB) and is logarithmic, so values cannot be totalled by simple addition (an increase of 6 dB at any point in the scale represents a doubling of sound pressure, a decrease of 6 dB represents halving). Readers are advised to consult the references given below for introductions into the nature and measurement of sound. The sound insulation of a floor is measured by the dB reduction from one side to the other.

BS 8233:1987, Code of practice for sound insulation and noise reduction (contains the detailed theoretical basis for sound measurement)

BS 8204 Part 1: 1987, Code of practice for concrete bases and screeds to receive in situ floorings

BS 4727 Part 3: Group 08 1995, Acoustics and electro-acoustics (includes glossary)

BS 2750 Part 4: 1980 (1993), Field measurements of airborne sound insulation between rooms

BRE Digest 337: 1988, Sound Insulation: Basic principles

BRE Digest 333: 1988, Sound insulation of separating walls and floors, Part 1: Walls

BRE Digest 334: 1988 (rev. 1993), Sound insulation of separating walls and floors, Part 2: Floors

BRE Digest DAS 51 Floors: cement based screeds – specification (design)

BRE Digest 347: 1989, Sound insulation of lightweight dwellings

BRE current papers:
BRE 293 1985: Improving the sound insulation of separating walls and floors
BRE 347 1989: Sound insulation of lightweight dwellings

Acoustics and Noise Control, B. J. Smith, R. J. Peters and S. Owen. Longman, 1996.

The Building Regulations Technical Booklet G: Sound 1990, and G1: Sound (conversions) 1994

Mitchell's Building Series: Environment and Services, Chapter 6, Sound, Peter Burberry. Longman, 1997.

The Building Regulations 1991 Document E relates only to sound transmission between dwellings and from other purpose groups to dwellings. Regulation E2 and E3 concern floors and stairs and state that certain categories of floor must resist the transmission of airborne and impact sound. Examples of how this can be achieved in new buildings is given in Section 2, and in refurbished buildings, in Section 5

6.1 Airborne sound insulation

Because sound exists as a vibration, of air or objects, the amount of airborne sound transmitted (either upwards or downwards) through a floor is for all practical purposes related to its weight. Timber joisted floors can be made to achieve high standards of noise reduction in timber framed houses, but in traditional structures high standards are difficult to achieve with timber joisted floors because of flanking transmission. The normal method of reducing airborne sound through a timber joisted floor is to increase its weight by filling in the spaces between joists with absorbent material or pugging (often 50 mm of clean dry sand). This is usually combined with a floating floor on battens resting on a 25 mm resilient quilt of glass or mineral wool (density 35 kg/m³) laid over the joists. Sand pugging is difficult to handle and keep dry on site as well as causing joist sizes to increase to carry the extra load. In addition, ceilings need to be fixed before floor boards.

The main principles emphasized in the Regulations are:

1 achievement of a high mass of construction;
2 selection of an absorbent material;
3 isolation of the ceiling layer;
4 airtightness of the elements to avoid airborne noise.

The main path for airborne sound transmission is through holes in the floor such as around pipes and ducts and at floor/wall junctions. Special attention must be paid where battens, boards and skirtings abut the wall.

Sound stops over partitions will be necessary where suspended ceilings provide part of the sound reduction precautions.

6.2 Impact sound

Unlike airborne sound impact sound is normally one way, down or sideways through the building fabric. Impact sound transmission can be reduced by the use of resilient materials which will reduce the force of the impact. The most economic method uses resilient floor finishes. If this is not possible, a 'floating' floor finish can be used. The isolating quilt must be turned up all around the edges of the floating floor in order to separate it from the surrounding structure.

Floating floors can rarely reach their potential if not used in conjunction with a resilient floor finish. This presents particular problems where access galleries pass over bedrooms. Flexible and foamed polymeric sheets or tiles are recommended to solve this problem. Partitions should be built off structural floors because floating floors will crack or deflect under load.

7 Thermal insulation

Insulation is necessary where it is important to restrict heat loss or gain through a floor from one compartment to another. This normally means those cases where the floor divides different users, or is over (or extends over) an external or ventilated space.

Solid concrete ground floors are now provided with insulation because even though below ground temperatures tend to stay constant at about 13°C, heat losses through ground floors can account for a significant proportion of the total heat loss. Where ground levels fall away leaving exposed corners or areas of foundation walls, or where floor slabs extend to or beyond the external wall face, there should be sufficient protection against cold bridges. The standard U-value for an exposed ground floor is 0.35 W/m² K, unless the building has a SAP (Standard Assessment Procedure) energy rating of over 60 when 0.45 W/m² K will be allowed. (Method of calculation in Document L of the Building Regulations 1991, 1995 edition.)

Suspended concrete and timber ground floors will require thermal insulation if over a ventilated space. The Building Regulations require domestic floors in these positions to achieve the U-values described above. For buildings other than dwellings, Section 2 of Document L1 states that floors with their under surface exposed to the external air or a ventilated space must not have a U-value above 0.45 W/m² K.

As it is advisable to ventilate the space under suspended timber ground floors they will require some form of rigid or quilt insulation. Where a glass or mineral wool quilt is suspended over joists and under floorboards it should not contain a vapour barrier as this would trap water spillage and could cause deterioration of both insulant and timber.

Intermediate floors are sometimes required to restrict heat loss or gain – usually where heated and unheated compartments cannot be separated by planning methods. The insulant can be placed above or below the floor. When located above the floor slab it must have sufficient crushing strength to support any sub-floor, screeds and finishes. Rigid foamed polymers are appropriate for this position. They are often used below intermediate floors, directly applied or combined with suspended ceilings. They should not be exposed to flame and recent feedback from fires shows that it is essential for designers to check thoroughly the spread of flame, smoke emission and drip characteristics of proposed insulants in this location. See item 5 for references. Vapour barriers to prevent surface and interstitial condensation must be considered whichever location is chosen for thermal insulation. See **Roofs: General Section 8**, item 6.4, Condensation risk.

Intermediate floors sometimes project to or through (in the case of balconies) the external wall face. Very careful and sometimes expensive detailing is necessary if cold bridges are to be avoided (see BRE BR 262: Thermal Insulation: Avoiding Risks, 1994).

BS 8207:1985 (1995), Code of practice for energy efficiency in buildings

BS 8211 Part 1: 1988 (1995), Code of practice for energy efficient refurbishment of housing

BS 5250:1989 (1995), Code of practice for control of condensation in dwellings

BRE Digest 110: 1972, Condensation

BRE Digest 145: 1972, Heat losses through ground floors

The Building Regulations 1991, Document L1 Conservation of Fuel and Power

8 Moisture resistance

The Building Regulations 1991, Document C, Site preparation and resistance to moisture, require the ground floors of most classes of buildings to be protected from ground moisture. The ground below a suspended timber floor must be effectively sealed and the space ventilated at 1500 mm^2 per metre run. According to the Building Regulations sealing can be achieved by a dense layer of concrete sealing at least 100 mm thick, and made up of 50 kg cement to not more than 11 m^3 of fine aggregate and 0.16 m^3 of coarse aggregate or BS 5328 mix ST2. If the mix contains steel 50 kg cement to fines of 0.08 m^3 and 0.13 m^3 of coarse aggregate should be used, the top of which must not be lower than the surrounding ground or paving level. However, it should be borne in mind that concrete cannot be regarded as a vapour or water barrier in this location. See **Floors: Specific Factors Section 7**, for alternatives.

Concrete ground floors are normally protected by (a) sheet membranes such as bituminous felt or 1200 gauge polythene sheet with sealed joints, or (b) in situ liquid membranes such as hot bitumen (3.2 mm thickness required by Building Regulations) or cold applied bituminous compositions (applied in not less than three coats). Alternatively the Building Regulations will accept specifications to BS 102:1990, Code of practice for protection of structures against water from the ground.

Damp-proof membranes can be placed either above or below the concrete slab. The main advantage in placing a dpm below the slab is that it keeps the concrete dry thus allowing the slab to act as a thermal storage medium – it also prevents loss of fines when the concrete is being poured. In situ liquid membranes are usually placed above the slab because they require a good surface to be effective. They then need to be protected by a 'loading' screed which must be at least 50 mm thick because it cannot be bonded to the concrete slab.

Whatever the form of the floor damp-proof membrane it must be effectively connected to the wall damp-proof course and where these are of dissimilar materials effective detailing and supervision are essential. (See diagram for item 47 in **Floors in Detail Section 7**)

The moisture resistance of intermediate floors is mostly associated with protection against internal spillage and containment of liquids from particular wet areas such as kitchens or bathrooms, or a manufacturing process or specialist storage facility. In these cases protection is normally achieved by careful specification and detailing of floor coverings and floor/wall junctions.

Interstitial condensation might also be a problem – see item 9, Durability.

BSCP 102:1973, Code of practice for protection of buildings against water from the ground (amended 1978)

BRE DAS 45 Suspended timber ground floors: remedying dampness due to inadequate ventilation

BRE Digest 54: 1971, Damp proofing solid floors

BRE Digest 364: 1991, Design of timber floors to prevent decay

BRE Digest 163: 1974, Drying out buildings

The Building Regulations 1991, Document C

9 Durability

Floors should have the same life expectancy as that of the other structural elements of a building. The suitability and quality of the sub-base together with the floor finish will determine the durability of floor coverings.

Timber floors are liable to fungal and insect attack from damp and insufficient ventilation. Timber must be protected from water vapour, rising damp (see item 8), constant seepage or spillage from bathrooms or broken pipes and other leaks. Where the moisture content of untreated timber floor components (including boards, joists, battens and fixing fillets in or on concrete floors) is more than 20%, fungal and insect attack are almost inevitable as the wood becomes digestible by these forms of life. Treatment includes pressurized chemical impregnation, or full immersion of all floor timbers if advisable, particularly if floor joist ends are built into walls.

Concrete ground floors must be protected from ground moisture (see item 8) and must not come into contact with harmful chemicals in the ground or in base course materials such as hardcore, clinker, pulverized fuel ash etc. Where these materials contain more than 0.2% of soluble sulphates, a 1200 gauge polythene isolating membrane (also a dpm) or sulphate resisting cement should be used. Site surveys must now allow for chemical analysis of the soil if the land has been previously used by former industries, or utilities or used as a landfill site. Section C2 of Document C of the Building Regulations has useful checklists and advice on courses of action. Base courses and fill must be laid strictly in accordance with standard specifications (see **Floors: specific factors Section 7**) in order to provide adequate support to solid (non-suspended) concrete ground floors.

Reinforcement in concrete floors suspended over damp or marshy ground must be adequately protected from corrosion by sufficient concrete cover.

Concrete intermediate floors are rarely damaged by dampness but in certain building types (or rooms) the risk of damage from water or chemical spillage or of interstitial condensation must be allowed for and appropriate protection given to concrete and reinforcement.

It should be noted that the use of high alumina cement has been excluded from codes of practice.

BS 7543:1992, Guide to durability of buildings and building elements, products and components

BS 1282:1975, Guide to the choice, use and application of wood preservatives

BRE Digest 364, Design of timber floors to prevent decay

BRE Digest 363, Sulphate and acid resistance of concrete in the ground

BRE AP 65: Timber preservation and remedial treatment in buildings. Literature Package 1993

BRE 296: Timbers: their natural durability and resistance to preservative treatment

BRE 345 1989: Wet rot: recognition and control

BRE 299 1985: Dry rot: its recognition and control

BRE 307 186, rev. 1992: Identifying damage by wood boring insects

10 Services accommodation

Small diameter withdrawable services such as electricity and communications cables can be laid within the structural floor or screed. Cable ducts can be buried, covered only by the floor finish or exposed with movable plate covers.

To save costs, small diameter heating pipes are sometimes laid within the screed. This is not recommended as it often produces problems of access for repairs, increased depth of screed to accommodate joints and pipe crossover points, cracks in the screed (and deformation and excessive wear of floor finishes) at thin points or through thermal movement of pipes.

Galvanized wire mesh reinforcement can be used to reduce the risk of cracking in screeds, which should in any case provide a minimum cover of 25 mm over service pipes.

Holes and notches in timber joists should be kept within the safe limits recommended in BS 5268, particularly in view of the current use of stress-graded timber.

Larger services such as waste pipes and air ducts are usually accommodated in suspended ceilings or between structural configurations such as downstand beams etc. Special cavity or elevated sub-floors can be used for computer rooms or laboratories etc.

11 Finishes

General factors (floor finishes in detail are covered in **Floors: specific factors Section 7**):

1 Appearance. Patterns, colours and textures should be chosen from as large a sample as possible and viewed in similar lighting conditions to those that will exist in the completed building.

2 Wear resistance: Because foot traffic causes greatest wear where it is concentrated, stops, starts or turns, it is worth considering finishes that can be partially renewed. Indentation and impact wear might be far greater for certain types of buildings and particular areas such as lift lobbies or offices. Deterioration through water or chemical spillage might occur in certain rooms or buildings.

3 Acoustics: Soft finishes can absorb some airborne sound and help to reduce the reverberation time of a room. Hard finishes act as reflectors and tend to increase noise levels.

4 Sound transmission: Floor finishes can help to reduce the transmission of impact sound through a floor – see item 6.

5 Warmth: This is not only a matter of actual temperature as some materials, such as carpets and cork,

feel warmer at lower temperatures than others. This is because of their thermal conductivity characteristics (i.e. how much heat they absorb from the body).

6 Resilience: Non-yielding hard or rigid floors are more tiring to walk upon than soft or 'springy' floors (which are necessary for certain activities such as dancing or gymnastics).

7 Safety: Slippery floors are a major hazard. Non-slip polishes and seals are available for most hard floor finishes which have an inherent slipperiness. It is worth noting that although gloss and slipperiness are not necessarily related, a dull slippery floor can be very dangerous because it will be unexpected. The frictional resistance of the floor surface will change according to footwear and flooring specifications must allow for the floor use and location.

8 Crack resistance: Floor finishes should have sufficient flexibility to accommodate the expected movements (thermal, shrinkage, deflection and settlement) of the sub-base and structural floor and be resistant to fracture and able to absorb stress.

9 Water resistance: Floor surfaces subject to constant wetting should not contain magnesite or be fixed with a form of adhesive that will not be waterproof. Linoleum, cork and wood products should not be used. Careful detailing at skirtings and upstands is essential.

10 Chemical resistance: It is important to know the type of chemical to be resisted; these are often classified as acids, alkalis and solvents or oils. Some floors will require to be washed down regularly and will require special drainage and falls. It is normal practice to include a second line of defence in the form of a sheet membrane in the sub-floor.

BS 8204 Screeds, bases and in-situ floorings. Parts 1–5 cover concrete, polymer modified cementitious wearing surfaces, terrazzo and mastic asphalt.

Mitchell's Building Series: Finishes, Yvonne Dean. Longman, 1996 (floorings in every materials section).

Mitchell's Building Series: Internal Components, Alan Blanc. Longman, 1994 (includes suspended floors, raised floors).

References to specific floor finishes are given in **Floors: specific factors Section 7**.

Trade and research organizations

Fire Protection Association, 140 Aldersgate Street, London EC1A 4HX (tel. 0171-606 3757, fax 0171-600 1487).

Fire Research Station (BRE), Bucknalls Lane, Garston, Herts WD2 7JR (tel. 01923-664000).

Floors in Detail Section 7

SMM7: E in situ concrete, G Structural carcassing M Surface finishes

(See Section 6 for Floors: general)

Notes and references

Items are cross-referenced from the diagrams and divided into sections with a general comment followed by technical references and the Building Regulations in context. Addresses of relevant trade and research organizations are given at the end of the section. British Standards and BRE Digests should be checked for current amendments

   This section (containing specific factors 12 to 69) should be read in conjunction with **Floors: General Section 6** (general factors 1 to 11).

12 Path of damp and heat loss if no barrier

A vertical damp-proof barrier must be used to prevent moisture reaching the floor zone using either:

(a) flexible sheet materials such as reinforced bituminous felt, plastics sheet or metal such as lead or zinc;
(b) applied waterproof coatings such as bitumen paints (emulsion type paints allow moisture vapour to escape from the concrete). Shrinkage cracks in concrete can lead to cracks in a painted barrier and so this form of barrier is not recommended for exposed conditions;
(c) an unbridged cavity of at least 50 mm width.

Where a cavity is used as a moisture barrier, it will also be likely to contain thermal insulation and detailing has to ensure that both characteristics are catered for. Where a sheet material or an applied waterproof coating is used as a moisture barrier in conjunction with solid wall construction, horizontal thermal insulation should be applied to both top and bottom surfaces of the concrete floor to avoid cold bridges. Bottom insulation can be rigid boards recessed into the soffit in perimeter strips of not less than 300 mm width. Top insulation can be used in conjunction with an insulating lightweight concrete screed, rigid board or an insulation quilt under the floor finish.

13, 14, 15 Flanking, impact and airborne sound

See **Floors: General Section 6**, item 6, for general comments and references. Specifically, the Building Regulations, Document E Section 2, give requirements that satisfy different densities of construction. If the wall mass is less than 375 kg/m² then the floor base should pass through the construction to provide a barrier for sound transmission; if greater, then either the wall or floor could pass through. Cavities should not be bridged.

16 Fire resistance

See **Floors: General Section 6**, item 5, for comments and references.

17 Bearing and lateral bracing

As structural elements, all floors are used to provide lateral support to walls and also reduce the slenderness ratio of the wall by lowering its effective height. The Building Regulations define lateral support to a wall as adequate when a concrete floor (or roof) slab has a minimum of 90 mm bearing on walls irrespective of the direction of span (see Diagram 18 of Document A of the Building Regulations). Where lateral bracing of the wall is required but the bearing is less than 90 mm or where the floor slab butts against the wall, or where joists are running parallel to a wall, 30 × 5 mm galvanized mild steel straps must be used at recommended spacings. This ensures that all walls will receive some lateral support. See Document A, Section 1C, paragraphs 34, 35 and 36.

   Where floor slabs rest upon inner leaves of cavity walls check that concrete block or brick strengths are adequate to carry floor loadings. See item 28 for comments relating to floors supported by columns with brick infill panels between.

BS 5628 Part 1: 1992, Structural use of unreinforced masonry, Part 2: 1995, Structural use of reinforced and prestressed masonry
The Building Regulations 1991, Document A Sections 1/2

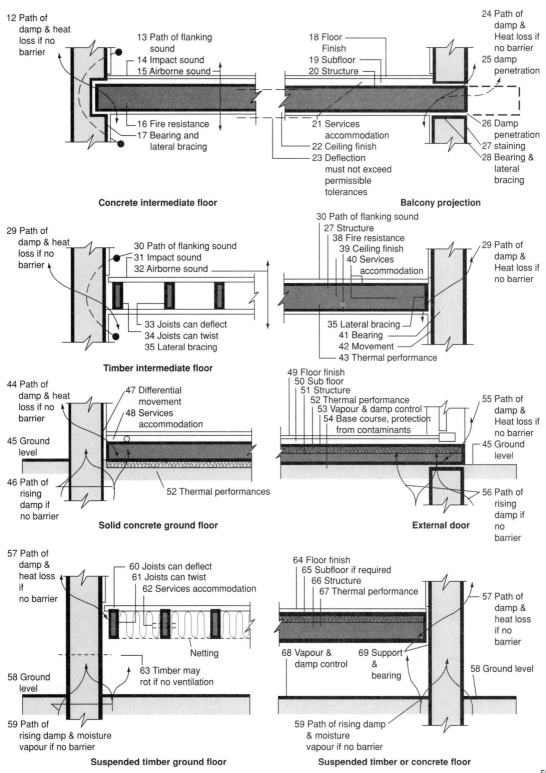

12 Path of damp & heat loss if no barrier

13 Path of flanking sound
14 Impact sound
15 Airborne sound

18 Floor Finish
19 Subfloor
20 Structure

24 Path of damp & Heat loss if no barrier
25 damp penetration

16 Fire resistance
17 Bearing and lateral bracing

21 Services accommodation
22 Ceiling finish
23 Deflection must not exceed permissible tolerances

26 Damp penetration
27 staining
28 Bearing & lateral bracing

Concrete intermediate floor

Balcony projection

29 Path of damp & heat loss if no barrier

30 Path of flanking sound
31 Impact sound
32 Airborne sound

30 Path of flanking sound
27 Structure
38 Fire resistance
39 Ceiling finish
40 Services accommodation

29 Path of damp & Heat loss if no barrier

33 Joists can deflect
34 Joists can twist
35 Lateral bracing

35 Lateral bracing
41 Bearing
42 Movement
43 Thermal performance

Timber intermediate floor

44 Path of damp & heat loss if no barrier

45 Ground level

47 Differential movement
48 Services accommodation

49 Floor finish
50 Sub floor
51 Structure
52 Thermal performance
53 Vapour & damp control
54 Base course, protection from contaminants

55 Path of damp & Heat loss if no barrier
45 Ground level

46 Path of rising damp if no barrier

52 Thermal performances

56 Path of rising damp if no barrier

Solid concrete ground floor

External door

57 Path of damp & heat loss if no barrier

60 Joists can deflect
61 Joists can twist
62 Services accommodation

64 Floor finish
65 Subfloor if required
66 Structure
67 Thermal performance

57 Path of damp & heat loss if no barrier

Netting

58 Ground level

63 Timber may rot if no ventilation

68 Vapour & damp control
69 Support & bearing

58 Ground level

59 Path of rising damp & moisture vapour if no barrier

59 Path of rising damp & moisture vapour if no barrier

Suspended timber ground floor

Suspended timber or concrete floor

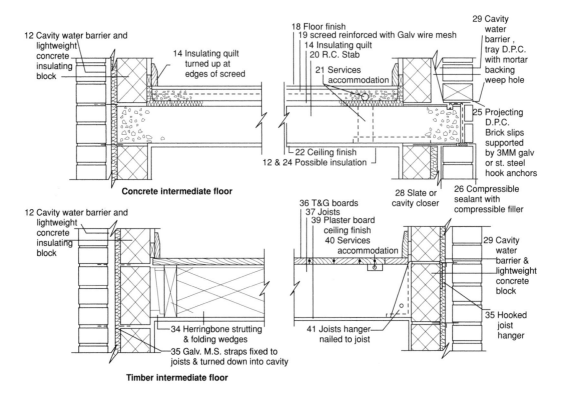

Concrete intermediate floor

Timber intermediate floor

18 Floor finish

See **Floors: General Section 6**, item 11, for general comments and references. The range of possible floor finishes suitable for suspended concrete floors is so wide that only the principle and some sub-categories can be mentioned here. For comprehensive lists readers are referred to the following: *Mitchell's Building Series: Finishes*, Yvonne Dean. Longman, 1996. In this book floorings are dealt with under Chapter 7 (Composites), and every chapter deals with floorings under their generic material classifications, for example ceramics (tiles, marble, concrete) or polymers (rubbers and plastics) or composites (timber).

However, floor finishes may also be classified in an elemental way as follows:

1 Hard continuous floorings laid in situ such as concrete, granolithic, terrazzo, asphalt, pitch mastic, plastics and rubber compositions, epoxy or acrylic resins.
2 Hard tiles made of similar materials to those in group 1 but, in addition, clay and ceramic tiles, mosaics, slate, marble, stone.
3 Wood in strip, block or sheet form.
4 Soft, continuous floorings including thin tile or sheet made from rubber or rubber-based compositions, cork, linoleum, thermoplastics, vinyl compositions, pvc.
5 Carpets are available in woven, tufted, corded or needle-loom form, as well as in various forms of tiles. The piles and proportions of wool, nylon, acrylic, rayon, sisal, coir, jute, felt are so varied that expert advice is necessary from manufacturers and trade associations directly.
6 Rigid plates, usually metal in the form of steel anchor plates, metal clad concrete flags, iron paving tiles.

BS 8201:1987, Code of practice for flooring of timber, timber products and wood based panel products
BS 5385 Part 3: 1989, Code of practice for the design and installation of internal ceramic and natural stone wall tiling and mosaic in normal conditions
BS 5385 Part 5: 1994, Code of practice for the design and installation of terrazzo tile and slab, natural stone and composition block floorings
BS 8203:1987, Code of practice for the design and installation of sheet and tile flooring (cork, linoleum,

rubber) thermoplastic; semi-flexible pvc and flexible pvc flooring

BS 8204 Parts 1, 2 and 4: 1993, In situ floor finishes (includes concrete bases and screeds, terrazzo and mastic asphalt)

BS 776:1972, Materials for magnesium oxychloride (magnesite) flooring

BS 1711:1975 (1991), Specification for solid rubber flooring

BS 3187:1978 (1991), Specification for electrically conducting rubber flooring

BS 3260:1969 (1991), Specification for semi flexible PVC floor tiles

BS 3261 Specification for unbacked flexible PVC flooring. Part 1: 1973 (1991), Homogeneous flooring

BS 6431 Ceramic wall and floor tiles. Note: 23 Parts, Part 7 deals with sizes

BS 7263 Part 1: 1994, Pre-cast concrete flags

BS 1297:1987, Specification for tongued and grooved softwood flooring

BS 1187:1959, Specification for wood blocks for floors

BS 4050 Specification for mosaic parquet panels. Part 1: 1977, General characteristics, Part 2: 1966, Classi-fication and quality requirements

BS 3655:1974 (1991), Recommendations for informative labelling of textile floor coverings

BS 1006:1978, Methods for colour fastness of textiles and leather

BS 4051:1987, Method of determination of thickness of textile floor covering

BS 4098:1975 (1988), Method for the determination of thickness compression and recovery characteristics of textile floor coverings

BS 4131:1973, Specification for terrazzo tiles

BS 4682 Part 2: 1988, Determination of dimensional changes due to changes in ambient humidity, Part 3: 1987, Determination of dimensional changes after exposure to heat, Part 4: 1987, Determina-tion of dimensional changes after immersion in water

BS 4790:1987, Determination of flammability of textile floor coverings

BS 5442 Classification of adhesives for construction. Part 1: 1989, Classification of adhesives for use with flooring materials

BS 5669 Part 2: 1989, Specification for wood chipboard

BRE Digest 33: 1971, Sheet and tile flooring made from thermoplastic binders

BRE DAS 51 Floors: cement based screeds – specifica-tion (design)

BRE DAS 51 Floors: cement based screeds – mixing and laying (site)

Timber in Construction, TRADA. Batsford, 1985.

Timber intermediate floors for dwellings, TRADA AD1, 1992

Concrete Ground Floors, R. C. Deacon. British Cement Association, 1986

Laying Floor Screeds, G. Barnbrook. British Cement Association, 1979

19 Sub-floor

An intermediate material is normally necessary between the structural slab and the floor finish. This is usually in the form of a cement-based screed but other materials are used. The purpose of the sub-floor is to:

1 produce a smooth level and sound surface upon which to support or fix the floor finish;
2 provide falls for drainage if necessary;
3 accommodate services;
4 help prevent heat, sound and fire transmission (only when screed bonded to slab) from one compartment to the other;
5 transfer loading uniformly from floor finish to struc-ture.

Floor screeding, like wall plastering, is an important stage in the process of rough-to-smooth finished construction. Floor screeds cover up the rougher workmanship on the structural slab as well as any superficial damage inflicted during construction.

Screeds can be classified as:

1 *Monolithic*, meaning laid on 'green' concrete to ensure a good bond, and so minimize differential shrinkage. Protection during the remainder of the building process is essential. Can be between 12 mm and 25 mm thick.
2 *Bonded*. These are laid after the structural concrete has hardened. Screeds may need to be fully bonded, especiallly where thin (under 50 mm) screeds support thin flexible floor surfaces; or partially bonded where they are thick and/or support rigid units such as stone or clay quarry tiles. Bonding can be achieved by exposing the aggregate in the structural slab when not fully hardened, or by a textured finish. On precast or cured concrete, a proprietary bonding agent, or a textured finish can be used.

3 *Unbonded*. Here a minimum thickness of 50 mm is essential. When laid on a resilient material for sound or heat insulation, screeds should be at least 65 mm thick and 75 mm thick when they contain heating installations. Galvanized wire mesh reinforcement is often used to prevent screeds cracking when shrinking during the hardening process. Resilient insulants should not be reduced to less than 10 mm under the load of the screed and finish.

Materials used for screeds are:

(a) *Cement and dense aggregate*, most widely used but shrinkage is a common fault and mixes should not be richer than 1 part of Portland cement to 3 parts of fine aggregate. A more normal mix is 1 to 5. See references in the British Standards.

(b) *Cement and lightweight aggregate*. Reduces floor loading. Aggregate can be expanded clay, shale, slate foamed slag, sintered pulverized fuel ash, exfoliated vermiculite etc. These materials improve the insulating value but being less dense then give poor sound insulation. Minimum thickness 40 mm.

(c) *Aerated concrete*. Fine sand and cement with a foaming agent introduced in order to produce a screed containing tiny air pockets. Usually requires a specialist firm as success depends on very careful control of proportions of ingredients.

(d) *Gyproc (alpha hemi-hydrate)*, has the advantage of very low drying shrinkage and can be laid in thicknesses of 25 mm or 40 mm when on a resilient layer. Bonding to the structural floor is not necessary. A disadvantage is that it loses strength in damp conditions; floors must be very dry before being screeded.

(e) *Modified cement and sand (with additives)*. There are many proprietary screeds containing materials which include bitumen, polyvinyl acetate, acrylic resins, synthetic rubbers etc. These materials can allow screeds down to 13 mm thick. Their performance regarding bonding, workability, shrinkage etc. should be checked as installation often relies on use of a specialist contractor – preferably the same one handling the floor finish.

(f) *Asphalt*. Can be laid in a single coat 13 mm thick and be either of mastic asphalt or pitch mastic (BS 8204). Has the advantages of providing a damp-proof membrane, no drying time, no shrinkage problems and provides a very smooth true surface to receive the floor finish.

To be successful all screeds require a thorough specification, site preparation and execution as well as good supervision. It is essential to follow the good practice recommendations contained in the references given below.

BS 8203:1987, Code of practice for the installation of sheet and tile flooring
BS 8204 Screeds bases and in situ floorings
BS 8204 Part 1: 1987, Code of practice for in situ concrete bases and screeds to receive in situ flooring
BS 8204 Part 2: 1987, Code of practice for concrete wearing surfaces
BS 8204 Part 3: 1993, Code of practice for polymer modified cementitious wearing surfaces
BS 8204 Part 4: 1993, Code of practice for terazzo wearing surfaces
BS 8204 Part 5: 1994, Code of practice for mastic asphalt underlays and wearing surfaces

20 Structure

For general comments and references concerning strength and stability see **Floors: General Section 6**, item 3. Specifically, concrete suspended floors are most widely used where sound and fire compartmentation is needed.

Reinforced concrete floors can be classified in a number of ways but generally they fall into two broad categories (a) cast in situ and (b) precast. Each have a number of sub-categories, some of which overlap, such as precast units which have a structural in situ topping. There is so much variety with many advantages and disadvantages, that only the basic forms can be mentioned here and readers are advised to consult the standard references given below.

1 *Solid concrete slab*. In its simplest form spanning in one direction only. For larger spans (over 5 m) or heavier than domestic loadings a two-way spanning slab is often used. This form of floor requires supporting on formwork (normally for at least 7 days) until strong enough to carry loads.

2 *In situ plate floor*, used over columns with reinforcement designed in a concentrated grid within the depth of the slab and avoiding the need for exposed beams.

3 *In situ flat slab floor*, similar to (2) but using 'mushroom' or 'flared' columns.

4 *In situ ribbed floor*, consisting of a series of ribs or tee beams integral with a thin floor slab.

5 *In situ hollow block floor.* Hollow blocks of concrete, clay etc. are laid on formwork, reinforcement placed between the blocks and concrete poured to form a series of small beams. Where slip tiles are used between blocks to provide a uniform key for plastering, there should be adequate covering to steel reinforcement.

6 *In situ rectangular diagonal grid floor* (coffered), consisting of a thin floor slab spanning between a reinforced regular grid of main and subsidiary beams.

7 *Precast beams* – either hollow or solid, laid close together with reinforcement and in situ concrete poured to form a structural topping.

8 *Precast ribs and filler blocks.* Concrete ribs span between supports and concrete, clay or wood wool blocks between the ribs. Some forms require a structural topping – others only a non-structural screed. No shuttering is required.

9 *Precast large panels.* Panels up to approximately 2.70 m wide and the height of four storeys can be lifted by crane and supported on precast beams, wall panels or in situ frames. This form of construction is used when there is a need for speed of erection and then the use of a large crane can be economic.

10 *Prestressed floors.* Pre-tensioned reinforcement is normally used in precast components of concrete floors. Tensioning the reinforcement (done in the casting factory) puts the surrounding concrete in compression and so limits deflection, it also induces a camber which must be taken into account when considering screed thicknesses. Prestressing allows longer spans for any given depth of slab, plank or rib.

11 *Composite floors.* This form of construction employs steel in various ways in addition to or other than as straightforward reinforcement bars e.g. in situ concrete on ribbed expanded metal supported over steel joists; ribbed expanded metal arched between steel filler joists; hollow steel trough sections supporting an in situ slab. New slimmer slab constructions can be achieved saving on overall height of a building by integrating the floor slab with the flanges of supporting steels.

Slim Floor Construction using Deep Decking, D. Mullet. The Steel Construction Institute, 1993.

Mitchell's Building Series: Structure and Fabric, Part 2, Jack Stroud Foster and Raymond Harrington, Chapter 6, Floor Structures. Longman, 1994.

21 Services accommodation

See comments in **Floors: General Section 6**, item 10. Small diameter services such as electric and telecommunication cables can be run within in situ floors by placing conduit and all accessories on the formwork before the concrete is poured. In this location they are vulnerable to damage or misalignment by following trades. They must not reduce the efficiency of the reinforcement by reducing the specified minimum concrete cover. Alternatively, conduit can be laid on top of the slab, holes having been made to receive vertical connections. Screeds should cover conduits by at least 25 mm. Normally where conduit is laid within a structural concrete topping it can only run parallel to the main reinforcement. Larger diameter pipes for water, gas etc. require access for maintenance and are usually laid on top of the structural slab or are suspended from the soffit.

When on top, crossover points and large radius bends must be allowed for or avoided. Thick screeds might be necessary and lightweight screeds (see item 19) are often used to reduce loading.

The location of holes through concrete floors should be decided before slabs are fixed or poured. Precast floors require concrete or steel trimmers around holes and in situ floors will require timber, plastics or cardboard roll formwork for small holes and adjustment or additional reinforcement around larger holes. See Building Regulations 1991 Document B3 Internal fire spread (structure), Section 10 Protection of openings and fire stopping.

Check on fire stopping requirements around pipes passing through floors. Vertical duct construction should be of a similar fire resistance standard as the floor through which the pipes pass.

22 Ceiling finishes

Suspended ceilings are considered to be outside the scope of this book as they are not normally used in domestic construction.

Plastering on dense concrete floor slab soffits requires thoroughness in specification and execution. Failures are common, due mainly to the concrete not being thoroughly set and not having completed its initial shrinkage; or to it having high water absorption preventing a good bond with the plaster. If the initial bond is poor, then differential thermal expansion between concrete and plaster can cause a breakdown in bonding later. Mechanical keying by using surface retarders on the formwork or special grooved formwork linings are both available. Hacking of the concrete to provide a key is not recommended. Bonding agents are also available. Ceiling boards fixed to concrete soffits should be checked for their surface spread of flame and smoke emission. Under high temperatures they may fall as hot molten material.

BS 5492:1990, Code of practice for internal plastering
BS 6100 Part 6: Section 6.6 1990, Plaster: Terms applicable to plasters, plasterwork and gypsum plasterboard
BS 4049:1966, Glossary of terms applicable to internal plastering, external rendering and floor screeding

23 Deflection must not exceed permissible tolerances

See **Floors: General Section 6**, item 4, for comments and references. Deflection values relate to the material chosen for the structure.

24 Path of damp and heat loss if no barrier

Generally as item 12, but in this case the slab continues to or extends beyond the external wall face. This means that the damp-proof barrier, whatever its form and location, must be positioned to protect the top of the floor slab. In cavity wall construction a cavity tray dpc is used to collect cavity moisture and lead it to the external wall face protecting the floor slab. Cavity tray materials must be flexible, particularly for complex folding and detailing. To prevent the cavity tray from being punctured during cavity cleaning, a solid mortar backing is usually provided for the tray to lie against (see diagram).

Methods to reduce heat losses are described in item 12.

25 Damp penetration (top of slab)

Where the floor slab extends close to or flush with the external wall face, the dpc should be taken out and project slightly to reduce the chances of bricks spalling just above the dpc. The dpc should always be laid on a bed of mortar. Where the slab extends to form a balcony, the cavity tray or other form of dpc must be taken to the external face and effectively connected with the balcony waterproof membrane, which should have a minimum of 150 mm upstand against the wall face.

Good Site Practice, BDA BN1, Brick Development Association

26 Damp penetration (under slab)

Differential movement between the concrete slab and the brickwork results in hair cracks at this point and a non-ferrous metal flashing or pointing with sealant should be provided to protect the joint. Where the floor slab is cast in situ over a supporting cavity wall, proprietary plastics or metal cavity closers are available which incorporate a water bar and drip centrally placed over the cavity.

Where the floor slab is cast before the external wall is built (as in the case of brick infill panels, see item 28) a drip can be cast in the concrete soffit and placed centrally over the cavity. Where brick slips are required to cover the edge of the concrete floor slab great care is necessary in detailing and execution if they are not to buckle or be dislodged. Brick slips are difficult to bond successfully but if used they should have a mechanical fixing. Galvanized or stainless steel supporting plates or clip anchors should be used. These are discussed and illustrated in *Mitchell's Building Series: Structure and Fabric*, Part 2. Brick slips often weather differently to surrounding brickwork because of their different thickness and manufacturing process.

27 Staining

Differential moisture absorption as well as chemicals from the exposed concrete slab can lead to staining of brickwork below the slab. As absolutely flush detailing is difficult to obtain designers sometimes recess the floor slab; this is best avoided but where it is done the top of the brickwork should be protected by a metal flashing. It is better to project the floor slab and incorporate a drip on the underside and a splayed top edge.

28 Bearing and lateral bracing

Comments generally as item 17. Where the floor is supported independently of the external wall, e.g. by columns or cross walls, shrinkage of the concrete, particularly RC frames, and expansion of clay brick panels must be carefully considered. Proprietary sliding metal anchors are available which allow vertical movement whilst resisting lateral loads from wind. A compressible sealant should be used in the top joint between concrete and brickwork.

29 Path of damp and heat loss if no barrier

Generally as item 12, except that heat losses in the case of timber joisted floors should be avoided by uninterrupted wall insulation. Where joists run parallel to the wall this presents little problem but where joists are at 90° to the wall their method of support may make uninterrupted insulation difficult. Joist hangers and brackets avoid this problem – see item 41. Where joists are built into external walls they must be treated against insect and fungal decay.

Exposed joist ends in unventilated cavities should be avoided if possible and in any case should not project into the cavity as mortar droppings could form a cavity bridge.

(Joists are rarely built into party cross walls because of the fire risk and the mandatory requirement to have at least 100 mm of solid incombustible material between ends of joists on opposite sides of a 215 mm wall.)

30 Path of flanking sound

See **Floors: General Section 6**, item 6, for general comments and references.

The Building Regulations have specific requirements relating to flanking sound for timber floors which separate one dwelling from another. Although there are no requirements for timber floors within a single dwelling, for conversions Section 5 of Document E gives comprehensive guidance to achieve satisfactory resistance to airborne and impact sound which could be used to improve the specification for a single dwelling. Section 2 of Document E gives guidance on floor bases (density 365 kg/m², and the detailing with junctions for external and internal walls. The mass of the wall must be at least 120 kg/m². Refer to items 13, 14 and 15 of **Floors: General Section 6** for additional guidance.

The BRE have a number of very good publications for design guidance for new buildings as well as advice for improving the sound insulation of existing structures including DIY advice for householders.

BRE Improving sound insulation in your home, Ref: XL4
BRE Digest 387: 1989, Sound insulation of lightweight dwellings
BRE Current Papers: BRE IP 6/88: Methods for improving the sound insulation between converted flats

31 and 32 Impact and airborne sound

See **Floors: General Section 6**, items 6.1 and 6.2, for general comments and references.

33 Joists can deflect

See **Floors: General Section 6**, item 4, for general comments and references.

34 Joists can twist

Timber joists are subject to twisting (rotation) as the result of changes in moisture content during and after construction.

This can cause unevenness of floor and ceiling finishes as well as weakening the floor as a whole. The effects of twisting are reduced by the use of lateral stiffening in the form of herringbone strutting, solid blocking or mild steel bolts. The floor deck can change to give greater stiffness. For example, plywood screwed to joists can provide an overall stiffer structure. Care should be taken if these structures (stressed skins) are used that services are not inaccessible for future repair/replacement. Stressed skins should be calculated and the application of adhesives and fixings supervised, together with the laying of the plywood in the correct direction to optimize strength. See *Timber Designers' Manual*, Ozleton and Baird, Crosby Lockwood Staples, 2nd edn, 1984.

The breadth to depth ratio of solid and laminated members (beams and joists) should comply with Table 17 of BS 5268. A ratio of 7 is acceptable only for members with ends held in position and both edges held firmly in line. The most common form of stiffening joists with spans over 2.5 m 150 mm is herringbone strutting. See Table 3 of Document A: Structure of the Building Regulations for joist span and number of rows of strutting. Struts should be at least 38 mm in thickness (but more normally 50 × 38) 'extending at least 0.75 times the depth of the joists'. See item 35 on lateral bracing to fix the last laid joist (parallel to the wall) directly to the wall.

BSCP 5268 Part 2: 1984, Structural use of timber

35 Lateral bracing

Floors should be used to provide lateral support to walls, see item 17 for reasons.

The Building Regulations (Document A: paragraphs 1C 33–39) lay down the method, frequency and the conditions under which timber joisted floors must be connected to walls in order to obtain adequate lateral support. These include 5 mm $\times$ 50 mm wide galvanized mild steel anchors taken over and carried over to at least three joists and securely fixed to the wall at intervals not exceeding 2 m. BS 5628 Part 1: 1992 and Part 2: 1995 show various recommended methods.

Similar anchors can be used where joists are at 90° to the wall or special galvanized pressed steel hooked joist hangers turned down over the inner leaf and into the wall cavity.

Joists should always be nailed through joist hangers to provide positive fixing.

BS 5628 Part 3: 1985, Code of practice for use of masonry. Materials and components, design and workmanship

The Building Regulations 1991 (Document A: paragraphs 1C 33–39, Schedule 7.

36 Floor finish

See **Floors: General Section 6**, item 11, for general comments and references.

Timber flooring can be obtained in a wide variety of forms and species, see references. Board and sheet materials provide both support and wearing functions whilst other forms provide decoration and wearing qualities only. In addition to the criteria listed in **Floors: General Section 6**, item 11, consideration should also be given to methods of access to services, especially when using sheet forms of floor finish. Strip boarding (normally 19 mm thick spanning over joists at 400 mm centres) should be tongued and grooved making sure the tongues are kept low down to enable future resurfacing. T and G boards and sheets allow for shrinkage, reduce curling and help prevent the passage of air and dust. These boards also help spread point loads from one board to another as well as enabling the use of slightly thinner ceiling finishes to obtain mandatory floor fire resistance up to half-hour standard (see item 38). Boards can be surface nailed or secret nailed through tongues. T and G boarding must be tightly 'cramped' before fixing to avoid large shrinkage gaps at joints with seasonal moisture loss and movement.

Timber sheet flooring such as plywood, chipboard etc. should be tongued and grooved or have butt joints supported by joists or battens at all edges. Various tongue and groove profiles are available, see manufacturers' literature.

An important aspect of timber flooring is its moisture content before, during and after construction. BS 1297:1987 recommends a moisture content of 22% for air-dried timber and 15% for kiln-dried timber, whilst BS 8201:1987 gives 18%. It should be remembered that 21% is the dry rot safety line.

When the building is occupied the moisture content may be between 14–18% with no heating, 12–15% with intermittent heating and 11–12% with continuous heating. Underfloor heating will reduce the moisture content of timber floor finishes still further, to between 5 and 10%.

Flooring grades of chipboard can vary in quality and manufacturers' recommendations should be followed regarding storage, moisture content prior to and during installation, as well as tolerances around all edges for movement. Special nails for fixing are needed. There are special requirements for using resin-bonded wood chipboard flooring, for loading, fixing and span limitations. Wet areas including toilets, bathrooms, kitchens and showers should have a flooring grade of chipboard that can satisfy these conditions, or a moisture resistant or waterproof grade of plywood should be specified.

Boards and sheets are normally suitable as a sub-floor for carpets and linoleum. Where cork, thermoplastics or other thin sheet materials are to be used as a finish on top of a boarded floor, an underlayer of hardboard or thin plywood is needed to provide a level surface preventing differential wear.

It is possible to lay a sand and cement screed on top of a timber boarded floor and this is sometimes done where the floor finish requires a very smooth sub-floor as in the case of epoxy resins etc. BS 8204 Part 1: 1987 gives guidance.

See item 18 for references.

BS 5669 Part 2: 1989, Specification for wood chipboard, and Part 4: 1989, Code of practice for the selection and application of particleboards for specific purposes

BRE Digest 373: 1992, Wood chipboard.

37 Structure

See **Floors: General Section 6**, item 3, for general comments and references.

Spans and loads for normal domestic softwood joists are given in the Building Regulations 1991, Document A, Appendix A for various joist sizes at centres up to 600 mm and spans of approximately 5 m (check current availability of sizes and lengths before specifying). See **Floors: General Section 6**, item 4, Deflection.

Large spans can be divided by laminated beams, plywood box and I beams; manufacturers should be consulted for spans, loadings and fixing methods. Stressed plywood panels of either single or double skins are also available. Another form of structural timber floor is thick (50 mm to 75 mm) softwood T and G boarding.

For normal domestic loadings (1.5 kN/m²) joists are usually spaced up to 500 mm centres for 16 mm thick T and G boards; for up to 600 mm centres, 19 mm thick T and G boards will have to be used (see Table A1 of Document A, Structure). Joists should not be narrower than 50 mm (nominal) as nailing of floorboards tends to split narrow joists. Note that where sheet flooring is butt jointed over joists, two lines of nails are needed. Structural timbers should normally be treated against insect and fungal attack – see **Floors: General Section 6**, item 9, for references.

BS 5268 Structural use of timber. Part 2: 1996, Code of practice for permissible stress design, materials and workmanship

BS 4978:1988, Specification for softwood grades for structural use

BS 4471:1987, Specification for dimensions for sizes of sawn and processed softwood

Span tables for one-family houses of not more than three storeys. Metric span tables for domestic floor and roof joists – Nordic Timber Council, (also useful factfile leaflets on timber).

TRADA – various publications particularly: Timber joist and deck floors – avoiding movement WIS1-36, 1995, Stress-graded British softwood, structural uses and span tables to BS 5268 WIS 2/3 29, rev. 1996.

American Plywood Association: Design and construction guides available on all aspects of building

The Building Regulations 1991, Document A Section 1B

38 Fire resistance

See **Floors: General Section 6**, item 5, for general comments and references as well as item 16 of this sheet for additional references. Building Regulations require timber floors within a single two-storey dwelling to have a 'modified' half-hour fire resistance i.e. stability 30 minutes, integrity 15 minutes and insulation 15 minutes (see Table A1 of Document B of the Building Regulations). Such floors should be designed to act independently of compartment walls in the event of their collapse during fire. For timber floors forming a compartment floor between separate dwellings 1-hour fire resistance is required. In dealing with party cross walls, the structure should be regarded as separating two compartments, which for domestic buildings is likely to be 1-hour fire resistance. Accordingly where joists span between party cross walls the structure in between must comply with this requirement. A separation of a minimum 90 mm of solid non-combustible material (masonry) is likely to comply. Junctions between floors and walls should be detailed to allow for compliance. The use of joist hangers gives bearing without risk to integrity of maintaining compartmentation. See also item 42; continuity across the wall and ceiling junction is vital to prevent fire spread.

The Building Regulations 1991, Document B Section 8, Compartmentation

39 Ceiling finishes

Ceiling finishes on timber joisted floors are usually of plaster or plasterboard. Plastering is no longer applied to wood laths (except for repair work) and it is now common practice to use Gypsum plasterboard finished with one coat of plaster. Where one coat is used it should be not less than 5 mm thick. Gypsum lath (9.5 mm and 12.7 mm thick and 406 mm wide) has rounded longitudinal edges that do not require jute scrim at the joints (except at ceiling/wall junctions). The laths are fixed across the joists with joints in straight lines.

The specification for plaster applied to Gypsum plasterboards must be carefully matched to the board. See references. Gypsum wallboard and plank are designed for direct application of the decorative finish. They have tapered edges ready to receive paper reinforcing tape. A thin primer is applied to the board and joint before decoration. Another simple method is to butt-joint square-edged boards and fill joints with tape or filler before decorating with a flexible textured coating.

Gypsum wallboard is made in 9.5 mm and 12.7 mm thicknesses to various widths and lengths. Gypsum plank is made in 19 mm thickness, 600 mm widths to various lengths. See references for insulating fibre boards, metal lathing, woodwool slabs, etc. Plasterboard has a low spread of flame rating (Class 1 to BS 476) and contributes to the fire resistance of floors.

BS 5492:1990, Code of practice for internal plastering

BS 1230 Part 1: 1984 (1985), Specification for plaster-board excluding material submitted to secondary operations

Mitchell's Building Series: Finishes, Yvonne Dean. Chapter 5 Applications of ceramics materials. Longman, 1996.

Gypsum White Book, published annually by British Gypsum Ltd

40 Services accommodation

Holes and notches in timber joists must not weaken the structure and in view of the use of stress-graded timber it is essential to follow the recommendations of BS 5268. Briefly these are that no notch should be at the bottom of a joist, notches should be no deeper than 0.125 of the joist depth and should be kept between 0.07 and 0.25 of the span from the support. Holes through joists should only be on the neutral axis, i.e. at the centre of depth, not exceed 0.25 of the joist depth in diameter and should be positioned between 0.25 and 0.4 of the span from the centre of the support. Feed or waste pipes carrying cold water should be lagged to avoid condensation within floor spaces.

41 Bearing

The bearing of timber joists needs to:

1 provide lateral bracing to walls – see item 35;
2 maintain the thermal barrier;
3 keep the floor construction dry – see comments under item 29 relating to building joists into walls.

The standard methods of achieving these aims are:

1 Non-ferrous metal brackets (minimum size 50 mm × 6 mm extending 215 mm into wall) built into the wall at 750 mm centres carrying a wall-plate treated against fungal attack. This method produces the difficulty of concealing the wall-plate at the wall/ceiling junction.
2 Galvanized metal angles (minimum size 50 mm × 50 mm × 6 mm) bolted to the wall at 600 mm centres. Joists can be notched slightly to produce a flush soffit. Nogging pieces should be fixed in between the joists and the joists fixed to the metal angle. This method is good for existing or concrete walls.
3 Galvanized pressed metal joist hangers. This method is now most widely used. Hangers must be nailed to

joists to provide a positive fixing. Bearing should be a minimum of 75 mm. Hooked hangers can also provide lateral wall bracing – see item 35.

42 Movement

Cracks at the ceiling line are a common fault caused by differential movement between the floor and the wall as well as drying shrinkage between ceiling and wall finishes. The wall/ceiling junction should be well-taped with heavy duty jute scrimming tape at least 90 mm wide. It is difficult to eradicate entirely this problem and it is customary to make good the cracks at the end of the maintenance period. Traditional cornices were installed after some movement had taken place and covered any shrinkage gaps between wall and ceiling, as well as providing continuity of fire protection.

Preformed plaster or plastics coves are sometimes used to cover the ceiling junction. Strips of corrosion resistant expanded metal should be used to form a key over exposed timber wall-plates.

43 Thermal performance

Thermal insulation for suspended timber floors in dwellings is required to be 0.35 W/m^{2}K for a SAP energy rating less than 60 and 0.45 W/m^{2}K if the rating is over 60. Semi-exposed floors between heated areas and enclosed but colder areas such as garages should attain a U-value of at least 0.6 W/m^{2}K. Attainment of the recommended U-values will normally help to reduce impact and airborne sound transmission.

44 Path of damp and heat loss if no barrier

See item 12 for comments relating to the path of dampness from above ground; also item 24 for comments relating to the protection of the floor slab where it extends to or beyond the face of an external wall.

See **Floors: General Section 6**, item 7, Thermal insulation for general comments and references relating to heat losses from solid ground floors.

The main heat losses through solid ground floors are sideways through walls to the colder ground outside. The Building Regulations require solid ground floors to be insulated and perimeter (horizontal) and/or edge (vertical) insulation should be detailed to avoid thermal bridging. This can be achieved by a horizontal strip of

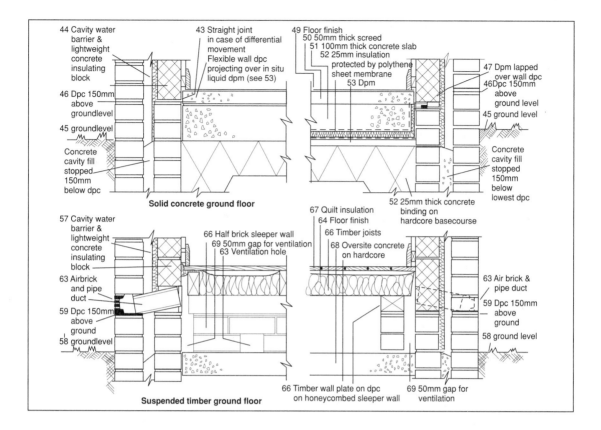

Solid concrete ground floor

Suspended timber ground floor

insulation around the edge of the floor and/or vertical insulation extending from the floor slab down to the top of the foundations.

BRE Digest 145: 1972, Heat losses through ground floors
BRE IP 7/93: The U-value of solid ground floors with
   edge insulation

45 Ground level

The relationships between finished external ground level, finished internal floor level and existing site levels are important. Solid floors (i.e. continuously supported by the ground or hardcore 'fill' etc.) are usually chosen where the existing and final levels would not require more than about 500 mm and 600 mm of fill. Over this depth it is normally more economic to use a suspended floor.

However, each case requires careful analysis, taking into account the difference between existing site levels and finished floor levels (sloping ground, loading bays

etc.); availability, type and cost of fill; floor loadings; flood water levels; bearing capacity of soil; risk of ground subsidence; nature of foundations.

Finished ground levels should be carefully calculated around the perimeter of a building to ensure that the Building Regulation requirement of 150 mm from ground to dpc is maintained (see item 46). Wherever possible finished floor levels should be fixed so that the floor damp-proof membrane lines through with the horizontal wall dpc, so avoiding short lengths of vertical dpcs. In cavity walls this need apply only to the inner leaf dpc; the outer leaf dpc can be at a different height as the cavity acts as a vertical water barrier.

Where finished ground level is unavoidably above finished floor level special vertical waterproofing precautions are necessary. See reference for basements below. Ground levels should slope away from buildings.

Mitchell's Building Series: Structure and Fabric, Part 1,   Chapter 8 Floor Structures, Part 2, Waterproofing of   Basements. Longman, 1994.

46 Path of rising damp and moisture vapour if no barrier

Ground dampness will be transmitted to walls and solid floors by capillary attraction unless prevented by correctly specified, detailed and installed impervious barriers. See **External Walls, General Section 3**, item 13, Rising damp, for comments and references to technical literature and Building Regulations relating to walls.

See **Floors: General Section 6**, item 8, Moisture resistance, for general comments and references relating to floors. The merits and demerits of locating floor damp-proof membranes in various positions are discussed under item 53.

Whatever the form and materials of wall damp-proof courses and floor damp-proof membranes they must be effectively continuously-welded or overlapped to form a permanent and flexible continuous barrier in order to protect insulants, sub-floors and finishes. In addition these barriers prevent moisture vapour from the ground penetrating into the building.

47 Differential movement

The junction between external walls and solid ground floors is vulnerable to movement because of either:

(a) expansion or contraction of concrete floors and sub-floors, or
(b) differential settlement between the wall and floor.

Solid floors must then be free to move in relation to walls. This is achieved by a straight joint or, for large areas of concrete floor, by a water-resistant compressible expansion joint (e.g. polyurethane foam sealing strips or 20 mm thick bitumen impregnated fibre board). Designers must provide for permanent continuity of dpcs and dpms at this junction, and the use of PVC waterstops may need to be incorporated. Wall dpcs should be projected over floor dpms where they are level with each other, or wall dpcs overlapped with the floor dpm where there is a level difference.

48 Services accommodation

Comments generally as for upper concrete floors, see item 21. Services on ground floor slabs must not damage damp-proof membranes either during their installation or subsequent screed or concrete laying.

Effective screed cover of 25 mm must be maintained. Consider access for repairs. Some water authorities will insist on continuous access over cold water feed pipes.

49 Floor finish

See **Floors: General Section 6**, item 11, for general comments and references and item 18 for specific comments and references relating to finishes suitable for concrete floors.

50 Sub-floor

See item 19 for specific comments and references to sub-floors and screeds.

Concrete ground floor slabs are sometimes 'power floated' using mechanical rotary surfacers to produce a reasonably level and smooth surface ready to receive floor finishes. This method eliminates the need for a sub-floor but is not always suitable or economic for certain site conditions (e.g. disconnected small floor areas) or certain floor finishes.

51 Structure

The main functions of a solid concrete ground floor are to transmit uniformly distributed and point loads to the supporting ground and to provide an adequate base for sub-floors and/or finishes. The slab thickness, concrete quality and whether or not reinforcement is required will depend on the type of soil, fill or hardcore material and expected floor loadings.

For domestic floors the Building Regulations require a minimum thickness of 100 mm containing 300 kg cement for every m^3 of concrete. Thicker (120 mm to 150 mm) slabs are required (a) where the soil is less than 'very stable', (b) to spread point loads such as those from partition walls, and (c) where the water table is within 600 mm of ground level. Industrial floor slabs must be properly calculated taking into account all loading and bearing conditions.

Reinforcement in solid concrete ground floors is used: (a) to prevent cracks or minimize their thickness, (b) to resist bending movements under or over local loads, (c) to avoid unevenness across construction joints, and (d) where the soil type is less than of average bearing capacity.

Reinforcement is usually in the form of rolls or sheets of square (about 203 mm) mesh weighing from 1.54 to

6.16 kg/m². A minimum bottom cover of 40 mm must be provided where concrete is in contact with the ground but cover should be adequate for the severity of exposure of the ground conditions. The same minimum cover should be provided at the top of slabs to prevent the reinforcement coming to the surface during concreting. BS 8110 Structural use of concrete, Part 1: 1985, gives guidance on concrete shrinkage and bay size.

Anti-crack reinforcement for domestic ground floors is usually in the form of a lightweight mesh placed in the centre of the slab. But this decreases the effective depth of the slab and for industrial or heavily loaded floors, or where uneven settlement is expected, reinforcement is best placed at both top and bottom of slabs. Concrete ground floor slabs must be protected from harmful chemicals. See **Section**, item 9, Durability.

See **Floors: General Section 6**, item 3, for structural references.

BS 8110:1985, Structural use of reinforced concrete

52 Thermal Performance

See **Floors: General Section 6**, item 7, Thermal Insulation for general comments and references. See item 44 above relating to heat losses around edges of solid concrete floors. As it is necessary to use a continuous layer of thermal insulation combined with a solid ground floor to reduce heat losses it is important to choose an insulant that will be unaffected by water, e.g. polystyrene. Insulants will get wet during the construction process, and their thickness required must be checked by calculation. In addition, the insulation should be protected from ground moisture and vapour. See **Roofs: General Section 8**, item 6.4, Condensation risk, for explanation and references.

53 Vapour and damp control

See **Floors: General Section 6**, item 8, Moisture resistance, for general comments and references.

The Building Regulations Document C require floors resting upon the ground to be protected from ground moisture. This is normally achieved by using continuous sheet membranes of bituminous felt or plastics such as 1200 gauge polyethylene, in situ liquid membranes such as hot bitumen (3.2 mm minimum thickness required by Building Regulations) or cold applied bituminous compositions (applied in not less than three coats). Damp-proof membranes can be placed on top, under or at the centre of concrete slabs. Consider the following:

1 On top of slab:
(a) To avoid puncturing, sheet membranes must have a smooth surface (trowelled finish costs extra).
(b) Concrete base must be as dry as practicable before in situ liquid membranes can be applied, particularly if site is wet. (If this is the case, a sheet dpm would be more suitable).
(c) Screed thickness should be 50 mm minimum (for sand and cement) and provide a smooth surface and falls if required. A lightweight screed assists with thermal insulation as well, although at the expense of thermal capacity.

2 Bottom of slab:
(a) Must have a smooth surface (25 mm of rolled sand or blinding concrete).
(b) Care required when casting slab, particularly if reinforced.
(c) dpm will protect slab from some contaminants that may cause deterioration of the concrete but sulphate-resisting cement may still need to be specified depending on the soil conditions. See Table 2 of Section C2 of the Building Regulations for guidance on contaminants and actions.
(d) The concrete slab can only harden upwards, therefore there could be a longer wait before floor finishes can be applied (100 mm thick floor slab with 50 mm thick screed can take at least six months to harden fully, i.e. one month per 25 mm of thickness).
(e) Concrete slab not subject to moisture and therefore the thermal mass provides better insulation.
(f) Screed thickness can be reduced because it is possible to use a fully or partially bonded screed (this could mean a cost saving on both screed thickness and not having to trowel smooth the slab surface).
(g) A power floated slab is possible.

3 Centre of slab:
(a) Loss of strength between normal thickness slab or the necessity of increasing slab thickness.
(b) Will decrease hardening time before application of floor finishes.
(c) Extra cost of casting two slabs.
(d) Often used as a 'sandwich' floor to combat positive water pressure – see references to basement construction, item 45.

Sheet membranes must be well lapped at joints and turned up and secured to pipes and ducts etc. Permanently effective connections to horizontal dpcs are important.

Asphalt membranes should have special sleeves or flashings to continue protection around pipes and ducts. Brush-applied membranes should be well coated around pipes and ducts.

See **Floors: General Section 6**, item 8, for references.

54 Base course, protection from contaminants

Solid concrete floors must not be laid directly upon organic matter and it is normal practice to strip off the first 150 mm of topsoil. A suitable base course is then laid to receive the concrete slab.

Base course functions are to (a) make up levels as necessary, (b) spread point loads, (c) provide a level dry surface to receive the concrete slab, (d) reduce upward ground moisture movement by reducing capillary attraction, and (e) may incorporate insulation.

Base course thicknesses may vary from 125 to approximately 300 mm. Greater depths can be made up with 'fill'. Base course and fill are often specified as the same material but not all fill materials are suitable for base courses. This is because a base course material should achieve a lateral interlocking strength after compaction. This implies that such materials as shale, pfa (pulverized fuel ash), dolomite and clinker, whilst suitable for fill, will not be suitable for a base course.

Both base course and fill materials must be chemically inert, physically stable (wet or dry), free from organic matter, sulphates and other harmful chemicals. The material must also be capable of full compaction, be angular shaped and small enough to pass through a 125 mm diameter ring. Ideally, materials should be tested before use. Where untested or where they contain more than 0.2% soluble sulphates, the concrete slab should be protected by a sheet of 1200 gauge polyethylene or by the use of sulphate-resisting cement.

Types of material include:
(a) Hardcore (broken brick, tile etc.) must be free from metal, glass, plastics, tree stumps and other building waste matter. Suitable for both fill and base course.
(b) Blast furnace slag (by-product of steel manufacturing) may contain soluble sulphates. Suitable for both fill and base course.

(c) Clinker, unless well burnt, will contain sulphates. Unsuitable for base course.
(d) Colliery shale must be well burnt, otherwise may swell when wet; may contain sulphates. Unsuitable for base course.
(e) Concrete rubble. Usually large lumps requiring finer infill material. Suitable for both fill and base course.
(f) Hoggin (natural mixture of gravel and sand). May contain sulphates. Suitable for both fill and base course.
(g) Pulverized fuel ash (pfa), a by-product of larger boiler installations. Unsuitable for base course.
(h) Dolomite (soft broken limestone), unsuitable for base course.
(i) Stone. Broken stone or quarry waste. Suitable for both fill and base course.

BS 5930:1981, Code of practice for site investigation
BS DD 175:1988 (1992), Code of practice for the identification of potentially contaminated land and its investigation
BRE Digest 276: 1992, Hardcore

55 Path of damp and heat loss if no barrier

Generally as item 44. See **External doors Section 18**, item 24: example detail 2 shows a door threshold, dpm and insulation.

56 Path of rising damp if no barrier

As item 46.

57 Path of damp and heat loss if no barrier

Comments generally as for item 12 and 29. For comments relating to joists at right angles to walls see item 69.

58 Ground level

The relationship between existing site and finished floor levels is usually the dictating factor when choosing a suspended floor in preference to a solid floor. Where depths of fill over approximately 500 mm to 600 mm (depending on cost and availability) would be necessary it is often more economic to use a suspended floor. See also item 45 above.

Building Regulations Document C require all dpcs to be at least 150 mm above finished ground level as well as the top of any oversite concrete being not lower than the highest level of the ground or paving adjoining. See item 68 and related note on diagram. The minimum height from top of oversite concrete to underside of joists is also laid down (paragraph 3.10) as 150 mm, i.e. one course of bricks, dpc and timber wall-plate. See item 66.

59 Path of rising damp and moisture vapour if no barrier

Generally as item 46. In addition, the ground under suspended timber floors must be sealed to restrict moisture vapour rising into the air space between ground and floor.

See item 68 for comments and references.

60 Joists can deflect

See **Floors: General Section 6**, item 4, for comments and references.

61 Joists can twist

See item 34 and example for comments and references.

62 Services accommodation

See item 40 for comments and references.

63 Timber may rot if no ventilation

Humid air favours the growth of dry rot and the Building Regulations (paragraph 3.9) require the space between the ground and a suspended timber floor to be constructed to prevent any part of the floor being adversely affected by moisture or water vapour. A figure of 1500 mm² is given to ventilate every metre run of wall, with a proviso that the opening should be a least 100 mm in diameter for adequate through ventilation, but no figures for airflow rates are given. Air bricks should be well clear of the ground and one placed within one metre of corners to avoid dead air pockets. In cavity wall construction air bricks must not allow water to bridge the cavity. This can be achieved by sloping the air brick (or pipe duct) to the outside leaf, forming a sloping slate duct between leaves or forming a metal or felt cavity tray dpc over a horizontal air brick.

Cross ventilation is essential and ventilation holes must be formed through all partition and supporting walls to allow venting to opposite external walls. The 'sleeper' walls (see item 66) supporting joists should be honeycombed by holes half a brick long by one brick course high, see example. All timbers should be treated to resist fungal and insect attack. For comments and references see **Floors: General Section 6**, item 9, Durability.

BRE Digest 18, Design of timber floors to prevent decay
BRE DAS 136: 1989, Domestic draughtproofing: balancing ventilation needs against heat losses (design)
BRE BR 12: 1989, Background ventilation of dwellings: a review

64 Floor finish

1 For finishes on timber suspended floors see item 36 for comment and references. On timber ground floors tongued and grooved boards or sheets should be used to prevent draughts. Sheet flooring must be adequately supported and joints sealed by nogging pieces at right angles to joists.
2 For finishes on concrete suspended floors see item 18 for comments and references.

65 Sub-floor

For sub-floors on concrete suspended floors see item 19 for comments and references.

66 Structure

1 For timber suspended floors see item 37 for comments and references relating to joist sizes and spans etc. Ground floors offer the opportunity to support joists (via walls or columns) off of the ground or oversite concrete, thus reducing joist spans and allowing the use of smaller timber sections.

For domestic loadings (1.5 kN/m²) a joist depth of 100 mm is normal when joists are supported by dwarf 'sleeper' walls placed 1.20 m to 1.80 m apart. Joists should be skew nailed to timber wall-plates. The wall-plates are normally 100 mm wide × 75 mm high (being a similar size to bricks) in order to line through with brick wall courses; they are sometimes reduced to 75 mm × 50 mm if this is not a requirement. Wall-plates are bedded in mortar on a dpc which in turn is bedded in mortar on top of the sleeper walls. Wall-plates are not normally fixed down to low sleeper walls. Galvanized ms straps can be used where the floor is required to provide horizontal bracing to high sleeper walls. (See paragraph 1C 36 of Document A of the Building Regulations, 'walls should be strapped to floors above ground level. . .'). For methods of trimming around openings and chimney breasts see standard text books (e.g. *Mitchell's Building Series: Structure and Fabric*, Part 1). See also diagram 35 of Document B of the Building Regulations.

2 For concrete suspended upper floors see item 20.

   On ground floors the construction may take a number of different forms depending on site levels, soil bearing capacities and floor loadings. On a level site with good ground conditions the concrete floor slab can be supported by sleeper walls with strip foundations or span from external or partition walls without the use of sleeper walls. On poor ground sleeper walls may have to be supported off a concrete raft or pile beams and piles. In this case the economics of spanning without sleeper walls should be checked.

   On sloping sites sleeper walls may be of different heights and raft foundations may have to be stepped. Where sleeper walls become high their height/slenderness ratio should be calculated and their width increased to a stable thickness where necessary. The concrete floor slab may be precast or cast in situ (see item 20). A disadvantage of the latter is that it requires formwork which may have to be permanent as removal is often impossible. Impermeable insulation boards are often used as permanent formwork. Where the floor slab rests on walls it must be protected from rising damp by dpcs.

67 Thermal performance

See **Floors: General Section 6**, item 7: Thermal insulation, for general comments and references.

1 Suspended timber ground floors in dwellings are required by the Building Regulations (Document L Section 1) to have a U-value of 0.35 W/m^2 K for a SAP (Standard Assessment Procedure) rating of 60 or less and 0.45 W/m^2 K for a SAP rating of over 60. The final insulation thickness can only be arrived at in conjunction with calculating the ratio of the floor perimeter to area (P/A) but the tables in Appendix A are clear and helpful.

   If designers wish to increase insulation to existing floors, it can be added in the form of a glass or mineral wool quilt between the joists and held in place by pea netting stapled to joists. There are proprietary foamed products which can also be squeezed in between joists. Quilts should not contain an integral vapour barrier as this would trap water spillage and cause deterioration of both insulant and surrounding timber. An air space should be left between the insulant and the underside of floorboards in order to allow some ventilation and so decrease condensation risk.

2 Suspended concrete ground floors must also reach a minimum U-value of 0.35 W/m^2 K for a SAP rating of 60 or less and 0.45 W/m^2 K for a SAP rating of over 60. This can be achieved by placing insulation either above or below the slab.

   Below slab insulation is more suitable for permanently heated buildings because the concrete mass of the floor, once heated, provides a good thermal storage medium. There is also less condensation risk with this form of 'warm floor'. For complete safety from interstitial condensation a vapour barrier should be placed above the floor slab.

   Above slab insulation is more suitable for intermittently heated buildings because the mass of the slab does not absorb heat so that room air temperatures are quicker to respond to intermittent heat inputs. This form of 'cold floor' increases the risk of condensation and a properly specified, detailed and installed vapour barrier may, under some circumstances, be necessary (see **Roofs: General Section 8**, item 6.4, Condensation risk). The vapour barrier must be on the warm side of the insulant.

   This form of construction results in an unbonded screed which needs to be a minimum of 50 mm thick on rigid insulants and at least 64 mm thick, and reinforced with galvanized wire mesh, on compressible insulants. See item 19, Sub-floor for comments and references relating to screeds.

Building Regulations 1991, Document L (1995 edition)

68 Vapour and damp control

See **Floors: Section 6**, 11 item 8: Moisture resistance, for general comments and references.

1 The ground below a suspended timber floor must be effectively sealed from rising ground damp and moisture vapour (Building Regulations Document C) as well as being ventilated (see item 63). The Building Regulations require the ground to be sealed by a

minimum thickness of 100 mm of oversite concrete 300 kg of cement per m³, laid on clean hardcore, the top of the concrete must not be lower than the surrounding ground or paving level (to prevent the underfloor space being flooded).

However, concrete cannot be regarded as a vapour or water barrier in this location and there must be effective cross ventilation. On wet sites the oversite concrete mix quality can be improved and for guidance refer to Clause 11 of CP 102:1973, Protection of buildings against water from the ground, and BS 8102:1990, Code of practice for protection of structures against water from the ground.

2 The topsoil below a suspended concrete ground floor should be removed and the ground sealed to prevent organic regrowth. Sealing against moisture vapour and damp will depend on the nature of the floor slab construction and materials, particularly if an insulant is placed on the underside of the floor as described in item 67.

Building Regulations 1991, Document C.

69 Support and bearing

1 Suspended timber floors are normally supported on half-brick honeycombed 'sleeper' walls as described in item 66. Ground floor joists are no longer built into external walls and it is normal practice to build the first sleeper wall a minimum of 50 mm away from external and partition walls where they are parallel and to leave a similar space where they are at right angles. This is to allow for free air movement.

(If high sleeper walls require support from external walls this would not apply but partial bonding and honeycombing could be used.) The bedding of timber wall-plates and dpcs are explained in item 66.

2 Suspended concrete ground floors. See item 17, Bearing and lateral bracing, for general comments relating to suspended concrete floors. See item 66 for comments relating to sleeper walls supporting suspended concrete floors.

Trade and research organizations

British Carpet Manufacturers' Association Ltd, 5 Portland Place, London W1N 3AA (tel. 0171-580 7155, fax 0171-580 4854).

British Ceramic Tile Council, Federation House, Station Road, Stoke-on-Trent, Staffs ST4 2RU (tel. 01782-747147, fax 01782-747161).

British Cement Association (BCA), Century House, Telford Avenue, Crowthorne, Berks RG11 6YS (tel. 01344-762676, fax 01344-761214).

British Plastics Federation, 6 Bath Place, Rivington Street, London EC2A 3JE (tel. 0171-457 5000, fax 0171-457 5038).

Gypsum Products Development Association, c/o KPMG Peat Marwick, 168 Queen Victoria Street, London EC2V 4DD (tel. 0171-583 2104).

Nordic Timber Council, 33 Rosebery Road, London N10 2LE (tel. 0181-365 2700, fax 0181-663 6700).

TRADA Technology Ltd (Timber Research and Development Association), Stocking Lane, Hughenden Valley, High Wycombe, Bucks HP14 4ND (tel. 01494-563091, fax 01494-565487).

Roofs: **General** Section 8

SMM7: G Structural carcassing, J Waterproofing

(See Section 9 and Section 10 for Flat roofs and Section 11 for Pitched roofs)

Tortoise
*Animals find natural shelters, below leaves, under rocks, some
have adapted in areas with little protection to retreat into
their own shell.*

*Thatched roof,
Shaftesbury, Dorset
(Dean)*

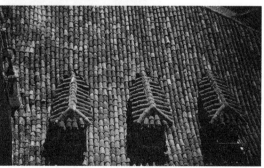

Tiled roof Italy (Rich)

Notes and references

Items are cross-referenced from the diagrams and
divided into sections with a general comment followed
by technical references and the Building Regulations in
context. Addresses of relevant trade and research
organizations are given at the end of the section. British
Standards and BRE Digests should be checked for
current amendments.

General references

Mitchell's Building Series: Structure and Fabric, Part 1,
Jack Stroud Foster. Section 7, Roof Structure.
Batsford, 1994.
Mitchell's Building Series: Finishes, Alan Everett. Section
7, Roofings. Batsford, 1994.
A *Practical Guide to Roofing*, ed. P. Roper. E & F N Spon,
1987.
Flat Roofing: Design and Good Practice. British Flat
Roofing Council with CIRIA, 1993.
Building Failures, Lyall Addleson. Architectural Press,
1992 (3rd edition).
Roof Construction and Loft Conversions, Mindham.
Blackwells, 1994.
Principles of pitched roof construction, TRADA WIS 1–10,
1993.
Trussed rafters, TRADA WIS 1–29, 1991.

1 Roof form and type of weatherproof covering

Criteria for choosing the particular form and weatherproofing materials of a roof are considered outside the
scope of this checklist. See the general references for
examples of the wide variety of roof systems available.
It is extremely important that choice of form and covering should be based on a balance between appearance
(internal and external), cost and the achievement of a
fully compatible assembly of interactive components
(covering, insulation and vapour barriers if necessary,
structural support and ceilings). (See Flat and pitched
roofs: BRE publication AP63 of 25 Defect Action Sheets.)

At an early design stage check the Building Regulations for any restrictions of form or covering in relation
to the 'purpose group of building' tables.

Key Factors	Action	Counteraction
Gravity	Downward pull	Support
Wind	Motive force (suction), destructive, penetrative	Rigidity, resilience, sealing
Rain	Moisture deposition	Deflection, impervious skin, absorption and drainage, sealing
Snow	Moisture deposition, loading	Deflection, impervious skin, absorption and drainage, sealing
Sun	Temperature variation, movement, heat gain, chemical decomposition	Movement joints, insulation, shielding, invulnerable materials, reflection
Dirt and dust	Infiltration, deposition, surface pollution	Repulsion, exclusion, shielding, cleaning
Chemicals	Corrosion, disintegration, decomposition	Invulnerable materials, exclusion
Sound	Noise nuisance	Insulation

1   Roof form and type of weatherproof covering

2   Structural strength and stability

3   Weather shield

3.1 Rain

3.2 Snow

3.3 Wind

3.4 Sun

3.5 Dirt and dust

4   Drainage

5   Durability

6   Thermal performance

6.1 Thermal movement

6.2 Heat gain

6.3 Heat loss

6.4 Condensation risk

7   Sound

8   Maintenance

8.1 External

8.2 Internal

9   Security

10   Fire, penetration

11   Natural light

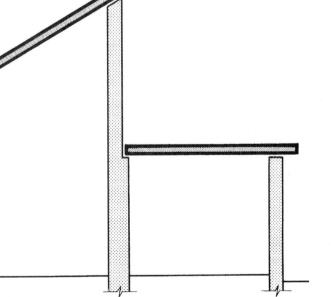

6.3 Heat loss

6.4 Condensation risk

8.2 Maintenance, internal

10   Fire, spread

12   Roof access and safety

13   Ventilation

Building Regulations 1991, Document A, Tables in Appendix A

2 Structural strength and stability

In most cases the main purpose of structural roof elements is to support with elegance and economy relatively thin skins of waterproofing and insulating materials plus the various loads falling upon the complete system. The structure must be designed to do this in a way that will let the roof covering maintain its waterproofing and be easily maintained. This means the designer must understand all likely structural and thermal movements, and make sure that the structure and finishes are compatible. A roof should be considered as a single system, with components that are interactive and which may move dynamically through the seasons.

Loading: dead loads are self-weight of structure and coverings plus all other static loads carried or hung from the structure. Weights of materials are calculated in accordance with BS 648:1964.

Imposed loads: wind (item 3.3); snow (item 3.2); miscellaneous loads include items such as cranes, lifting tackle, water tanks, etc. Traffic access decks, spectators, etc., will require special consideration.

For all spans it is essential to minimize the ratio between dead and live loads and to keep within safety factors.

Distortion and deflection can upset drainage falls, crack glazing and split flashings and coverings. Certain building types might require roof structures to be marked to indicate the location and size of loading suspended from the roof structure which should be taken into account at the design stage.

Wind loading – see item 3.3.

BS 648:1964, Schedule of weights for building materials (metric and imperial)
BS 6399 Part 1:1984, Code of practice for dead and imposed loads
BSCP 8110 Structural use of concrete. Part 1: 1985, Code of practice for design and construction, materials and workmanship, Part 3: 1985, Design charts for singly reinforced beams, doubly reinforced columns and rectangular columns, Part 2: 1985, Code of practice for special circumstances
BS 8297 Code of practice for design and installation of non loadbearing precast concrete cladding
BRE BR 235: High alumina cement concrete in existing building superstructures

BS 5268 Part 2: 1984, and BS 5268 Part 3: 1985, Code of practice for structural use of timber
BSCP 5950 Part 3: 1990 Section 3.1, Code of practice for design of simple and continuous composite beams
BSCP 118:1969, The structural use of aluminium (replaced by BS 8118 Part 1: 1991, and BS 8118 Part 2: 1991, but remains current for overlapping knowledge)
BS 449 Specification for the use of structural steel in building. Part 2: 1969, (amendments up to November 1995)
BS 1161:1977 (1991), Specification for aluminium alloy sections for structural purposes
Design guides and information sheets published by TRADA and CONSTRADO.
Building Regulations 1991, Document A: Structure

3 Weather shield

3.1 Rain

The amount of rainwater penetration is related to a combination of total volume of water with accompanying wind pressure, rather than to quantity or duration of rainfall alone. On sloping roofs, where dry jointed overlapping units are used, it is essential to match roof pitch to the overlap requirements of roofing units; manufacturers' advice should be followed. On flat roofs (0° to 10°) a continuous waterproof membrane should be laid sloping, termed 'to falls', to avoid ponding which through local differential stresses and chemical deposits at the pond edges can sometimes result in the deterioration of bitumastic membranes. Ponding also provides an unwanted reservoir should a leak occur, as well as making the detection of leaks difficult – see item 4 Drainage.

BRE DAS 33 Flat roofs: built-up bitumen felt – remedying rain penetration (design)
BRE Reports: *Driving Rain Index*, R. E. Lacey, 1976; *Climate and Weather in Britain*, R. E. Lacey, 1977
BS 8104:1992, Code of practice for assessing exposure of walls to wind driven rain

3.2 Snow

Loading should be calculated with regard to location and exposure, including possible drifting (fresh snow weighs approx 100 kg/m^3, wet compacted snow approx 320 kg/m^3).

On steeply pitched roofs consider the use of snow guards to protect gutters, windows, doorways and balconies. On pitched roofs wind-driven fine snow (and rain) can penetrate between the joints and overlaps of tiles and slates. Sarking felt is used over the rafters to collect snow and water and lead it into gutters at eaves.

BRE 332 1988: Loads on roofs from snow drifting against vertical obstructions and in valleys
BS 6399 Part 1: 1984, Code of practice for dead and imposed loads (includes snow loading)

3.3 Wind
Loading depends on roof pitch, height of building, geographical location and exposure. Special considera-tion must be given to roofs of buildings on high, exposed ground or near the sea. Wind exerts pressure and produces suction to varying degrees over various parts of the roof. The type of roof most vulnerable to suction is a monopitch – especially if it incorporates a large overhang at the eaves.

Where light claddings and lightweight supporting structures are used, special care must be taken by designers and contractors to ensure that the roof is firmly anchored to the building. (In some cases of lightweight industrial structures the building itself might have to be anchored to the ground.) All edges of sheet roof coverings should be sealed. Flashings must be securely tucked into the surrounding structure and held in place with adequate clips, wedges, etc.

BS 5534 Code of practice for slating and tiling (includ-ing shingles): Part 1: 1997, Design
BS 6399 Part 2: 1997, Code of practice for wind loads
Windloading Handbook: Guide to the Use of BS 6399 Part 2, Tom Lawson. Architectural Press, 1996
BRE Digest 346 Parts 1 and 2: 1989 rev. 1992, The assessment of wind loads. Part 1: background and method, Part 2: classification of structures
BRE AP63: Wind Loading Digest Package, 1990 (contains 12 BRE Digests)
BRE 346 1989: The assessment of wind loads. Part 6: loading coefficients for typical buildings
BRE BR 248: 1993, The gales of January and February 1990: Damage to buildings and structures
BRE BR 138: 1991, The October gale of 1987: Damage to buildings and structures in the south east of England
Building Regulations 1991, Document A. Controls loadings for various categories of roofs and for wind loading refers to CP 3 Chapter V, Part 2 up to Amend-ment 6028

3.4 Sun (solar radiation)
Solar reflective treatments are used to reduce surface temperatures and protect coverings from ultra-violet radiation (which can cause the breakdown of some mastic materials). They also help to limit the 'flowing' of bitumastic materials as well as reducing heat gain and overall movement of coverings, and also bases. Upstands and gutter walls should have an integral or applied reflective coating to avoid differ-ential stresses between horizontal and vertical surfaces.

In certain circumstances a designer will have to strike a balance between appearance and reflectivity. Alter-native types of treatment are referred to in **Flat roofs, Section 9**.

Reflective roofs should be well drained and maintained to keep them clean for continued efficiency.

Solar radiation can cause the delamination of some types of slates and tiles as well as the bubbling and splitting of waterproof membranes through water vapour pressure produced by residual construction water, rain penetration or condensation.

Windows adjacent to reflective roofs may have to be fitted with anti-glare devices.

See also item 6.1 Thermal movement and 6.2 Heat gain.

BSCP 8217: 1994, Code of practice for built-up felt roofing
BSCP 144 Part 4: 1970 (rev. 1990), Mastic asphalt

Principles of Modern Building, HMSO, 1961, Vol 2 page 134, gives Reflection coefficients for different surfaces as below. The figures in brackets are from *Design Primer for Hot Climates* by Allan Konya, Architectural Press, 1984. The lower the reflection coefficient, the higher the absorption of solar radiation. Higher absorption might be engineered for useful solar gain, but could be undesirable because of the thermal stress on some materials leading to movement and failure. Manufac-turers of specific materials should be able to supply this data.

Material	*Reflection Coefficient*
Weathered asphalt	0.19
Aluminium paint	0.46
(Bright aluminium)	(0.80)
Limewash	0.79
(White paint)	(0.80)

3.5 Dirt and dust

On pitched roofs the sarking felt laid over rafters prevents excessive dust being blown into roof spaces but cuts down ventilation. On flat roofs dirt and dust are harmful to reflective treatments, see item 3.4. In areas of atmospheric pollution roof covering materials will have to be chosen with a knowledge of the expected chemical interaction between covering and local pollutants. Flat roofs and gutters of pitched roofs near trees will require regular maintenance. Flat roofs should be cleaned of dirt and debris at least once a year.

4 Drainage

Water should be drained from roofs in the simplest and most direct manner possible. On pitched roofs with dry jointed units, internal or hidden gutters should be avoided because of the difficulty of construction and maintenance as well as the risk of severe consequential damage if they fail. On flat roofs, designed falls are generally 1 in 80 but some localities may recommend using 1 in 60. Any falls specified should take account of site inaccuracies, possible deflection or distortion due to drying out.

BRE DAS 33 Flat roofs: built-up bitumen felt remedying rain penetration (design)
BRE DAS 55: 1988, Roofs: eaves, gutters and downpipes – specification (design)
BSCP 6367:1983, Code of practice for drainage of roofs and paved areas
Flat roof covering problems: a guidance note. RICS, 1995.

5 Durability

If a roof is to endure the external elements as well as possible internal attack from humidity, rot and insects, a high degree of efficiency and compatibility must be achieved in the design, choice of materials (including such accessories as nails, clips, flashings, outlets, etc.), workmanship and site supervision. Reductions in costs, design knowledge and site craftsmanship, combined with increases in new roofing materials and components (often with only partially understood interactions) have led to the reduction, if not elimination, of safety factors. This is particularly so in the case of flat roofs (see **Flat Roofs, Basic Types Section 9**). Points to check:

1 *Roof support structures.* All non-durable wood should be treated against fungal and insect attack, the latter

being mandatory in some geographical locations – see references.

Timber roofs should be ventilated (see item 6.4 Condensation risk) above the insulation layer. Ventilation requires airflow generated by local air movement and temperature differentials from one side of the building to another, called cross flow ventilation. Permanent vents encouraging cross-ventilation should be equivalent to continuous slots of 10 mm in width along eaves level on either side of the roof. See Document F2 of the Building Regulations, Ventilation.

Reinforcement in lightweight concrete and thin concrete roofs should be protected by specifying the correct depth of cover (BRE IP 14/88, BRE Digest 389). Steelwork must be protected against corrosion (see 8.2 internal maintenance).

BRE 389 1993: Concrete: cracking and corrosion of reinforcement
BRE IP 14/88: Corrosion protected and corrosion resistant reinforcement in concrete

2 *Waterproof coverings and sub-bases.* Allow for adequate differential movement between components of a roofing system (see item 6.1). Check that any likely movement can be accommodated horizontally and vertically and is adequate at upstands, changes in level, perimeter detailing, flashings, gutters and where pipes or supports carry up through coverings.

Allow for decay of coverings due to atmospheric pollution (see item 3.5, Dirt and dust), frost action (delamination) or ultra-violet radiation (see item 3.4, Sun) and bubbling and splitting of membranes due to water vapour pressure from entrapped water or condensation. Various moisture venting systems are available either within the waterproof covering or underneath it, or both.

In all cases care must be taken to obtain uniform venting over the whole roof and to avoid dead pockets such as corners. Wet screeds should be avoided because of drying-out problems. Sub-bases and insulation boards should be chosen for thermal stability as well as their insulating qualities.

Building Regulations 1991, Document F2 Condensation
BS 7543:1992, Guide to the durability of buildings and building elements, products and components
BS 5493:1977, Code of practice for protective coating of iron and steel structures against corrosion (Amd 1993)

BS EN 100155:1993, Structural steels with improved atmospheric corrosion resistance

BS 7079 Preparation of steel substrates before application of paints and related products. (This has a great number of parts. It is important to stress that for coating steel, the preparation is critical.)

BS 6150:1991, Code of practice for painting of buildings

BS 5589:1989, Code of practice for the preservation of timber

BS 5707 Solutions of wood preservatives in organic solvents. Part 3: 1980 (1990), Methods of treatment

BRE 305 1986: Zinc coated steel

BRE 263 1982: The durability of steel in concrete. Part 1: mechanism of protection and corrosion

BRE Digest 144, Asphalt and built-up felt roofings – durability

BRE 296 1985: Timbers: their natural durability and resistance to preservative treatment

BRE 378 1993: Wood preservatives: application methods

Building Regulations 1991, Document A, Structure.

Timber preservation treatment is normally required to all new softwood timber. Different areas may have particular requirements. For example, in the original Building Regulations all softwood used in roof construction in the South East had to be treated against attack by Longhorn beetle which could cause major structural damage due to the size of the tunnel emergence holes (6–10 mm diameter).

Recognising Wood Rot and Insect Damage in Buildings, BRE Report, HMSO, 1987.

6 Thermal performance

6.1 Thermal movement

All forms of construction and finishes are liable to thermal movement and most roof failures are caused by poor allowance for expansion and contraction between various parts of a roof system. Pitched roofs suffer less because their covering materials are more often able to absorb movement in multiple joints and overlaps.

Flat roofs and their weatherproof coverings are particularly vulnerable; extremes of surface temperatures must be avoided (see item 3.4) and the movements which are bound to occur seasonally must be accommodated. The technical references given below (and in **Flat roofs basic types Section 9** and **Flat roofs specific factors Section 10**) show standard details for expansion, sliding and day work joints; isolating membranes between different materials; movement allowances at edges, abutments and upstands. All these details should be followed. As insulation standards improve, so for a given roof covering and given reflective surface the range of surface temperatures experienced will increase.

BSCP 8217:1994, Code of practice for built-up felt roofing

CP 144 Part 4: 1970 (rev. 1990), Mastic asphalt

Mitchell's Building Series: External Components, M. McEvoy. Longman, 1994.

6.2 Heat gain

Normally the amount of insulation required to retain heat within a building will be sufficient to exclude heat again, but the location of insulating materials is of vital importance (see item 6.3).

6.3 Heat loss

Various forms of insulating materials are used to control the amount of heat passing through the roof system.

Roofs of dwellings must attain 0.2 W/m^2 K for SAP energy ratings of 60 or less or 0.25 W/m^2 K for SAP energy ratings of 60 and over, see references below. With the increased mandatory insulation values now required designers are warned to check that fire hazards are not increased together with insulation thickness. For commercial and industrial projects, designers and clients may carry out cost benefit analysis to compare the reduced capital and running cost of a heating plant compared with the cost of achieving higher than normal values. However, as the demand for energy savings continues in an effort to meet EC targets, the energy efficiency of running a building will also now impact on the overall energy input into making products and it is advisable always to optimize possible energy savings given current technologies and materials.

The location of insulation within the roof system is an important factor. Generally it will be found more effective if the insulation is placed in a single layer under the waterproofing covering and on top of the supporting structure, keeping the whole structure warm.

Because of site conditions theoretical insulation values are sometimes not reached in practice due to poor installation or damage – especially by water during construction.

BS 8207:1985 (1995), Code of practice for energy efficiency in buildings (gives recommendations for the main procedures to be followed in obtaining efficient use of energy in the design and management of buildings)

BRECSU Guide 155: Energy efficient refurbishment of existing housing, 1995

BS 5803 Thermal insulation for pitched roof spaces in dwellings. Part 1: 1985 (1994), Specification for man-made mineral fibre thermal insulation mats

BRE 355 1990: Energy efficiency in dwellings

BRE BR 150: 1989, Building Regulations: Conservation of fuel and power – the 'energy target' method of compliance for dwellings

Mitchell's Building Series: Environment and Services, Peter Burberry, Chapter 5, Heat. Longman, 1992.

Building Regulations 1991 (1995 edn), Document L: Conservation of fuel and power

6.4 Condensation risk

Modern forms of construction and living patterns have greatly increased the risk of condensation, especially in roof systems. This should be thought of as a source of internally created damp, and is preventable. Traditional roof construction allowed moisture vapour to pass into the roof space and then out of the building through dry jointed covering units. In addition there was less water vapour to be vented at roof level as domestic living temperatures were lower combined with much greater ventilation from air bricks and flues from other parts of the building. Document F of the Building Regulations (1991) gives requirements to limit risk of condensation in roof spaces.

This checklist can only underline the importance of the subject and note the general principles. Designers must consult the references given below. Avoidance of condensation will rely on a combination of the following points depending on particular circumstances:

1 *Keeping the internal surfaces at the temperature above the dew point.* This is the temperature at which air becomes saturated, condenses and then deposits moisture. Warm air can carry more vapour than cool air. In general this means placing insulation above the roof structure and below the weatherproofing covering.

2 *Reducing the moisture content* of the air reaching the vulnerable parts of the roof system. Ventilation must be provided at source (kitchens, bathrooms, laundry rooms, etc.) and ventilation provided within the roof.

3 *Vapour barriers* must be positioned correctly (usually close to the warmest side of the construction) and be effective (made continuous, taped and sealed so there are no gaps).

The vapour barrier must be located on the warm side of the insulation layer where it will prevent moisture vapour reaching a point within the construction where the lower temperature would cause the air to become saturated and deposit moisture, where the dew point would have been reached. (When the dew point is reached inside building materials it is known as interstitial condensation and will cause material failure.) In practice vapour barriers are often less efficient than in theory because they become discontinuous through gaps between boarded materials having integral vapour barriers, or because of holes for lighting fittings and services, or through poor fitting around ducts and junctions. There is also an argument for designing the fabric of a building to be breathable and to allow for the evaporation of any moisture build-up.

Practical detailing and good site supervision are essential. Condensation is a health risk as it produces an environment for micro-organisms and fungi to survive, creating respiratory problems and other health risks.

BS 5250:1989, Code of practice for the control of condensation in dwellings

BRE Digest 110: 1972, Condensation (deals with principles and methods of estimating risk in roofs)

BRE AP 58: Condensation checklist, 1991 (packs of 20 for use when investigating dwellings)

BRE Digest 180: 1986, Condensation in roofs

Ventilation: Document F of the Building Regulations 1992 (1994 edn) (F2, condensation)

Mitchell's Building Series: Environment and Services, Peter Burberry. Longman, 1997 (condensation, general principles).

7 Sound

Special precautions may be needed against either airborne or impact sound. Airborne sound will be a factor for most building types adjacent to airports, flight paths, busy roads, industrial areas and in some cases close to existing or proposed motorways. It should be emphasized that noise is a recognized form of stress and affects health.

Glazed roof areas must not be a weak point in an otherwise protected roof. Factory sealed double glazing should be a minimum specification and is advisable with an additional sealed air gap of at least 100 mm.

Specialist advice will be required for concert halls and similar buildings.

Impact sound can be a factor in certain forms of lightweight roof systems (especially if ceilings are omitted) where drumming rain can be a nuisance.

Special isolating precautions are necessary where roofs are used as access decks, or house machinery, or carry tracks for window cleaning cradles.

BS 8233:1987, Code of practice for sound insulation and noise reduction for buildings

BRE BR 238: 1993, Sound control for homes

BRE IP 12/89: The insulation of dwellings against external noise (deals with special ventilating problems connected with buildings in noisy areas)

BRE Digest 337, Sound insulation: basic principles (outlines the physical principles used in other digests)

BRE IP 21/93: The noise climate around our homes

BRE Digest 187, Sound insulation of lightweight dwellings

8 Maintenance

8.1 External maintenance

Roofs need regular maintenance and client attitudes as well as design decisions will usually determine the future maintenance requirements of a roof's weatherproof covering. The designer should present the client with as clear a picture as possible of the merits and demerits of initial high or low expenditure against future high or low maintenance costs.

Maintenance of traditional pitched roofs is often limited to replacement of individual small units and clearance of gutters.

On built-up felt and asphalt roofs a policy of regular inspections should be followed and the possibility of a roof maintenance contract explored (preferably with the original roofing contractor). This is particularly important where high consequential damages could result from water penetration.

Large glazed areas usually require high maintenance as well as special access provision. Vulnerable roof coverings and insulation materials might require special protection and access on decking; see item 12, Roof access and safety, and item 5, Durability.

BRE Digest 280: 1983, Cleaning external surfaces of buildings

8.2 Internal maintenance

All roofs should be inspected occasionally. Closed spaces thought to be uninhabitable are highly desirable to wasps, bees, flies, squirrels and rats.

Steel trusses will require treatment to prevent corrosion (see item 5, Durability).

Cost is always related to ease of access and whether temporary plant or scaffolding may be needed (especially in the case of complex roof forms composed of angles and tees.) Maintenance could be a decisive factor in choosing the material and form of a roof, particularly for some types of corrosive industrial process. Check that access is possible for cleaning and maintaining all glazed areas, service runs and light fittings. It is worth incorporating permanent lighting runs for inspection and power sources for maintenance, and avoids the unsafe use of long and temporary cable runs later.

9 Security

Roof systems must prevent illegal entry. Glazing on roof lights can often be easily removed from the outside (glazing bars, clips and frames can have internal screws or external vandal-proof fixings such as 'one-way' screws). Special locks should be provided on roof fire escape, maintenance and plant room doors. Advice on security measures can be obtained from police officers as well as insurers.

10 Fire

The general principles and main points are listed below but mandatory controls and recommendations are always being revised from the most recent experiences in fire fighting, loss of life and loss from property. Buildings are at their most vulnerable just before completion, when firefighting systems are not fully operational and there is packaging left around from materials delivery.

General principles were gained originally from *Fire and the Architect No 12: Construction of Roofs*, the fire prevention design guide issued by the Fire Protection Association.

Three risks were identified in roof construction and are summarized below:

1 *Ignition from a fire within the building* and the possible spread of fire throughout the building.
2 *Fire heating the supporting structure*, overstressing the structure to the point of collapse and causing extensive damage. There is a risk to the life of occupants and firefighters, and even fixed firefighting systems such as automatic sprinklers could be destroyed. Structural collapse will cause fire spread, internally and externally.
3 *Ignition by a fire in a neighbouring building* could be an identifiable hazard.

Fire-CD combines information on fire information from Home Office, Loss Prevention Council, Fire Protection Association and Fire Research Association. BRE, FPA, Home Office and Loss Prevention Council, January 1996 version. Obtainable from HMSO
LPC Design Guide for the Fire Protection of Buildings. Loss Prevention Council, 1996

Points to check:
1 *Insurance*. Insurers often have different standards to those embodied in mandatory controls and the technical references listed below. Compliance with their standards sometimes results in discounted premiums. Fire officers also have their own rules for the guidance of insurers, clients and architects.
2 *Penetration* by heat radiation and flame, measures extent of surface ignition (BS 476 Part 3: 1975, External fire exposure, roof test).
3 *Surface spread of flame*, including ceilings in certain cases (BS 476 Part 3: 1975).
4 *Supports to internal linings* – Building Regulations Approved Document B, Section 6.0.
5 *Compartmentation, cavities within roofs and fire stopping* – Building Regulations Approved Document B, Sections 8.0. and 9.0.
6 *Venting of gases and smoke stopping* – Building Regulations Approved Document B, Section 18.
7 *Performance of materials and structures in fire stopping* – Building Regulations Approved Document B, Appendix A.

For roof coverings and rooflights generally, refer to Building Regulations Approved Document B, Section 14.

BS 5588 Part 1: 1990, Code of practice for residential buildings
BS 5588 Part 5: 1991, Code of practice for fire fighting stairs and lifts
BS 5588 Part 8: 1988, Code of practice for means of escape for disabled people
BS 476 Part 4: 1970 (1984), Non-combustibility test for materials
BS 476 Part 7: 1987, Method for classification of the surface flame of products
BS 476 Part 20: 1987, Methods for determination of the fire resistance of loadbearing elements of construction
BS 5268 Part 4: Section 4.1 1978, Recommendations for calculating fire resistance of timber members
Fire from first principles, P. Stollard and J. Abrahams. E & F N Spon, 1995.

11 Natural Light

Since this part of the building has the greatest exposure to unobstructed sky, it should be used for natural daylighting and possibly useful solar gain. There are many proprietary products that can be bought complete with flashings and blind systems for shade, solar control and prevention of night-time heat loss. Calculation of rooflighting has to be looked at in conjunction with the overall thermal and energy performance of the building, complying with Document L of the Building Regulations.

BS 8206 Part 2: 1992, Code of practice for daylighting
Building Regulations 1991, Document B, Section 14 Roof Coverings

12 Roof access and safety

Safe access is required for maintenance and any roof coverings that are liable to deformation should be protected with permanent decking that will also allow for drainage of rainwater. Insulation materials may also need protection and permanent crawl boards may need to be left in roof spaces. Access should be easy for washing down rooflights which otherwise can cut down daylight and increase the unnecessary use of artificial lighting. Roofs are sometimes used as means of escape by others and if there is permanent access needed for any other purpose then railings and parapets will need to be at heights that conform to the Building Regulations.

13 Ventilation

Ventilation is required to roof spaces and structure as well as providing routes for air changes from the building. Although there are proprietary roof vent details available for eaves and ridges that require little maintenance, ducts and systems that have any mechanical parts need to be inspected and will have to be accessible. See item 9 for security, item 10 for fire and smoke venting and item 6.4 for condensation ventilation.

BS 5720:1979, Code of practice for mechanical ventilation and air conditioning in buildings
BRE 108: 1975 (rev. 1991), Standard U-values

Trade and research organizations

British Board of Agrément, PO Box 159, Bucknalls Lane, Garston, Watford, Herts WD2 7NE (tel. 01923-670844, fax 01923-662133).
British Cement Association, Telford Avenue, Crowthorne, Berks RG11 6YS (tel. 01344-762676, fax 01344-761214).

British Wood Preserving and Damp-Proofing Association, 6 Office Village, 4 Romford Road, Stratford, London E15 4SF (tel. 0181-519 2588, fax 0181-519 3444).
Building Maintenance Information, 85–87 Clarence Street, Kingston upon Thames, Surrey KT1 1RB (0181-855 7777, fax 0181-547 1238).
Building Research Establishment (BRE), Bucknalls Lane, Garston, Watford, Herts, WD2 7JR (tel. 01923-894040, fax 01923-664010).
Cement and Concrete Association, Wexham Springs, Slough, Berks SL3 6PL (tel. 028-16 2727).
Constructional Steel Research and Development Organisation (CONSTRADO), NLA Tower, 12 Addiscombe Road, Croydon, CR9 3JH (tel. 01-688 2688).
Fire Research Station (BRE), Bucknalls Lane, Garston, Watford, WD2 7JR (tel. 01923-894040).
Loss Prevention Council, Melrose Avenue, Borehamwood, Herts WD6 2BJ (tel. 0181-207 2345, fax 0181-943 4705).
TRADA Technology Ltd (Timber Research and Development Association), Stocking Lane, Hughenden Valley, High Wycombe, Bucks HP14 4ND (tel. 01494-563091, fax 01494-565487).

Flat Roofs: Basic Types Section 9

SMM7: G Structural carcassing, J Waterproofing

(See Section 8 Roofs: General and Section 10, Flat roofs, in detail)

Notes and references

Items are cross-referenced from the diagrams and include comments followed, where appropriate, by technical references and relevant Building Regulations. Addresses of relevant trade and research organizations are given at the end of the section. British Standards and BRE Digests should be checked for current amendments. General guides for flat roofs include: BRE Digest 312, Flat roof design: the technical options.

14 Insulation above structure and under waterproof covering

This is known as a 'warm' roof system as it results in a structure being kept close to room temperature. The main advantages of this form of roof are: (a) the structure is protected from extremes of external temperature which can cause various types of unwanted movement (see **Roofs: general Section 8**, item 6.1) and fatigue; (b) the structure can provide a good (and practical) surface upon which to place the vapour barrier; (c) heavy structures such as concrete provide heat storage.

Disadvantages are: (a) heavy warm roofs are slow to heat up to room temperatures where insufficient or intermittent heating is used (as in many domestic situations, especially in bedrooms); (b) as the insulation is trapped under a waterproof layer it must not become wet. If wet, from leaks or rain during laying, it can become saturated so lowering its insulation value and thus producing a spiral effect of condensation and higher U-values – the dew point moves up into the insulation so producing interstitial condensation. Vapour barriers are placed under the insulation to avoid this, but they are often not perfect. Various venting systems have been devised to allow vapour pressure to escape from the cold side of the insulation.

Points to watch:
Sufficient insulation and a correctly specified and laid vapour barrier are essential if condensation is to be avoided. In this case the vapour barrier must be under the insulation and on top of the structure.

This thickness of insulation must result from calculation (see **Roofs: general Section 8**, item 6.4, for general discussion of condensation and references to calculation methods) in order to avoid the temperature at the vapour barrier falling to the dew point of the air inside the building. The insulation must be dry when laid.

Where the structure of a 'warm' roof contains wood joists and boards, it is important to keep their moisture content as low as possible to avoid decay and warping; they should also be treated with preservative (see **Roofs: general Section 8**, item 5). General practice for timber 'warm' roofs is to place a vapour check, in addition to the vapour barrier, under the joists and above the ceiling.

BRE 324 1986: Flat roof design: the technical options

14.1 Solar control

For general discussion see **Roofs: general Section 8**, item 3.4. Reduction of surface temperatures can be achieved by the following methods:

14.1.1 Reflective coatings

These must be chemically compatible with the waterproof covering and are useful on all vertical surfaces to reduce differential stresses between horizontal and vertical planes. On horizontal surfaces they tend to lose their efficiency as they become dirty and re-coating at about three- to four-year intervals is recommended. The main advantage of reflective paints is that sources of leaks and deterioration of coverings are more easily detected than with chippings.

14.1.2 Stone chippings

Light coloured chippings of 'limestone, granite, gravel or calcined flint calcite or felspar retained on a 6 mm mesh 56 sieve and passing a 10 mm mesh sieve' (quoted from BSCP 144 Part 4: 1970 (and 1990), Mastic asphalt, para 4.7.9.3; for built-up felt roofs see BS 8217:1994.

The advantages claimed for chippings are that as a prominent texture they have a relatively large surface area with voids so that they:

(a) allow an airflow and thus cool the surface of roof coverings;

14 Insulation above structure and under waterproof covering

'Warm roof'

14.1 Solar control
.2 Water barrier
.3 Thermal performance and energy conservation
.4 Vapour barrier
.5 Structure

Insulation below structure

'Cold roof'

15.1 Solar control
.2 Water barrier
.3 Structure
.4 Thermal performance and energy conservation
.5 Vapour control

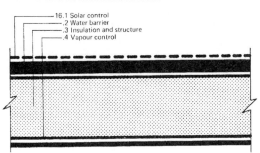

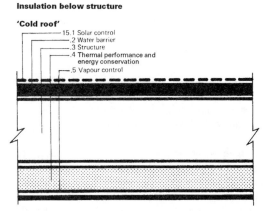

16 Combined insulation and structure

16.1 Solar control
.2 Water barrier
.3 Insulation and structure
.4 Vapour control

17 Insulation above waterproof covering

17.1 Solar control, wind and traffic protection
.2 Thermal performance and energy conservation
.3 Water and vapour barrier
.4 Structure

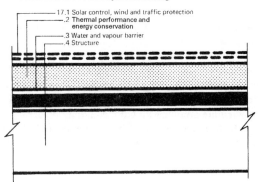

18 Falls–basic types

18.1 Raking structural support

18.2 Sloping top surface or top structural member

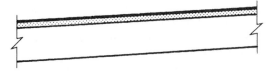

18.3 Sloping sub-base, screed or firrings

18.4 Shaped insulation

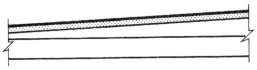

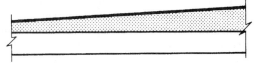

(b) provide shade and protection from ultra-violet radiation;

(c) collect dust and dirt which protects the roof covering by slowing the cycle of wetting and drying.

The disadvantages are they:

(a) prevent the early detection of deteriorating coverings and leaks;

(b) sometimes block rainwater outlets;

(c) may cause the waterproof covering to be punctured.

The disadvantages in points (b) and (c) can be safeguarded against by preventative detailing and a better choice of materials. The practice of using a much thicker 50 to 100 mm layer of rounded chippings is better than using a 10 to 12 mm thickness bedded in bitumen. The added advantage of a heavier layer of chippings is that they overcome the problem of uplift where felts are unbonded or partially bonded to roof decks.

14.1.3 Tiles made from glass reinforced cement or concrete

These provide good protection against traffic as well as forming reflective surfaces. They can either be bedded in hot bitumen or, in the case of concrete slabs, placed upon felt or plastics pads. Some thin composite tiles may require priming with bitumen primer before laying (see BS 8217 Code of practice for built-up roofing, and BSCP 144 Part 4: Mastic asphalt). Composite tiles with smooth surfaces can be slippery.

14.1.4 Self-coloured or materials having an integral reflective surface

Mineral surfaced roofing felts are available for use on pitches over 5° (BSCP 144 Part 4: Mastic asphalt). Light-coloured sheet plastics and sheet metals also provide a reflective surface. Non-bituminous plastics roof materials can be pigmented to produce a desired degree of reflection.

14.2 Water barrier

Waterproof coverings for flat roofs (BSCP 144 Part 4: Mastic asphalt – 0° to 10° pitch) are listed below together with their appropriate British Standards and information sources. Metal sheet systems are more often used on small roofs, or on larger roofs with pitches above 10°, rather than to cover substantial flat areas.

Asphalt, built-up bituminous felt and various polymeric sheet materials are now the most frequently

used materials for flat roofs. Choice of a roof finish cannot be made without considering the total roof system. Finish and sub-base must be compatible in terms of support, movement, cost, falls and durability. Other considerations which might affect the final choice of waterproof covering are:

(a) roof shape and configuration,

(b) site conditions,

(c) craft availability,

(d) building exposure,

(e) maintenance requirements.

Appearance, particularly where flat roofs are overlooked, should always be considered and is usually the basis for making the overall decision about the roofing material.

BRE 372 1992: Flat roof design: waterproof membranes

14.2.1 Mastic asphalt

BSCP 144 Part 4: 1970 (and 1990), Mastic asphalt metric units

BS 6925:1988, Specification for mastic asphalt for building and civil engineering (limestone aggregate)

BRE Digest 144: 1972, Asphalt and built-up roofings: durability

BRE IP/91: Mastic asphalt for flat roofs: testing for quality assurance

14.2.2 Built-up bitumen felt roofing

BS 8217:1994, Code of practice for built-up felt roofing

BS 747:1994, Specification for roofing felts

BRE Digest 144: 1972, Asphalt and built-up roofings: durability

14.2.3 Sheet aluminium

BSCP 143, Sheet roof and wall coverings – aluminium. Part 1: 1958, Aluminium, corrugated and troughed

BS EN 485 Parts 1–4: Aluminium and aluminium alloys: sheet, strip and plate

BS EN 515: 1993, Aluminium and aluminium alloys. Wrought products. Temper designations

BS EN 573 Parts 1–4: Aluminium and aluminium alloys. Chemical composition and form of wrought products

14.2.4 Sheet copper

BSCP 143 Part 12: 1970 (1988), Copper, metric units

BS 2870:1980, Specification for rolled copper and copper alloys, sheet, strip and foil.

14.2.5 Sheet lead
BS 6915:1988, Specification for design and construction of fully supported lead sheet roof and wall coverings

BS 1178:1982, Specification for milled lead sheet for building purposes

14.2.6 Sheet zinc
BSCP 143 Part 5: 1964, Zinc

BS 849:1939 and 1985, Code of practice for plain sheet zinc roofing. Partially replaced by BS 6561:1981 (1991), Specification for zinc alloy sheet and strip for building

14.2.7 Stainless steel
No standards for roofing. Some constructions using welded seams have taken place on the continent and in Japan. The material has such an even oxide coating that the finish is mirror-like and very little dirt can attach to the surface, consequently it is self-cleaning.

14.2.8 Profiled sheeting
This is more likely to be used in conjunction with insulation as a composite panel for roofing as well as cladding. This increases the ability of the panels to span large distances (up to 4 m) and provide high quality finished cladding and good thermal performance. Not normally used for pitches below 10°.

14.2.9 Polymers used as single layer flexible sheeting
Many systems have received an Agrément Certificate. See manufacturers' literature. Single layer roof coverings place an enormous responsibility on the quality and practicality (in terms of site conditions and workmanship) of the joints between sheets. Manufacturers can give long-term guarantees on the actual material used but care should be taken that all edge details and fixings have the same life.

14.2.10 Liquid finishes of either synthetic or bitumen compounds
BS 6949:1991, Specification for bitumen based coatings for cold application excluding use in contact with potable water

14.3 Thermal performance and energy conservation
See the general references above and **Roofs: general, Section 8**, item 6, for general factors relating to insulation and thermal behaviour.

The standard U-value required by the 1991 Building Regulations (1995 edition) is 0.2 W/m² K for dwellings for a SAP Energy Rating of 60 or less, and 0.25 W/m² K for a SAP Energy Rating over 60. Some of the many materials with which heat control can be achieved with warm roofs are listed below. The thicknesses required in each case must be the result of calculations for heat loss and condensation risk (see **Roofs: general Section 8**, item 6.4). Fire ratings should be checked.

14.3.1 Screeds
Aerated concrete and cement aggregate screeds have been used to combine an insulant with an infill to achieve roof falls – see item 18.4. Because of problems with entrapped moisture and difficulties with drying out buildings this form of insulation requires great care in laying, ensuring that any trapped moisture or water can drain (see BRE Digest 163: 1974, Drying out Buildings). Proprietary systems of combined screed, ventilation and drainage should have evidence of long-term performance in practice. It is now more common to use board insulants that are shaped to fall which are then covered by the roofing material.

BS 3797:1990, Specification for lightweight aggregates for masonry units and structural concrete

14.3.2 Expanded polystyrene
Any board products should be checked for alternative compounds to the use of CFCs in the production process.

Two types are available, bead board and extruded, the latter having a lower absorption rate. Obtainable in various grades (densities) and fire ratings, board sizes and thicknesses. Can also be sawn in the factory to provide tapered sheets for falls. A good insulator with a low water absorption rate, its main disadvantage is its high rate of thermal expansion and contraction. Waterproofing materials and adhesives must be chemically compatible with polystyrene, and bitumen or asphalt above 80°C must not come into contact with it.

BS 3837 Expanded polystyrene boards. Part 2: 1990, Specification for extruded boards

BS 6203 Guide to fire characteristics and fire performance of expanded polystyrene EPS used in building applications

14.3.3 Foamed glass
Available in various grades (densities), board sizes and thicknesses. A good insulator and impermeable

(because of its 'closed cell' structure). Thermally much more stable than polystyrene but also more expensive; this is partially offset by not having to use a layer of felt as a vapour barrier as the hot bitumen upon which the slabs are laid is sufficient (its fire rating is 'incombustible'). Slabs of this material are now made from recycled glass as well and can be pre-ordered with falls.

14.3.4 Cork
Available in various densities, board sizes and thicknesses. A good insulator, now superseded by more modern materials. It is thermally more stable than polystyrene but has a higher absorption rate and is more expensive. (Fire rating 'combustible'.)

14.3.5 Fibre insulating board
Available in various densities, sizes and thickness. Also available as laminated or bitumen bonded board. (Fire rating 'combustible'.) Less likely to be used for roofing today.

BS 1142:1989, Specification for fibre building boards

14.3.6 Rigid polyurethane
Rigid polyurethane and boards based on polyisocyanurates are high strength materials and are more thermally stable than polystyrene as well as being able to stand higher temperatures during laying.

14.3.7 Wood wool slabs
Whereas the insulants above require continuous support, wood wool slabs (available pre-screeded or pre-felted) have the ability to span between joists or firrings, and are used as a combined insulant and roof deck either over firrings on timber joists or over firrings fixed to a concrete structural slab. (In both cases all timber must be protected against fungal decay – see **Roofs: general Section 8**, item 5.)

There is a difference of opinion about the ventilation of this type of roof space. Some experts insist that warm roofs should not have any through ventilation under the insulation; others maintain that a minimal airflow will hardly reduce the insulation value while getting rid of small amounts of moisture.

BS 1105:1972, Wood wool slabs up to 102 mm thick

14.3.8 Green roofs
It is becoming more common to specify a warm roof construction that uses slabs of insulation material

below a waterproofing layer or 'building protection' layer. Above this layer are mats for root barriers and then graded material for drainage and soils for planting. See 'Building Green', a guide to using plants on roofs, walls and pavements. J. Johnston, J. Newton. London Ecology Unit, 1993.

14.4 Vapour barrier
See **Roofs: general Section 8**, item 6.4, for general factors relating to vapour barriers. Designers, contractors and clerks of works must ensure that vapour barriers are completely sealed with no perforations. This is quite difficult given on-site conditions, but as a balloon is not effective if it contains a pinhole, a vapour barrier has to be continuous to be effective. Quality checks have to be made as the vapour barrier is being installed. A great throughput of ventilation is needed to evacuate moisture vapour that has escaped through a comparatively (in building terms) small hole.

See BRE IP 2/89 Thermal performance of lightweight inverted warm deck flat roofs. Warm roofs (item 14) lend themselves to the installation of efficient vapour barriers. A different theoretical and practical approach is demonstrated in the case of cold roofs (item 15).

The materials usually used for vapour barriers are bitumen felts bedded in hot bitumen, asphalt or bitumen coatings, and sheet plastics such as polythene and polypropylene. All these materials must be specified thick enough to reduce their vapour permeability as much as possible. Manufacturers' literature should be consulted.

14.5 Structure
See **Roofs: general Section 8**, item 2, for general factors and references relating to structural strength and stability.

The structural support for warm roofs can be from slab, joist or beam construction. The principal requirement, in terms of insulation and weatherproofing, is that it should adequately support the relatively lightweight layers of material placed upon it. All forms of movement must be anticipated at design stage in order to match finish with structure to produce a fully compatible roof system.

15 Insulation below structure
This is known as a 'cold' roof system as the temperature of structure and voids follows that of the external air.

The main advantages are:

(a) local conservation of heat;
(b) fast response to heat input.

In the past (and perhaps the future) this has made the cold roof an attractive proposition where insufficient or intermittent heating can be expected. Energy conservation has produced a new interest in the cold roof but designers are warned of the difficulties that must be overcome.

The main disadvantages are:

(a) the structural elements are subjected to the full range of external temperatures which can produce (seasonal) movement in the structure and thus fatigue or tearing of coverings;
(b) current practice (see item 14) requires that a vapour barrier is placed under the insulation, in this case at ceiling level. This is an impractical location for a barrier – the best that can be achieved is a vapour check (vapour control layer). Consequently, in solid structures, there is the high risk of interstitial condensation (see **Roofs: general Section 8**, item 6.4). In joist or beam structures the voids can be ventilated above the insulation and vapour brake in order to evacuate moisture vapour;
(c) it is difficult to ensure adequate ventilation to all parts of the structure and cross ventilation must be provided at the design stage and supervised to ensure proper installation stages.

For structures with large voids and for some building types (such as swimming pools), mechanical ventilation of voids above insulation level may be needed. The extra cost and risk of ensuring adequate cross ventilation should be taken into consideration when deciding which roof system to adopt. In these situations the amount of ventilation must be calculated, whether from natural ventilation or as part of a mechanical system.

15.1 Solar control
See 14 1.

15.2 Water barrier
See 14.2.

With cold roofs the evacuation of moisture vapour can be helped by the use of water barriers that allow the passage of air vapour. This category includes metal sheetings that allow ventilation through joints and some pvc sheet roofing systems. Waterproof coverings can also be laid on various forms of 'breather' or vented underlays, as well as having breather vents inserted through the waterproof barrier.

15.3 Structure
The structural support for cold roofs can be of slab, joist or beam construction. As the structure will be subjected to extremes of external temperature, it is essential that all forms of possible movement are estimated and allowed for in the design and choice of both internal and external finishes. In this roof system, the structure must accommodate the internal insulation lining. With joists and beams, this implies a compatibility between structural spacing and internal and external board or decking sizes.

15.4 Thermal performance and energy conservation
In addition to the boards and sheets listed in 14.3 above, cold roof systems can more easily use glass fibre mats or quilts (available in various grades, roll widths and thicknesses). Being compressible, quilts are more usually hung over, under or between joists than placed directly under waterproof coverings. When hung in this position, the location of roof void ventilation and any vapour barrier becomes highly critical. It is now considered best to place the quilt at ceiling level (between or below joists) and ventilate the voids above. A vapour check (vapour control layer) is then required on the warm side of the quilt to limit the amount of moisture reaching structure and voids.

All materials used as internal roof insulants must be checked carefully for fire grading, smoke and toxic gas emissions in the effects of fire as well as the likely 'gassing off' of compounds which may be a health hazard over the long-term use of the building.

15.5 Vapour control
Unless extraordinary precautions are taken, it is not practical to install a vapour barrier at ceiling level owing to its likely perforation by services, jointing problems or following trades. The term 'vapour check' describes best the action of an anti-vapour membrane in this location, for in effect it will reduce the amount of moisture into the structure and voids above. (Note: BS 5250 uses the term vapour control layer instead of vapour check.) In past, and some present circumstances (see **Roofs: general Section 8**, item 6.4) a check is all that was required to avoid condensation troubles. This is because a well-ventilated structure will

have a reservoir of potential absorbency from very dry materials which can take small amounts of moisture between drying out periods. Old-fashioned ceiling papers and decorative finishes probably acted in this manner.

Plastic sheet or ceiling boards with integral vapour barriers are usually used in this location.

Building Regulations 1991, Document F2, Condensation in roofs.

16 Combined insulation and structure

Various laminated, sandwich or deck systems are available; wood wool slabs (see 14.3.7) come into this category. The quality of joint between units will often determine the quality of the roof for they have to absorb movement and not place too great a strain on the waterproof covering above, or the vapour barrier below. The joint must not provide a cold bridge which will reduce the insulation of the deck.

This form of roof is open to the risk of damage caused by moisture vapour entering the insulant from below or from leaks in the waterproof covering (especially where fibrous or wood based materials are used). The degree of risk will depend on the moisture conditions expected (e.g. domestic, industrial, recreational, etc.) inside the building, and the quality of joint, deck, covering, insulant and workmanship.

16.1 Solar control
See 14.1.

16.2 Water barrier
See 14.2.

Extra care is required at joints and waterproof coverings should be vented.

16.3 Insulation and structure
Special care must be taken when detailing and installing light fittings and services.

16.4 Vapour control
See 15.5.

17 Insulation above waterproof covering

Because of new materials developed and used in the latter part of this century, this system is currently receiving much attention although the principles involved have been known and used since early building history (earth or sod roofs, also the fur on the backs of animals). It has been known variously as the 'upside-down roof', 'inverted roof' or 'protected membrane roof', and is now referred to commonly as a 'warm deck roof'.

The advantages which seem to outweigh the disadvantages are:

(a) all those claimed for a warm roof, see item 14;
(b) the waterproof membrane is permanently protected from traffic and solar (ultra-violet) radiation;
(c) the insulation thickness can be increased easily and cheaply;
(d) if the insulation is laid loose, then detection and repair of leaks is simplified;
(e) the waterproof membrane can be tested before the insulant is laid;
(f) it is more likely that condensation will occur in the insulation of a cold deck roof as water vapour can travel into the insulation.

The disadvantages are:

(a) it has been shown that during rain heat losses are higher, by anything up to 30 per cent – this is equivalent to an average additional heat loss of 6–8% depending on rainfall. To compensate for this, extra thickness must be added to the insulant (20% extra for 50 mm extruded expanded polystyrene – see Zimmermann);
(b) roof loadings may be increased by the weight of gravel or concrete pavings required to hold the insulant in position (this can be offset to some extent by using a lightweight waterproof membrane such as plastics sheet).

17.1 Solar control, wind and traffic protection
The warm deck roof requires that the insulant is protected from wind uplift, ultra-violet radiation, traffic and buoyancy. This is normally achieved by a deep layer of rounded gravel, the same depth as the insulant but not less than 50 mm, or by paving slabs laid on proprietary pads.

17.2 Thermal performance and energy conservation
See 14.3. Because of the positioning of this material above the waterproofing layer it must be impervious

and unaffected by moisture. Extruded polystyrene was first used for this purpose in the USA in 1951 and most expanded or extruded polymers will satisfy the criteria as well as foamed glass. Although boards can be laid loose it is also common practice to bed some insulants in a bitumen layer, especially the foamed glass.

17.3 Water and vapour barrier

Most common waterproof finishes can be used but they must be chemically compatible with the insulant. To avoid punctures, single layer plastics sheet should be laid over a protective membrane. Drainage outlets must be placed at the level of the membrane and fitted with grilles to prevent blockage. Close jointed paved areas should also have an outlet at the upper level.

17.4 Structure

Inverted roof systems usually have concrete slab structures but some experience exists with timber and metal decks.

A good quality top surface upon which to place the waterproof covering is essential.

18 Falls

For general factors and references to drainage, see **Roofs: general Section 8**, item 4. Waterproof roof coverings should be laid to the falls recommended for the materials covered by Codes of Practice for aluminium steel, lead, copper, zinc, glass reinforced cement and semi-rigid bitumen sheets, built-up bitumen felt and mastic asphalt.

Falls of not less than 1 in 80 are recommended for mastic asphalt and built-up felt roofs. As these are minimal, they should be increased if deflection or distortion of the sub-base is expected. Areas receiving foot or vehicle traffic should be laid to 1 in 40 if short-term ponding is to be avoided. Roofs without designed falls are not recommended unless their design is based upon considerable experience of the materials, design details and workmanship to be employed.

See **Roofs: Sections 10 and 11** for specific details relating to falls.

Basic methods of achieving falls are listed below.

18.1 Raking structural support

This method can be used for either warm or cold roof systems and the structure can be of slabs, joists or beams.

18.2 Sloping top surface or top structural member

Suitable for either warm or cold roofs, this method can be used with slabs over small spans or shallow trusses over larger spans.

18.3 Sloping sub-base, screed or firrings

Where a dense non-insulating screed is used to obtain falls there are severe risks connected with entrapped moisture and drying out, see item 14.3.1.

Both warm and cold roof systems can be used but the insulation should not be placed under a screed and on top of a structural slab. This is because the insulant can become saturated during drying out. Firring pieces can be used over joist or beam structures in warm or cold roof systems.

18.4 Shaped insulation

Factory tapered expanded polystyrene is available, see 14.3.2. To avoid expensive thickness of material, consider closer spacing of rainwater outlets.

Insulating screeds laid to falls were common in warm roof systems, although these have been largely replaced by slab insulation that can be cut to falls. See 14.3.1.

Trade and research organizations

Aluminium Federation, Broadway House, Calthorpe Road, Five Ways, Birmingham B15 1TN (tel. 0121-456 1103, fax 0121-456 2274).

British Plastics Federation, Plastics and Rubber Advisory Service, 6 Bath Place, Rivington Street, London EC2A 3JE (tel. 0171-457 5000, fax 0171-457 5038).

British Stainless Steel Association, Bridge House, Smallbrook, Queensway, Birmingham B5 4JP (tel. 0121-643 5064, fax 0121-643 5064).

British Steel Technical, Swinden Laboratories, Moorgate, Rotherham S60 3AR (tel. 01709-820166, fax 01709 825337).

Copper Development Association, Orchard House, Mutton Lane, Potters Bar, Herts EN6 3AP (tel. 01707-650711, fax 01707-642769).

European Panel Information Centre, 7a Albert Mansion Luxborough Street, London W1M 3LN (tel. 0171-224 0814, fax 0171-935 9464).

Expanded Polystyrene Cavity Insulation Association, 248 High Road, North Weald, Essex CM16 6E (tel. 0137-8882026, fax 0137-8883376).

Flat Roofing Contractors' Advisory Board, Felds House, Gower Road, Haywards Heath, West Sussex RH16 4PL (tel. 01444-4400027).

Lead Sheet Association, St John's Road, Tunbridge Wells, Kent TN4 9XA (tel. 01892-513351, fax 01892-535028).

Mastic Asphalt Council and Employers' Federation Ltd, Lesley House, 6–8 Broadway, Bexley Heath, Kent DA6 7LE (tel. 0181-298 0414, fax 0181-298 0381).

RAPRA Technology Ltd (Rubber and Plastics Research Association of Great Britain) Shawbury, Shrewsbury, Shropshire SY4 4NR (tel. 01939-250383, fax 01939-251118).

Wood Wool Slab Manufacturers' Association, 26 Store Street, London WC1E 7BT (tel. 0171-323 3770, fax 0171-323 0307).

Zinc Development Association, 42 Weymouth Street, London W1N 3CQ (tel. 0171-499 6636, fax 0171 493 1555).

Flat Roofs in Detail Section 10

SMM7: G Structural carcassing, J Waterproofing

(See Section 8 Roofs: general and 9 Flat roofs: Basic types)

Notes and references

Items are cross-referenced from the diagrams and include comments followed, where appropriate, by technical references and relevant Building Regulations. Addresses of relevant trade and research organizations are given at the end of the section. British Standards and BRE Digests should be checked for current amendments. General guides for flat roofs include: BRE Digest 312, Flat roof design: the technical options.

This section, which deals with the specific factors occurring at the perimeter of flat roofs, must be read in conjunction with **Flat roofs, Sections 8 and 9**, which also list the general references and general research sources.

19 Solar control

For flat roofs generally see **Flat roofs, Section 8**, item 3.4. For flat roofs, basic types, see **Flat roofs, Section 9**, item 14.1.

20 Water barrier

For roofs generally see **Flat roofs, Section 8**, items 1, 3 and 5. For flat roofs, basic types, see **Flat roofs, Section 9**, items 14.2, 15.2 and 17.3. These items also list the relevant British Standards and Codes of Practice.

As waterproofing is the prime function of roofing, all details, material specifications and workmanship must comply with the relevant Codes of Practice and the recommendations of the appropriate trade and research organizations. Any departures from the above standards should be investigated and new approaches tested before approval is given. Roofing problems are often the result of not specifying thoroughly relatively thin skins of material and then not spending enough time on their detailing, including their edges, which have to be as effective as water barriers. Another major cause of flat roof failure in this country is our persistent false assumption that due to our less extreme climate, we can build flat roofs at lower relative costs than most other countries in Northern Europe or Northern America (compare flat roof details used in Germany or America). It is worth noting that the bulk of the British Isles has an annual precipitation of between 500–750 mm with the west coasts of Ireland and Scotland, Wales and Cornwall having a higher rate of between 1000–2000 mm (source: *European Passive Solar Handbook*, 1992). Although this is comparable with parts of Europe, our Northern European maritime climate has lower air temperatures and greater cloud cover. After periods of saturation through rainfall, it can then take longer for our buildings to dry out.

21 Thermal performance and energy conservation

For general points see **Flat roofs, Section 8**, item 6. For detail see **Flat roofs, Section 9**, items 14.3, 15.4 and 17.2. In this case the insulation could be 'dry', such as shaped extruded polystyrene, cork slabs or glass fibre boards or foamed glass with in situ insulating screeds.

22 Vapour barrier

For general points see **Flat roofs, Section 8**, item 6.4. For detail see **Flat roofs, Section 9**, items 14.4, 15.5 and 17.3. Vapour barriers should protect the exposed edges of insulation by being folded over the insulation at roof edges. They must also be properly lapped at all joints.

BS 8217:1994, Code of practice for built-up felt roofing (see details)
BSCP 144 Part 4: 1970, fig. 6 Asphalt – standard detail

23 Structure

For general points see **Flat roofs, Section 8**, item 2. For detail see **Flat roofs, Section 9**, items 14.5, 15.3, 16.3 and 17.4. In this case the principles mentioned could apply to most structural materials.

24 Gutters

Water must be collected and carried to the ground by gutters and downpipes. Water will also flow if guided,

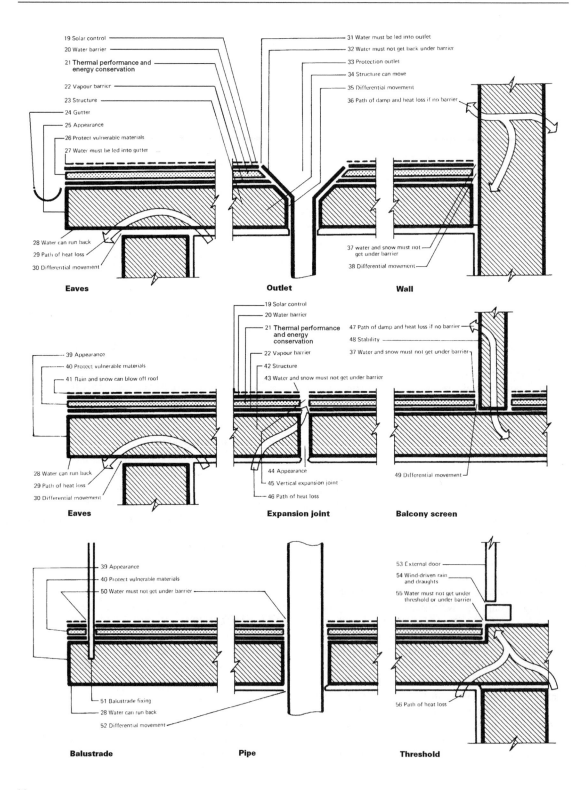

19 Solar control
20 Water barrier
21 Thermal performance and energy conservation
22 Vapour barrier
23 Structure
24 Gutter
25 Appearance
26 Protect vulnerable materials
27 Water must be led into gutter
28 Water can run back
29 Path of heat loss
30 Differential movement

Eaves

31 Water must be led into outlet
32 Water must not get back under barrier
33 Protection outlet
34 Structure can move
35 Differential movement
36 Path of damp and heat loss if no barrier
37 water and snow must not get under barrier
38 Differential movement

Outlet

Wall

19 Solar control
20 Water barrier
21 Thermal performance and energy conservation
22 Vapour barrier
42 Structure
43 Water and snow must not get under barrier
39 Appearance
40 Protect vulnerable materials
41 Rain and snow can blow off roof
28 Water can run back
29 Path of heat loss
30 Differential movement

Eaves

44 Appearance
45 Vertical expansion joint
46 Path of heat loss

Expansion joint

47 Path of damp and heat loss if no barrier
48 Stability
37 Water and snow must not get under barrier
49 Differential movement

Balcony screen

39 Appearance
40 Protect vulnerable materials
50 Water must not get under barrier
51 Balustrade fixing
28 Water can run back
52 Differential movement

Balustrade

Pipe

53 External door
54 Wind-driven rain and draughts
55 Water must not get under threshold or under barrier
56 Path of heat loss

Threshold

and simple vertical chains can also be used. Some roofing materials (notably thatch) will not be able to use a gutter detail and then the spillage of water should be routed at ground level through landscaping details that provide dished gulleys and keep water away from the walls, directing it to ground drainage or holding cisterns. Gutters will be fixed to falls, so fascias must accommodate fixings and allow for these level changes in the gutter. Where gutters are within easy reach or where ladders are likely to be placed against them, they should be strong and able to take this load. If the water is to be recycled, materials used should optimize cleanliness and full systems of downpipes and gutters should be made from materials that can ensure high purity of water collected (e.g. the use of copper).

25 Appearance

Fascia appearance is an important aspect of roof design. Consider proportion (depth), colour and texture in relation to remainder of design. Exposed concrete edges of roof slabs should be specified to have the required finish, not left to chance. Timber fascias should be designed and materials specified to avoid warping, or in the case of plywood, delamination and be easy to maintain. Gutter fixings, flashings and metal edge trim must not stain fascias. Joints in edge trim should have 'formers' or jointing sections to avoid water ingress and staining.

26 Protect vulnerable materials

The edge of the water barrier must be made impenetrable by wind-driven rain or standing water, for example by a flashing or the barrier itself turned down over the gutter – see item 27.

The insulation must be covered, usually by a timber fascia board projecting above the deck or structural slab; a timber batten or curb; or a small concrete or sand and cement upstand.

BS 8217:1994, Code of practice for built-up felt roofing
BSCP 144 Part 4: 1970, figs 7 and 9, Asphalt
BS 6915:1988, Specification for the design and construction of fully supported lead sheet roofing and wall coverings
BSCP 143 Part 12: 1988 figs 1 and 14, Copper, metric units
BS 2870:1980, Specification for rolled copper and copper alloys, sheet, strip and foil

BSEN 485 Parts 1–4: Aluminium and aluminium alloys: sheet strip and plate

27 Water must be led into gutter

Built-up felt roofing is turned down over the gutter with a welted felt drip of 50 mm minimum depth.

Asphalt roofing is finished with a non-ferrous metal flashing turned down over the gutter. All metals must be primed with a rubber bitumen emulsion to allow the asphalt to adhere to the metal.

Flashing materials must be chemically unreactive with the water barrier. Joints in flashings must be properly jointed, overlapped and fixed. Consider differential thermal movement between water barrier and flashing – see item 40.

Provide adequate flashing fixing blocks or battens in concrete structures.

BS 8217:1994, Code of practice for built-up felt roofing
BSCP 144 Part 4: 1970, figs 7 and 9, – Asphalt
BS 6915:1988, Specification for the design and construction of fully supported lead sheet roofing and wall coverings
BSCP 143 Part 12: 1988, figs 1 and 14, Copper, metric units
BS 2870:1980, Specification for rolled copper and copper alloys, sheet, strip and foil
BS EN 485 Parts 1–4: Aluminium and aluminium alloys: sheet strip and plate

28 Water can run back on soffit

Protect soffit from staining and limit amount of water blown onto vulnerable joints (see item 30) by providing a drip or check. Timber fascia boards should project below the soffit.

29 Path of heat loss

Provide edge insulation in concrete slab or detail joist and deck construction to provide a barrier against heat loss.

30 Differential movement

Estimate the degree of movement expected. Where concrete slabs are cast on loadbearing brickwork, minor movement can be allowed for by casting upon two courses of dpc.

Cavities should be protected by a course of slates. Larger movements can be accommodated by special preformed plastics strips placed between concrete and brickwork.

Where masonry is built up to the underside of previously cast concrete, there may be water penetration through cracks caused by differential movement and drying out. This can be prevented by incorporating small flashings or by detailing the concrete with a rebate to receive masonry.

31 Water must be led into outlet
The insulation or screed is usually slightly 'dished' to receive the outlet. The water barrier is then dressed down into the outlet. Cast iron, spun metal or plastic outlets are available with clamping rings which hold the water barrier in place.

BS 8217:1994, Code of practice for built-up felt roofing
BSCP 144 Part 4: 1970 (and 1990), fig. 17, Mastic asphalt
　– metric units

32 Water must not get back under barrier
Some details (especially if not perfectly executed) can allow water to creep back under the barrier by capillary attraction, e.g. BSCP 144 Part 4: 1970 and 1990, fig. 16.

33 Protection to outlet
Flat and domed gratings are available. Choose grating size to suit material to be held back; this means allowing for the diameter of chippings, or children's balls or acts of deliberate vandalism (gratings can be bolted in position). Depending on the proximity of trees, domed gratings are better if heavy leaf fall is expected.

BS 8217:1994, Code of practice for built-up felt roofing
BSCP 144 Part 4: 1970 (and 1990), fig. 17, Mastic asphalt
　– metric units
Mitchell's Building Series: Components.

34 Structure can move
If a structure is expected to move, then the joint between outlet and downpipe should be flexible. Timber joists can deflect or twist as their moisture content reduces or varies seasonally. Concrete can deflect, especially at mid-span where outlets are often positioned.

35 Differential movement – internal finishes
If appearance is important where internal finishes abut a pipe, provide a small cover plate or flexible head.

36 Path of damp and heat loss if no barrier
A horizontal dpc must be used to prevent moisture in the wall bypassing the roof water barrier. The structure behind the upstand must remain dry. This point is often overlooked when detailing parapet walls.

Insulation is usually provided on or by the inside face of the wall. See **External Walls Sections 4 and 5**.

BS 8217:1994, Code of practice for built-up felt roofing
BSCP 144 Part 4: 1970 (and 1990), fig. 17, Mastic asphalt
　– metric units

37 Water and snow must not get under barrier
Whatever the material, roof coverings must be carried up abutments for a sufficient height to overcome temporary flooding, splash back and snow. Codes of Practice recommend 150 mm as a minimum. The roof covering must be formed at its internal angle, supported in its height and tucked into the structure with a configuration compatible with the covering material.

Bitumen felt roofing is better when taken up over an angle fillet whether in timber or concrete. Felt should not be bonded with hot bitumen at the perimeter. It should be loose, allowing the whole roof covering to move slightly under thermal stress. Under layers should be only partially bonded to the deck and be taken up over the fillet which is also independent from the wall. A metal flashing should always be provided to cover the top of the felt and fillet.

Asphalt, where no structural movement is expected, is carried up to a minimum of 150 mm and a two-coat angle fillet of 50 mm width formed at the internal angle. The asphalt is supported against brickwork by raking out the joints to form a key. Concrete surfaces are hacked or left rough. Timber structures or curbs are provided with a key by bitumen-coated expanded metal lathing (to BS 1369) fixed by nails or staples. The top of the upstand or skirting is tucked into a continuous groove of not less than 25 mm × 25 mm and the top edge of the asphalt formed into a splay. A non-ferrous metal flashing (fixed with metal tacks or cleats) can cover the top of the skirting or the continuous groove can be pointed with mortar. When structural movement is expected, asphalt is dressed up over a timber curb which is separate from the wall. Metal flashings are used to cover the open edge. See *Appraising Building Defects*, G. Cook and Dr A. J. Hinks (Longman, 1992). Damp penetration at roof level p. 368, and accompanying observations about asphalt detailing.

Sheet metal roof coverings are turned up at abutments using a small radius bend and held in place with cleats and clips. A metal flashing is then placed over the open top edge of the upstand and held in place with cleats.

BS 8217:1994, Code of practice for built-up felt roofing
BSCP 144 Part 4: 1970, figs 7 and 9, asphalt
BS 6915:1988, Specification for the design and construction of fully supported lead sheet roofing and wall coverings
BS CP 143 Part 12: 1988, figs 1 and 14, Copper, metric units
BS 2870:1980, Specification for rolled copper and copper alloys, sheet, strip and foil
BS EN 485 Parts 1–4: Aluminium and aluminium alloys: sheet strip and plate

38 Differential movement
Where structural movement is expected or where timber joists are used, roof coverings should be separated from walls by the use of timber or concrete kerbs. See BSCP 144 Part 4: fig. 4 for asphalt, and BS 8217:1994, Code of practice for built-up felt roofing. (The angle fillet should be made large enough – like a curb – to hold felt away from wall.) Even where structural movement is not expected, insulation boards should be kept back around edges by approximately 25 mm (see *Application of Mastic Asphalt* from Mastic Asphalt Council & Employers' Federation).

39 Appearance
Comments as for item 25 but more pertinent as large fascias can result when upstands are added to prevent water and snow blowing off roof. To reduce fascia

depth or to make it match the fascia supporting the gutter, water checks can be placed slightly inward of the fascia edge – see BSCP 144 Part 4: fig. 13.

40 Protect vulnerable materials
The edge of the water barrier can be turned down over the fascia but this is not usually done where it can be damaged by ladders or where a permanent sharp 'skyline' edge detail is required. Various forms of roof edge trim are available – see *Mitchell's Building Series: Components*. Failures have occurred because of the differential rates of thermal expansion between metal (especially aluminium) roof trim and bituminous roof coverings. GRP or GRC eaves trim is recommended as it bonds well to asphalt and bitumen as well as having a coefficient of expansion closer to asphalt and bitumen felt than aluminium. Insulation is stopped short of the fascia edge as described in item 26.

41 Rain and snow can blow off roof
To avoid staining and damage to walls water checks are usually incorporated at the non-drained edges of flat roofs. These can be formed by dressing the roof covering over timber fillets, concrete upstands (BSCP 144 Part 4: fig. 13 – asphalt), or by a solid asphalt water check set slightly back from the edge. (See *Application of Mastic Asphalt* by Mastic Asphalt Council & Employers' Federation.)

42 Structure
Items 43 to 49 are only applicable to a concrete roof slab.

43 Water and snow must not get under barrier
Major thermal movements in concrete roof slabs are accommodated by expansion joints which usually run across roofs and down walls. Roof coverings are taken up (150 mm minimum) concrete up stands and detailed in a similar way to abutments. The tops of upstands are closed either by metal flashings or preformed hoods or, in the case of bitumen felt, taken over a timber board or metal plate fixed to one upstand only. Hoods or flashings should be well supported as they are often walked upon or damaged by maintenance equipment. Their shapes should also be simple as they often have

Typical details

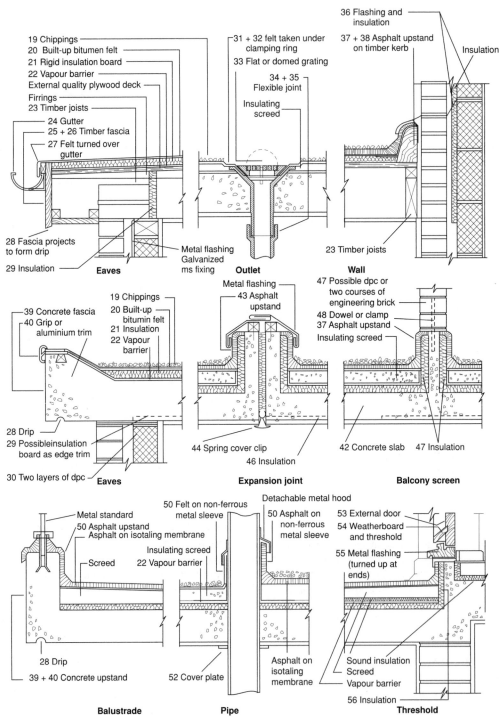

19 Chippings
20 Built-up bitumen felt
21 Rigid insulation board
22 Vapour barrier
External quality plywood deck
Firrings
23 Timber joists
24 Gutter
25 + 26 Timber fascia
27 Felt turned over gutter
28 Fascia projects to form drip
29 Insulation

Eaves

31 + 32 felt taken under clamping ring
33 Flat or domed grating
34 + 35 Flexible joint
Insulating screed
Metal flashing Galvanized ms fixing

Outlet

36 Flashing and insulation
37 + 38 Asphalt upstand on timber kerb
Insulation
23 Timber joists

Wall

39 Concrete fascia
40 Grip or aluminium trim
19 Chippings
20 Built-up bitumin felt
21 Insulation
22 Vapour barrier
28 Drip
29 Possibleinsulation board as edge trim
30 Two layers of dpc

Eaves

Metal flashing
43 Asphalt upstand
44 Spring cover clip
46 Insulation

Expansion joint

47 Possible dpc or two courses of engineering brick
48 Dowel or clamp
37 Asphalt upstand
Insulating screed
42 Concrete slab   47 Insulation

Balcony screen

Metal standard
50 Asphalt upstand
Asphalt on isotaling membrane
Screed
28 Drip
39 + 40 Concrete upstand

Balustrade

50 Felt on non-ferrous metal sleeve
Insulating screed
22 Vapour barrier
52 Cover plate

Pipe

Detachable metal hood
50 Asphalt on non-ferrous metal sleeve
Asphalt on isotaling membrane

53 External door
54 Weatherboard and threshold
55 Metal flashing (turned up at ends)
Sound insulation
Screed
Vapour barrier
56 Insulation

Threshold

to abut and be flashed into a vertical expansion joint at the junction of roof and parapet or eaves. See the typical details for walls and upstands in this section.

BS 8217:1994, Code of practice for built-up felt roofing
BSCP 144 Part 4: fig. 15 – Asphalt
Application of Mastic Asphalt. Mastic Asphalt Council and Employers' Federation (MACEF)

44 Appearance

Expansion joints attract a lot of water during the construction period. After the roof is finished they should be left open on the inside and allowed to drain out before decoration takes place. A system of cover plates or beads is usually used to cover and 'marry' horizontal and vertical joints. See the typical details for walls and upstands in this section.

45 Vertical expansion joint

Expansion joints must be designed and detailed in three dimensions. Sketch all horizontal and vertical junctions before deciding on roof joint details. Awkward corner details should not be left for site solution.

46 Path of heat loss

Insulation (where of a rigid non-compressive material) should be taken up the sides of the upstand leaving only the actual joint to be filled with a compressible insulation material. See the typical details for walls and upstands in this section.

47 Path of damp and heat loss if no barrier

Balcony screen walls require great care in detailing.

Usually made from half or single brick width, these can become saturated and need some form of horizontal damp-proof course above the skirting level of the roof covering. If normal dpcs are used, the screen wall may be unstable depending on its height and require structural restraints at either end. Sheet metal dpcs with welded cramps or dowels passing from the slab to the wall are a possible but expensive solution. Two courses of engineering bricks as a dpc plus vertical cramps or dowels are an alternative.

Insulation can be detailed as described for expansion joints (see item 46 and accompanying detail).

48 Stability (balcony screen walls)

Building Control officers should be consulted regarding their requirements. Where screen walls are placed upon cantilevered balconies they should have a movement joint at their junction with the main external wall of the building. This will add to the problem of lateral stability and some form of angle supports or dowels might have to be used. Stability can sometimes be obtained by gaining support from the balustrade.

BS 6399 Part 1: 1984, Code of practice for dead and imposed loads covers parapets and balustrades (see Table 4)
Building Regulations 1991, Document K Section 3, gives details for guarding of balconies and other places
See also BS 6180:1982, Code of practice for protective barriers in and about buildings

49 Differential movement

Structures may deflect, especially if on a cantilevered balcony. Place screen wall on an upstand in order to keep movement plane above the roof covering.

50 Water must not get under barrier at balustrades and pipes

Where movement is expected, either from structural deflection or by loading on the balustrade, roof coverings should be carried up around standards and pipes on metal flanged collars. This might also apply where tubular metal balcony privacy screens pierce roof coverings. The tops of roof coverings should be protected by detachable metal hoods. On no account should savings be made by compromising on detailing that will threaten weathertightness. Balustrades can also be fixed on the fascia to avoid piercing the water barrier.

BS 8217:1994, Code of practice for built-up felt roofing
BSCP 144 Part 4: fig. 15, Specification for mastic asphalt
Application of Mastic Asphalt, Mastic Asphalt Council and Employers' Federation.

51 Balustrade fixing

Balustrade standards must be firmly fixed to the structure in order not to allow cracks to occur around the base of the water barrier. Alternatively, standards can be fixed to the fascia. Pockets or drilled holes in concrete should not leave less than 50 mm of concrete around the standard. See Codes of Practice listed under item 50.

52 Differential movements
Comments as for items 34, 35 and 50.

53 External door
See **External Domestic Doors Section 18**.

54 Wind-driven rain and draughts
See **External Domestic Doors Section 18**, item 21.

55 Water must not get under threshold
This is a particularly vulnerable detail. The water barrier must be carried up to the underside of the threshold for a height of at least 100 mm which should be calculated from the highest point under the threshold. Designers often forget to allow for balcony or roof cross falls with the result that some thresholds have little or no upstand. Site operatives cannot make a good job if there is no room for their hands or tools under the threshold.

The upstand is either tucked into a groove on the underside of the threshold or turned over to meet a water bar, but this requires the threshold to be fixed after the roof covering (see BSCP 144 Part 4: fig. 10). Another alternative is to turn down a metal flashing after the roof covering has been formed into a skirting. These details should be sketched in three dimensions as they often produce a vulnerable junction where the jamb or reveal meets the threshold. Flashings should be turned up at the ends of timber thresholds.

Building Failures, Lyall Addleson. Architectural Press, 1992 (see sheets on flat roofs).
Look for External Doors: Thresholds, Architects Working Details Series. Architectural Press, 1988.
BRE DAS 67 Inward opening external doors: resistance to rain penetration (design)

56 Path of heat loss
Carry insulation up upstand or use insulation board edge trim as indicated for item 29.

Trade and research organizations
Mastic Asphalt Council and Employers' Federation (MACEF), Lesley House, 6–8 Broadway, Bexley Heath, Kent DA6 7LE (tel. 0181-298 0414, fax 0181-298 0381).

Pitched Roofs in Detail Section 11

SMM7: G Structural carcassing, J Waterproofing

(See Section 8 Roofs – General; Section 9 Flat Roofs – Basic types, Section 10 Flat Roofs – in detail)

Notes and references

Items are cross-referenced from the diagrams and divided into sections with a general comment followed by technical references and the Building Regulations in context. Addresses of relevant trade and research organizations are given at the end of the section. British Standards and BRE Digests should be checked for current amendments.

This sheet, which deals with specific factors for pitched roofs, must be read in conjunction with **Roofs: General Section 8** and **Flat Roofs: Basic Types Section 9** which also list the general references and general research sources

57 Roof appearance

Consider the following points:

1 The steeper the pitch the greater the roof area visible; check against the general massing of building.
2 Designers should be sensitive to local styles and experience. Roof shapes, 'grain' or 'texture', materials and details often demonstrate successful methods of coping with local building and climatic conditions.
3 Modern roofs usually neglect the importance of skyline; roofs, like other shapes, are visually determined by edges, and against a relatively bright background can have fine details. Crudely finished edges will be very noticeable.
4 Final choice of roof form will also have to balance economics against design and detailing as well as the successful assembly of components that include the roof coverings, insulation, vapour barriers, structural support and ceiling construction.
5 The intended (immediate or future) use of the roof space might be a major criteria in roof design.

58 Weather control

Dry lapped small units such as tiles and slates are not considered a weather barrier as wind, rain and snow can penetrate the joints under certain conditions.

Impermeable membranes such as asphalt, felt, polymeric and metal sheetings, and certain interlocking and/or sealed unit systems can be considered as water barriers. Criteria for choosing the particular form and weatherproofing materials of a roof are considered outside the scope of this checklist. See the general references **Roofs: general Section 8**. Covering materials and laying methods must be compatible with the roof pitch. Follow manufacturers' recommendations, paying particular attention to holding down methods, especially in exposed locations. At an early design stage check the Building Regulations for any restrictions of form or covering in relation to the 'purpose group of building' tables. Also check with the local Planning Authority for possible restrictions.

See **Roofs: specific factors Section 10**, item 14.2, for a general list of sheet membrane materials, together with their respective British Standards and technical references as well as trade information sources.

BS 5534 Code of practice for slating and tiling. Part 1: 1990, Design
BS EN 492: 1994, Fibre cement slates and their fittings for roofing. Product specification and test methods
BS 3083:1988, Specification for hot-dip zinc coated and hot-dip aluminium/zinc coated corrugated steel sheets for general purposes
BS 4868:1972, Specification for profiled aluminium sheet for building
BS 4154:1967, Corrugated plastic translucent sheets made from thermo-setting polyester resin (glass fibre reinforced). Part 1: 1985 (1994), Specification for material and performance requirements. Part 2: 1985 (1994), Specification for profile and dimensions
BS 4203 Extruded rigid PVC corrugated sheeting, Parts 1 1980 (1994) and 2: Specification for profiles and dimensions
BS 680 Part 2: 1971, Roofing slates (metric)
BS 402 Clay plain roofing tiles and fittings. Part 1: 1990, Specification for plain tiles and fittings (part replacement by BS EN 538: 1994)
BS EN 490: 1994, Concrete Roofing tiles and fittings. Product specifications

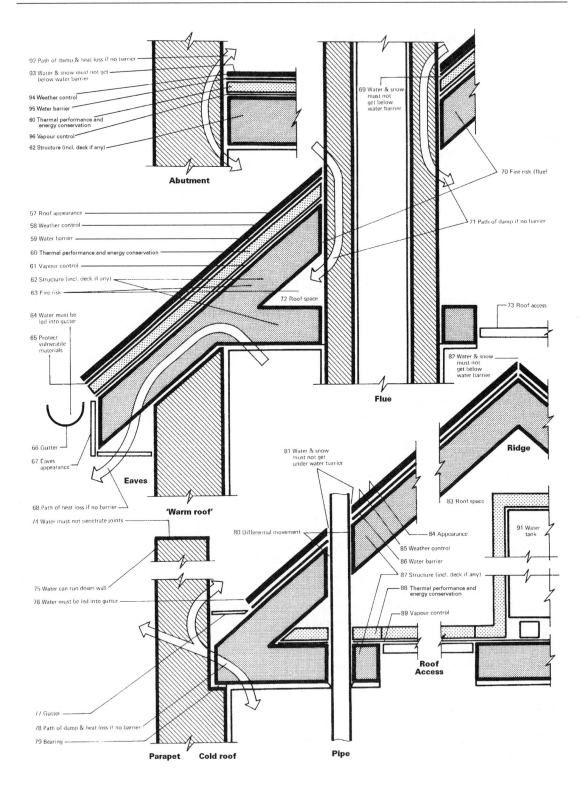

92 Path of damp & heat loss if no barrier
93 Water & snow must not get below water barrier
94 Weather control
95 Water barrier
60 Thermal performance and energy conservation
96 Vapour control
62 Structure (incl. deck if any)

Abutment

69 Water & snow must not get below water barrier

70 Fire risk (flue)

71 Path of damp if no barrier

57 Roof appearance
58 Weather control
59 Water barrier
60 Thermal performance and energy conservation
61 Vapour control
62 Structure (incl. deck if any)
63 Fire risk

72 Roof space

73 Roof access

64 Water must be led into gutter
65 Protect vulnerable materials

82 Water & snow must not get below water barrier

66 Gutter
67 Eaves appearance

Ridge

Eaves

81 Water & snow must not get under water barrier

83 Roof space

91 Water tank

68 Path of heat loss if no barrier

'Warm roof'

74 Water must not penetrate joints

80 Differential movement

84 Appearance
85 Weather control
86 Water barrier
87 Structure (incl. deck if any)
88 Thermal performance and energy conservation
89 Vapour control

75 Water can run down wall
76 Water must be led into gutter

Roof Access

77 Gutter
78 Path of damp & heat loss if no barrier
79 Bearing

Parapet   Cold roof

Pipe

BS 747:1994, Specification for roofing felts
See item 63, Fire risk.

59 Water barrier

Where dry lapped small units are used, a waterproof underlay should be integrated as a water barrier. Underlays can be of bitumen felt, with various fibres to make up a strong, flexible and waterproof composite. Various sheet polymers can be used and there are waterproof building papers. BS 747 lists different categories of felt.

Polymeric sheet underlays can be of thermoplastics (usually plasticized PVC sheet at least 0.13 mm thick or polyethylene film of at least 500 gauge, 0.13 mm thick chlorinated polythene CPE), or elastomers (usually butyl rubbers IIR, polyisobutylene PIB, or ethylene propylene diene monomer EPDM). Different manufacturers will supply different thickness, depending on whether the membranes are to be used for underlays or single sheet membranes for full waterproofing without additional cladding.

Certain qualities of waterproof building papers are sometimes used. See reference below.

Proprietary flexible underlays are available which combine a thermal insulation with a waterproof and vapour barrier.

Underlays must be properly lapped and supported in a way that will prevent 'troughs' of water or passages for water to be directed into the roof. Where rigid boards are used over rafters, counter battens (under normal tiling or slating battens) allow water to run down on top of the underlay.

BS 747:1994, Specification for roofing felts
BS 1521:1972 (1994), Specification for waterproof building papers

60 Thermal performance and energy conservation

See **Roofs: general Section 8**, item 6, Thermal performance for general factors. For 'warm' roofs, that is where the roof is to be used as a habitable space and to be maintained at a similar temperature to the rooms below the roof, the insulation is generally placed on top or below the rafters. Insulation quilts and rigid insulation boards can be used in both locations. See **Flat roofs, basic types Section 9**, item 14.3, for a brief list of insulants together with references. Proprietary

insulants are available that combine wall finishes, vapour barriers and insulation.

Increased U-values require materials to be checked for increased fire risk, smoke emission, and increased stresses in outer covering materials.

Thermal Insulation: Avoiding Risks, BRE. HMSO, 1994 (a good practice guide supporting the Building Regulations).
BS 5803 Thermal insulation for use in pitched roof spaces in dwellings. Part 1: 1985 (1994), Specification for man-made mineral fibre thermal insulation mats
The Building Regulations 1991, Document L, Conservation of Fuel and Power

61 Vapour control

See **Roofs: general Section 8**, item 6.4, Condensation risk, for general comments, and **Flat roofs, basic types Section 9**, item 14.4, for specific factors. A vapour barrier should be located on the warm side of the insulation and will therefore require protection from damage by building workers and occupiers.

BRE Digest 180:1986, Condensation in roofs

62 Structure

See **Roofs: general Section 8**, item 2, for general factors and references. For pitched roofs the structural support material is generally of timber and/or metal construction. Concrete frames can also be used and in hot climates concrete pitched slabs are often used as heat 'sinks' to absorb and moderate temperature differences between inside and outside. If these slabs are made hollow and cool air flows through them at night, they can be used to cool down the building fabric without the need for air conditioning. Timber and metal roof structures lend themselves to a wide variety of forms, either prefabricated on or off the site or assembled in situ. Consider the limiting effect of pitch, struts, collars and ties, etc., on the possible future conversion of the roof space into a habitable room. For comments and references on the durability of roof structures see **Roofs: general Section 8**, item 5, and item 2 for notes on structural strength and stability.

BS 5268 Structural use of timber. Part 3: 1985, Code of practice for trussed rafter roofs
Principles of pitched roof construction, TRADA WIS 1–10 rev. 1993 *Trussed rafters*, TRADA WIS 1–29 rev. 1991

The Building Regulations 1991, Document A, Appendix A Table A3 Ceiling joists, Table A5–A16 Common or jack rafters and purlins for roofs between 15 and 45°.

63 Fire risk

See **Roofs: general Section 8**, item, 10, for general summary of risks, references and sources of information association with roofs.

64 Water must be led into gutter

Roof covering materials should project well over the gutter and the water barrier (see item 59) lapped into the gutter to dispose of any water running down on top of the water barrier.

65 Protect vulnerable materials

Insulation materials (when on top of rafters) are usually stopped behind a protective batten or a fascia board is carried up to provide a stop.

66 Gutter

See **Roofs: general Section 8**, item 4, for general factors and references for calculating gutter and down pipe sizes. Gutters will be fixed to falls, therefore fascias must accommodate both fixings and falls. Where gutters are within easy reach they should be of stout materials. If water is to be recycled then the gutter materials should be chosen to control the purity of the water needed.

BS 2997:1958 (1980), Specification for aluminium rainwater goods
BS 460:1964 (1981), Specification for cast iron rainwater goods
BS 4576 Unplasticised polyvinyl chloride (PVC-U) rainwater goods and accessories. Part 1: 1989, Half-round gutters and pipes of circular cross section
BS 1431:1960 (1980), Specification for wrought copper and wrought zinc rainwater goods

67 Eaves appearance

Details around the edges of a pitched roof are of major aesthetic significance and deserve special study. See comments under item 57, Roof appearance. Check the local vernacular for a way of making roofs based on climatic need or a traditional use of local material.

Eaves details must prevent the entry into the roof of wind and dust. Fascia boards must be stout enough not to twist or warp (or in the case of plywood, delaminate). Fascias should project below soffits to form a drip. Soffits are often of thinner materials but must have adequate fixing battens to prevent sagging. Soffits can accommodate various forms of roof ventilation such as holes or slots, but must not allow the entry of vermin such as birds, bees or wasps. Bats and house martins are protected species.

68 Path of heat loss if no barrier

Link wall and roof insulation to form a barrier against a cold bridge.

69 Water and snow must not get below water barrier

Where chimneys and flues protrude through roof coverings standard flashing details must be followed. These are usually metal or plastic apron flashings turned up the chimney and dressed over the roof covering on the lower side. 'Back' or 'secret' gutters are turned up the chimney and dressed under the roof covering behind the chimney while systems of soakers and stepped flashings are fixed along the sloping abutments. Preformed flashings of metal, polymers or bitumen composites are available. All flashings must be securely fixed to avoid wind damage. Flashings fixed to brickwork should be turned at least 25 mm into brick joints and secured with clips or wedges and pointing. Special flashing fixing details might have to be devised in the case of precast or in situ concrete flues.

Refer to standard textbooks and manufacturers' technical information such as *Redland Tiles Technical Manual* or the Lead Development Association details.

70 Fire risk around chimneys and flues

The proximity of combustible materials to flues is controlled by the Building Regulations 1991, Document J Heat producing appliances. Flue pipes, chimneys, open-flued appliances and hearths have rigorous requirements for non-combustible adjacent materials and compartmentation.

71 Path of damp if no barrier

Provide a horizontal metal dpc tray in brick chimneys. See standard textbooks (e.g. *Principles of Modern Building, Vol 1* or *Mitchell's Building Series*).

72 Roof space

In the case of a 'warm roof' it is assumed that the roof space will be used for some form of accommodation. Consider natural lighting from rooflights, ventilation, floor and 'wall' finishes; loading on trusses and ceiling rafters and access to the roof for external maintenance, and easy access to tanks and long-term storage (see **Roofs: general Section 8**, item 12). To facilitate future conversion preplan:

1 location of access or stairs;
2 electrical layout;
3 plumbing;
4 location of water tank;
5 strength of ceiling joists for normal household roof loadings.

73 Access

If access is through a hatch or trapdoor consider:

1 ladder storage and fixing;
2 method of opening and securing trapdoor;
3 location of access for safety (ladder position should not foul lower stairs, headroom above access, etc.);
4 electric light switch at lower level;
5 detailing of finishes around opening to avoid water penetration and deterioration;
6 Maintenance of insulation in roof and vapour checks.

See accompanying part of diagram for item 90

74 Water must not penetrate joints

Tops of parapet walls should be protected against water lying in pools and penetration, particular attention being paid to the joints whether the coping is made of brick, stone, concrete, plastic or metal. Poor jointing in this location often results in wall staining as well as the deterioration of parapet walls. It is good practice to run a dpc under most forms of coping. Brick on edge copings are very vulnerable, the successful traditional detail incorporated a tile 'creasing' the denser tiled course acting as a dpc. Thermal movements of metal and plastic copings often result in water penetration between joints not protected by a dpc or not detailed to accommodate movement.

75 Water can run down wall

Copings should project slightly from the face of parapets in order to avoid haphazard wall staining.

76 Water must be led into gutter

Roof covering materials should project over the last batten or support (in the case of tiling and slating a tilting fillet is used) and the water barrier or underlay carried over the gutter lining and lapped into the gutter to dispose of water running down the roof.

77 Gutter

Parapet gutters must be wide enough to provide foot room (250 mm) as well as being laid to falls. The water-proof gutter lining is usually of non-ferrous metal, plastics or fibre cement, supported on timber-boards, bearers and uprights. The gutter lining must be taken up under the roof covering and over the tilting fillet or last support of the roof covering on one side and carried up the parapet wall a min of 150 mm on the other side. A 150 mm wide cover flashing is then fixed to the wall and dressed down over the top of the gutter lining.

78 Path of damp and heat loss if no barrier

Horizontal and vertical dpcs and cavity barriers must be located in order to prevent damp penetration. Cavities in masonry construction should be taken up to the coping. Solid parapets should not be rendered on one side only. Arrange the vertical and horizontal insulation barriers to link or overlap in order to avoid a cold bridge.

79 Bearing

Allow for adequate bearing, holding down and levelling of wall-plates. Lightweight roofs must be adequately fixed to wall-plates which in turn should be anchored to walls with galvanized mild steel straps (see Diagram 19 lateral support at roof level, Building Regulations 1991 Document A: Structure). Metal roof structures

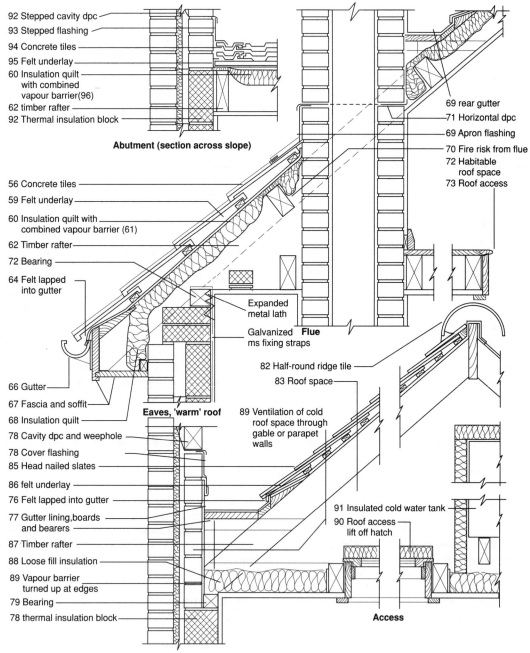

92 Stepped cavity dpc
93 Stepped flashing
94 Concrete tiles
95 Felt underlay
60 Insulation quilt
   with combined
   vapour barrier(96)
62 timber rafter
92 Thermal insulation block

Abutment (section across slope)

56 Concrete tiles
59 Felt underlay
60 Insulation quilt with
   combined vapour barrier (61)
62 Timber rafter
72 Bearing
64 Felt lapped
   into gutter

66 Gutter
67 Fascia and soffit
68 Insulation quilt
78 Cavity dpc and weephole
78 Cover flashing
85 Head nailed slates
86 felt underlay
76 Felt lapped into gutter
77 Gutter lining,boards
   and bearers
87 Timber rafter
88 Loose fill insulation
89 Vapour barrier
   turned up at edges
79 Bearing
78 thermal insulation block

Parapet, 'cold' roof

Eaves, 'warm' roof

Expanded
metal lath

Galvanized **Flue**
ms fixing straps

69 rear gutter
71 Horizontal dpc
69 Apron flashing
70 Fire risk from flue
72 Habitable
   roof space
73 Roof access

82 Half-round ridge tile
83 Roof space
89 Ventilation of cold
   roof space through
   gable or parapet
   walls

91 Insulated cold water tank
90 Roof access
   lift off hatch

Access

might require allowance for thermal movement at points of bearing.

80 Differential movement

Allow for movement between pipes and roof structures and coverings, see standard details for metal sleeves, 'slates' and preformed fittings.

81 Water and snow must not get under water barrier

Flashings and 'lead slates' etc. are dressed under the roof covering on the high side and over the covering on the low side and should be carried up pipes for a min of 150 mm and closed with 'hoods' or detachable collars. When using large diameter pipes check that adequate collars and fittings are available.

82 Water and snow must not get below water barrier

At ridges specially moulded ridge tiles and capping pieces are used to close off the roof covering. Ridge tiles should be continuously bedded in cement mortar. The underlay (if any) should be carried up one slope and slightly lapped down over the other to form a water-proof joint.

83 Roof space

In the case of 'cold' roofs the temperature of voids within the roof space and structure will be close to the external climate and heat gain should be allowed for and possible expansion and contraction, heat loss and freezing. Document L of the Building Regulations requires the active limitation of heat loss from hot water systems, and cold water pipes and overflows must be lagged. Boarding or walkways are needed for access to water tanks, and to prevent damage to ceilings. See item 89 for factors relating to roof ventilation and condensation risk.

84 Appearance

See item 57.

85 Weather control

See item 58.

86 Water barrier

See item 59.

87 Structure

See item 62, but note possible thermal movement of metal and polymeric roof structures.

88 Thermal performance and energy conservation

See **Roofs: general Section 8**, item 6, Thermal performance, for general factors but note that revised Building Regulations now stipulate a U-value of 0.2 W/m^2 K for domestic roofs (for SAP ratings of 60 or less), and 0.25 W/m^2 K for buildings other than dwellings. For 'cold' roofs the insulation can be placed on top, between or under the ceiling rafters. Rigid, or semi-rigid boards, quilts and loose fill between rafters are all possible insulants that may be used in this location. Some proprietary insulants incorporate a vapour barrier while others have a vapour barrier as well as a ceiling finish. Increased U-values require materials to be checked for increased fire risk and smoke emission.

See item 60 for reference.

89 Vapour control

See **Roofs: general Section 8**, item 6.4, Condensation risk, for general factors and 15.5 for comments relating to the difficulties of providing a vapour barrier at ceiling level.

Document F (Building Regulations 1991) sets out requirements to limit risk of condensation; see also BS 5250:1989.

For pitched roofs (square or rectangular plan) cross ventilation is required on opposite sides by maintaining a continuous 10 mm slot for roofs over 15°; if the pitch is less then the slot should be 25 mm.

90 Access

Comments as for item 73; in addition check that insulants and vapour checks are as continuous as possible.

91 Water tank

Points to check:

1 Insulation, lag tank, including pipes and connections.

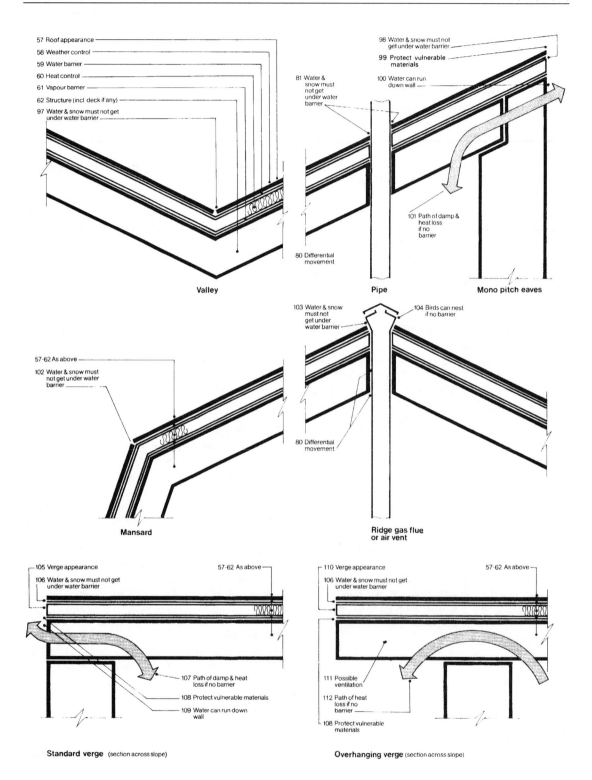

57 Roof appearance
58 Weather control
59 Water barrier
60 Heat control
61 Vapour barrier
62 Structure (incl deck if any)
97 Water & snow must not get under water barrier

81 Water & snow must not get under water barrier

80 Differential movement

Valley

98 Water & snow must not get under water barrier
99 Protect vulnerable materials
100 Water can run down wall

101 Path of damp & heat loss if no barrier

Pipe

Mono pitch eaves

57-62 As above
102 Water & snow must not get under water barrier

Mansard

103 Water & snow must not get under water barrier
104 Birds can nest if no barrier

80 Differential movement

Ridge gas flue or air vent

105 Verge appearance
106 Water & snow must not get under water barrier
57-62 As above

107 Path of damp & heat loss if no barrier
108 Protect vulnerable materials
109 Water can run down wall

Standard verge (section across slope)

110 Verge appearance
106 Water & snow must not get under water barrier
57-62 As above

111 Possible ventilation
112 Path of heat loss if no barrier
108 Protect vulnerable materials

Overhanging verge (section across slope)

2 Loading. Check loading on structure. Spread load across trusses and/or place tank over loadbearing partitions.

3 Bearers should be high enough to allow for access to pipe connections.

4 Leave room around tank for maintenance.

5 If possible locate tank for easy discharge of overflow pipe.

92 Path of damp and heat loss if no barrier

Provide a dpc to prevent damp bypassing the flashings described in item 93. On an external wall arrange the insulation to link with that of the roof. In very exposed conditions carry the dpc across the cavity.

93 Water and snow must not get below water barrier

At abutments provide either a secret gutter or a system of soakers and/or stepped cover flashings – see standard textbooks. In addition to the usual non-ferrous metals, preformed plastics and bitumen fibre composition flashings are available. Cover flashings must be securely fixed to walls (especially at corners of walls and chimneys, etc.) to avoid wind damage.

94 Weather control

Generally as item 58. Specifically roof coverings should be cut close to abutments to provide adequate support for soakers and flashings.

95 Water barrier

Generally as item 59. Specifically, where an underlay is used it should be turned up and over the fixing battens at abutments, or flashed into the wall.

96 Vapour control

Generally as item 61. Specifically, vapour barriers should be turned up and over the insulation at all edges.

97 Water and snow must not get under water barrier

Slated and tiled roofs can have 'open' or 'closed' valleys. Open valleys are constructed by forming metal or plastics lined troughs. Preformed plastics troughs and clay and concrete trough valley tiles are also available. Closed valleys are formed by various methods to provide a continuous roof covering; special valley units are available. See standard textbooks for details of 'laced', 'mitred' and 'swept' valleys. Open valleys should not be less than 150 mm wide to discourage blockages. Underlays should be continuous under closed valleys and lapped over the lining or trough in open valleys.

98 Water and snow must not get under water barrier

The edge of the weather and water barrier must be sealed, for example, by a special monopitch ridge tile, a metal or plastics edge trim or eaves filler for corrugated sheeting. Ridge tiles should not be solid bedded (except at joints) but thinned out with pieces of broken tile to reduce the mass of bedding to a minimum in order to avoid hair-line cracking in the mortar. Check that the colour of ridge tiles is compatible with that of the roof covering.

99 Protect vulnerable materials

Ridges of monopitch roofs are particularly vulnerable to wind damage, so roof coverings must be securely fixed down and good workmanship is essential in this location. Metal and plastics edge trim must be strong enough to withstand the impact of ladders, and be properly jointed to avoid water ingress and staining below joints. Insulation must be sealed, for example, by a timber fascia board or by the inner leaf of a cavity wall.

100 Water can run down wall

To avoid haphazard wall staining, ridge tiles and roof edge trim should project a maximum of 50 mm from the face of the wall to form a drip (too large a projection can result in wind damage).

101 Path of damp and heat loss if no barrier

Provide a dpc or cavity barrier to prevent damp penetration. Cavities in masonry construction should be carried up to the ridge. For 'warm' roofs, link or overlap roof and wall insulation to form a barrier against a cold bridge.

102 Water and snow must not get under water barrier

Where there is a change in roof pitch, for example, on a mansard roof, metal flashings are fixed under the roof covering on the high side and over the roof covering on the low side. To withstand local wind conditions, an adequate number of holding down clips or tacks are essential (normally at about 750 mm centres) but wind pressures should be checked. Underlays should be lapped over the flashing (but remain concealed) to direct water to the outside.

Lead Sheet in Building: a guide to good practice, Lead Development Association, 1989.

103 Water and snow must not get under water barrier

Gas flue terminal ridges are placed on a continuous bedding of cement mortar in the same manner as ordinary ridge tiles. The underlay should be cut back clear of the adaptor that connects outlet to flue.

Redland Tiles Technical Manual
Marley Technical Roofing Manual

104 Birds can nest if no barrier

Check that all grilles and vents are fixed with a bird barrier. This is essential where flues emit the products of combustion.

105 Verge appearance (standard)

Details around the edges of a pitched roof are of major aesthetic significance and deserve special study. See comments under item 57. Check local traditions. As with eaves details, verges must be carefully designed to protect entry into the roof of wind, dust, birds and insects. 'Standard' verges can be finished with timber or plastics barge boards, special verge clips and/or various cement mortar pointing and bedding details.

106 Water and snow must not get under water barrier

The edge of the weather barrier must be sealed, for example by using a tile or slate under cloak and cement mortar bedding, or by a preformed polymeric verge channel. The underlay should be cut short of the external face of the wall and, in the case of cavity wall construction, lapped slightly into the cavity.

107 Path of damp and heat loss if no barrier

Provide a dpc or cavity barrier to prevent damp penetration. Cavities in masonry construction should be carried up to the underside of the water barrier. For 'warm' roofs (see item 60) link or overlap roof and wall insulation to form a barrier against a cold bridge.

108 Protect vulnerable materials

Verges are particularly vulnerable to wind damage and so roof coverings must be securely fixed down. Good workmanship is essential in this location. Roof coverings should not project more than 50 mm from the face of the wall or barge board. Insulation should be stopped short of the external face of the wall, for example by a barge board or by the internal leaf of a cavity wall as shown on the diagram for 106.

109 Water can run down wall

Roof coverings at verges should be slightly canted inward to reduce the amount of rainwater overflowing the edge. To avoid haphazard wall staining 'standard' verges should be detailed to project between 38 and 50 mm from the wall face to form a drip.

110 Verge appearance (overhanging)

Comments as for item 105. Overhanging verges normally require special cantilever supports at right angles to the main rafters. They can be closed by a soffit or lined on the underside to expose the supporting sprockets or rafters. Barge boards can be ornamental or plain. Soffits must be well fixed to avoid sagging and barge boards stout enough to avoid warping as shown on the accompanying diagram.

111 Possible ventilation

Where 'cold' roofs are to be ventilated through soffits (see item 89 and **Roofs: general Section 8**, item 6.4) holes or slots must not allow the entry of birds, bees or wasps.

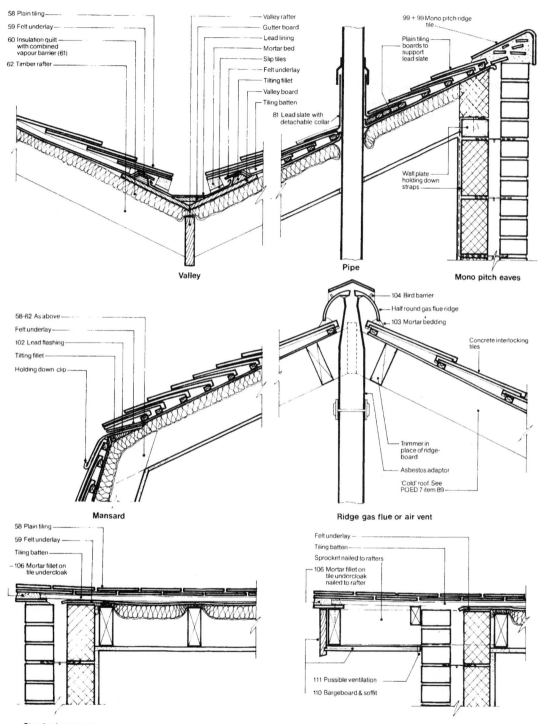

Valley

58 Plain tiling
59 Felt underlay
60 Insulation quilt with combined vapour barrier (61)
62 Timber rafter

Valley rafter
Gutter board
Lead lining
Mortar bed
Slip tiles
Felt underlay
Tilting fillet
Valley board
Tiling batten

Pipe

81 Lead slate with detachable collar

Mono pitch eaves

99 + 99 Mono pitch ridge tile
Plain tiling boards to support lead slate
Wall plate holding down straps

Mansard

58-62 As above
Felt underlay
102 Lead flashing
Tilting fillet
Holding down clip

Ridge gas flue or air vent

104 Bird barrier
Half round gas flue ridge
103 Mortar bedding
Concrete interlocking tiles
Trimmer in place of ridge-board
Asbestos adaptor
'Cold' roof. See POED 7 item 89

Standard verge (section across slope)

58 Plain tiling
59 Felt underlay
Tiling batten
106 Mortar fillet on tile undercloak

Overhanging verge (section across slope)

Felt underlay
Tiling batten
Sprocket nailed to rafters
106 Mortar fillet on tile undercloak nailed to rafter
111 Possible ventilation
110 Bargeboard & soffit

113

112 Path of heat loss if no barrier

For 'warm' roofs link or overlap roof and wall insulation to form a barrier against a cold bridge.

Trade and research organizations

Lead Sheet Association, St John's Road, Tunbridge Wells, Kent TN4 9XA (tel. 01892-51351, fax 01892-535028).

Marley Building Materials, Station Road, Coleshill, Birmingham B46 1HP (tel. 01675-462081, fax 01675-46544).

Redland Roof Tiles Ltd, Bedworth Works, Bayton Road Industrial Estate, Exhall, Coventry CV7 9E (tel. 01788 577166, fax 01788 537768).

Internal Walls: General Section 12

SMM: F Masonry, G Structural carcassing – timber, M Surface finishes,
K Linings/Sheathing/Dry partitioning

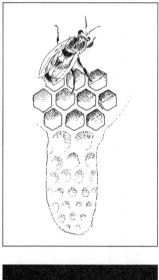

Honeycombs (bees)
Species that have individuals with different functions need to partition their habitat. The cellular divisions are for worker bees, the large hanging chamber for queen bees.

Japanese farmhouse, interior (Dean)

Notes and references

Items are cross-referenced from the diagrams and divided into sections with a general comment followed by technical references and the Building Regulations in context. Addresses of relevant trade and research organizations are given at the end of the section. British Standards and BRE Digests should be checked for current amendments.

This section contains general factors items 1 to 9; specific factors are contained in **Internal Walls: in Detail, Section 13.**

General references

Mitchell's Building Series: Structure and Fabric, Part 1 Jack Stroud Foster, 1994. Structure and Fabric, Part 2 by Jack Stroud Foster and Raymond Harrington 1994. Components, by Mike McEvoy 1979. Finishes by Yvonne Dean 1996. Longman.

Masonry Walls: Specification and Design, Kenneth Thomas. Architectural Press, 1995.

BS 5234 Partitions Part 1: 1992, Code of practice for design and installation of internal non-loadbearing partitioning

1 Wall categories

This information section deals with the general factors relating to most internal wall systems. As with external walls (see **External Walls Section 3**), internal walls have multiple functions and may be constructed in a wide range of materials and finishes.

1 *Partitions*. Internal walls which divide the space within a building into individual rooms or areas, the rooms being created to contain specific uses or activities within a single occupancy. Generally, 'partition wall' means any internal wall which is not a party wall or a division wall.

2 *Party walls or separating walls*. Internal walls used to separate different occupancies within the same building.

3 *Compartment walls*. Internal walls which divide a building into compartments for fire protection purposes.

Internal walls or partitions can be loadbearing or non-loadbearing, permanent or relocatable. The term

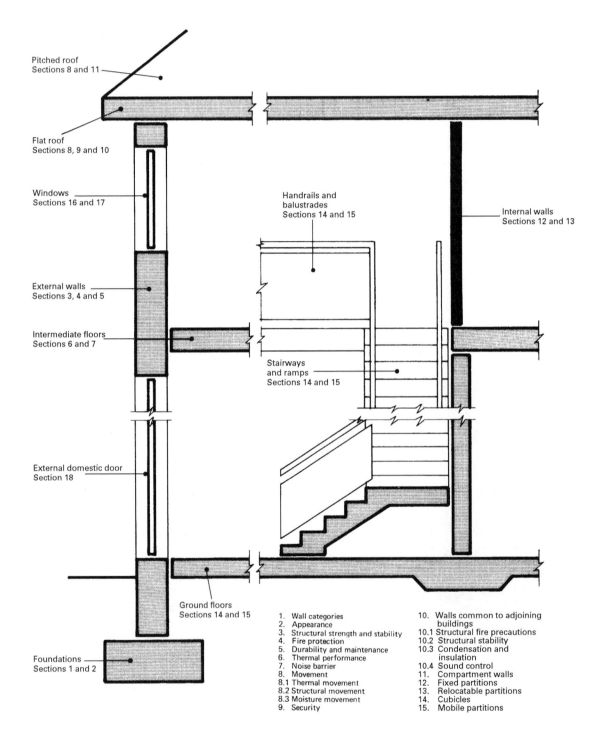

Pitched roof
Sections 8 and 11

Flat roof
Sections 8, 9 and 10

Windows
Sections 16 and 17

Handrails and
balustrades
Sections 14 and 15

Internal walls
Sections 12 and 13

External walls
Sections 3, 4 and 5

Intermediate floors
Sections 6 and 7

Stairways
and ramps
Sections 14 and 15

External domestic door
Section 18

Ground floors
Sections 14 and 15

Foundations
Sections 1 and 2

1. Wall categories
2. Appearance
3. Structural strength and stability
4. Fire protection
5. Durability and maintenance
6. Thermal performance
7. Noise barrier
8. Movement
8.1 Thermal movement
8.2 Structural movement
8.3 Moisture movement
9. Security

10. Walls common to adjoining
    buildings
10.1 Structural fire precautions
10.2 Structural stability
10.3 Condensation and
     insulation
10.4 Sound control
11. Compartment walls
12. Fixed partitions
13. Relocatable partitions
14. Cubicles
15. Mobile partitions

relocatable is preferred to the term demountable (BS 5234) as many partitions can be demounted or dismantled but not all can be reassembled and reused without substantial repair.

2 Appearance

Criteria for choosing a particular type of internal wall or partition are outside the scope of this information section. The designer must choose a wall system which achieves a balance between what may often be conflicting requirements: aesthetics, structural stability, durability, environmental performance, fire protection, sound control and cost effectiveness.

Appearance can be determined by the self-finish of the wall material, or by an applied new skin or decorative finish. Appearance is a fundamental to the choice of a proprietary partition system. This includes the texture and colour of surfaces and the arrangement of components. A great variety of finishes and surface materials are generally available within most systems.

The demand for adaptable partitions to subdivide internal spaces quickly, with minimum disruption and yet maximum choice of layout, has led to the development of wall systems which are now free-standing, mobile non-loadbearing screens. The wall has then made a transition to become an item of furniture. Materials, finishes and components of screens may be matched to those used for desks, chairs and other furniture as part of a complete office furnishing system. This trend away from the conventional fixed or relocatable systems of partitioning has been developed particularly for use in open plan office layouts. Appearance may also be affected by the restrictions placed on the use of certain finishes where fire protection requirements demand non-combustible surfaces or materials with specific surface spread of flame characteristics.

See general references.

3 Structural strength and stability

The structural roles performed by either permanent or relocatable internal walls and partitions can be classified as follows:

1 *Loadbearing.* Playing a positive part in a structural system by carrying dead and/or live loads (e.g. supporting floors and roofs), in addition to their own self weight. These walls may also have to resist lateral loading from wind pressures generated inside the building and/or stored material placed against one or both sides of the wall. Within a structural system the wall may be required to brace other walls or structural framework and resist vertical, horizontal and/or oblique forces being transmitted from and to other parts of the building structure.

Loadbearing internal walls combine the two primary functions of dividing space and supporting and transmitting loads. They can be an economical form of construction, reducing the need for an independent structural system, often limiting spans required for floor and roof members. However, in most cases the position of the loadbearing wall is fixed for the life of the building. It cannot be removed or relocated without endangering structural stability and unless a replacement structural supporting element is reintroduced.

2 *Non-loadbearing.* Walls which only have to carry their own weight plus certain live loads such as wind pressure, impact during use (either accidental or deliberate), fixings and fittings, maintenance operations, and loads applied during installation and handling (especially in the case of prefabricated walls or wall components).

Non-loadbearing walls may be either fixed or relocatable. Their main advantage is lightness of weight in comparison with loadbearing walls. This can reduce the total dead load of a building with consequent savings in structural elements including foundations. Their lightness and independence from the building structure enables these walls to be moved around to suit changing user activities and plan requirements.

Flexibility is especially useful when occupancy is expected to change during the building's lifetime, as in offices and other premises where space is leased to different tenants for varying periods. Where industrial processes or other commercial activities carried out within the life of the building are likely to change, particularly through advances in technology altering industrial production requirements, or plant installations, the building should be able to respond to change.

Internal walls can be constructed of a wide range of materials and/or components which may be grouped as follows:

(a) Individual brick or block units dry-jointed or bedded in mortar.

(b) Monolithic construction, principally concrete, either cast in situ or in precast components.

(c) Sheet material carried over or fixed within a supporting framework.

(d) Sandwich panels, with or without supporting elements.

Combinations of these general forms may be used and many relocatable non-loadbearing partition systems are available as proprietary prefabricated components.

See **Roofs Section 8**, item 2.

Windloading Handbook: Guide to the Use of BS 6399 Part 2, Tom Lawson. Architectural Press, 1996 (for effects of wind on internal partitions)

BS 6399 Part 2: 1997, Code of practice for wind loads

BS 648:1964, Schedule of weights of building materials

BS 4022:1970 (1994), Specification for prefabricated gypsum wallboard panels

BS 4046:1991, Specification for compressed straw building slabs (covers internal partitioning with wood or metal framing)

BS 5234 Partitions. Part 1: 1992, Code of practice for design and installation of internal non-loadbearing partitioning

Efficient Masonry Housebuilding – Detailing Approach, A. K. Tovey and J. J. Roberts. British Cement Association, 1990.

4 Fire protection

Certain internal walls are controlled by Building Regulations and by-laws to ensure the safety of people inside and outside the building. The controls are in the form of performance specifications or standards and codes of practice. Under the general heading of fire safety, in Document B of the Building Regulations, the following aims relate specifically to internal walls:

B1: that there is a satisfactory standard of means of escape for persons in the event of fire in a building.

B2: that fire spread over the internal linings is inhibited.

B3: to ensure the stability of buildings in the event of fire; to ensure there is a sufficient degree of fire separation; and to inhibit the unseen spread of fire and smoke in concealed spaces in buildings.

Internal walls to which the Building Regulations Document A apply may be loadbearing or non-loadbearing and include:

(a) walls common to two or more buildings;
(b) compartment walls;
(c) buttressing walls;
(d) supported wall.

They include walls enclosing a protected shaft and other loadbearing walls, or loadbearing parts of walls. Guidance relating to their requirements for fire spread come under Document B3 Internal fire spread (structure). In Document B of the Building Regulations (Fire safety) walls as structural elements are simply classified as 'a loadbearing wall or loadbearing part of a wall' and a 'compartment wall'.

Elements of structure must resist fire for minimum periods given in Table A of Appendix A of Document B according to the purpose group of the building (given in Table A2) or compartment and its height, area, volume and location (basement or not). The fire resistance is measured in accordance with BS testing methods set out in BS 476 Part 20: 1987, Method for determination of the fire resistance of elements of construction (general principles). It is useful to remember the broad requirements of a material or element in fire resistance which are as follows:

(a) Stability: resistance to collapse.

(b) Integrity: resistance to penetration of flame or hot gases.

(c) Insulation: resistance to temperature rise on unexposed face.

There are certain variations in the requirements under these headings to allow the use of existing traditional building methods/specifications and the method of test is altered to anticipate fire on one or both sides of the element (depending on degree and direction of assumed fire risk).

Some elements of structure are required to be non-combustible in certain conditions, in accordance with the test method given in BS 476 Part 4: 1970 (1980), as well as fire-resisting.

Walls in rooms, circulation spaces and protected shafts are also required to have minimum surface spread of flame properties. Ceilings sloping at 70° or more are considered to be walls, unless part of a rooflight. Protected shafts include stairways, lifts, escalators, chutes, ducts or other shafts which allow people, air or services to pass between compartments and which are enclosed by a protecting structure.

Specific factors for separating and compartment walls are given in **Internal Walls Section 13**, items 10 and 11.

Openings in walls enclosing a protected shaft are also controlled by the Regulations and include doors (Section 5 of Document B) and openings for pipes (Section 10 of Document B). Pipes passing through elements of structure are separately controlled in terms of pipe diameter and material and proximity to the element. Openings (for pipes, ducts, cables, etc.) in elements of structure and through cavity barriers must be as small as practicable and fire-stopped, but allow for thermal movement. Any junctions between, or gaps through, elements of structure must also be fire-stopped.

Cavities within internal walls must be closed around the perimeter of the wall, and barriers may be required within the cavity to prevent the movement of smoke or flames. Cavities within adjoining elements must not connect with one another, so wall cavities must not connect with floor and ceiling cavities. Junctions are particularly vulnerable to fire spread as often the details between elements do not continue the full fire resistance of a wall, floor or ceiling element.

See technical references to **Roofs, Section 8,** item 10 and **Stairways, Ramps, Handrails and Balustrades in Detail, Section 15**, item 3.

BS476 Part 2: 1987, Methods for determination of the fire resistance of non-loadbearing elements of construction (includes glazed elements)
BRE 230 1981: Fire performance of walls and linings
BRE 367 1991: Fire modelling
The Building Regulations 1991, Document B, Fire safety

5 Durability and maintenance

Loadbearing walls and the supporting framework of fixed non-loadbearing walls and partitions must last for the intended life of the building. Apart from finishes which can be renewed or replaced all materials used should be durable. Alternatively, cladding or infill panels can be designed for a shorter life than the structural or supporting framework, in which case details must allow for replacement without serious damage to the surrounding structure and fabric. Relocatable partitions may be designed for relatively shorter lifespans but must be detailed and constructed for removal and re-erection operations.

Maintenance includes the repair and replacement of materials or components damaged in use by impact or abrasion through normal wear as well as accidental damage. Materials may be repaired in situ or components

can be designed to anticipate damage, by allowing for easy removal, repair or complete replacement. Specially strengthened buffer rails and/or protective metal corner guards can be integrated into or mounted on wall surfaces. These are vital in areas of heavy circulation, where there are trolleys, wheelchairs or other wheeled vehicles. Materials must be able to cope with normal maintenance procedures and cleaning, which will vary according to the activities associated with the area defined by the wall or partition:

(a) In toilets, bathrooms, washing areas, kitchens, food storing, preparation and serving areas materials must be hygienic and easily cleaned with surfaces free from dirt retaining crevices or pores. This often means the use of inert materials such as ceramics, or stable metals like stainless steel.

(b) Cleaning may require the use of disinfectant or insecticide chemicals, detergents, polishes or other cleaning agents. At floor junctions details and skirtings must also resist floor cleaning operations which can involve chemicals and/or mechanical cleaners.

(c) Surfaces, materials and construction must be resistant to vermin. Avoid hollow cavities and voids which can encourage infestation, particularly when warmth, moisture and food are present in certain environmental conditions.

(d) Materials must not give off toxic fumes or irritants and this relates to the long-term potential of 'gassing off' from adhesives, coatings and other complex materials as well as airborne particulates from insulation materials (note the controls on use of certain asbestos and other fibrous materials).

See **External Walls Section 3**, item 5, and **External Walls Section 3**, item 11, for references and general references for this section.

BRE Digest 370: 1992, Control of lichens, moulds and similar growths
BRE Digest 238: 1980 (rev. 1992), Reducing the risk of pest infestation: design recommendations and literature review
Brickwork Durability, Harding and Smith, BDA

6 Thermal performance

The principles of thermal performance set out in **Roofs, Section 8**, item 6, for external walls also apply to internal walls. Note should be taken of special conditions, in particular:

(a) walls enclosing boiler rooms or other heat producing plant;
(b) walls enclosing cold stores;
(c) walls enclosing areas in which temperatures must be closely controlled and/or maintained to safeguard equipment, processes or people;
(d) semi-exposed walls or floors to unheated spaces (such as garages) in dwellings are expected to achieve a U-value of 0. 6 W/m² K.

Regulations for buildings other than dwellings give standard U-values for internal walls to ventilated spaces as either 0.6 to unheated spaces or 0.45 to sheltered areas and percentages of the exposed wall areas depend on the purpose group of the building.

As for external walls, the problems of cold bridging, surface and interstitial condensation must be avoided by careful choice of construction and materials. Cold bridges occur where materials with high thermal conductivity or capacity continue unbroken across a wall construction. Heat can then be transmitted directly across the wall thickness giving rise to surface condensation and pattern staining on the warmer side. Particular problem areas are structural frames, projecting floors and walls, jambs and lintels and cills to openings. Cold bridges can be avoided by using surface insulation or by incorporating thermal breaks within the element. The risk of condensation will be increased in areas in which moisture is produced, for example by washing or cooking activities, by people and during the drying-out period in new buildings. In some areas surface condensation must be accepted and surface finishes should be provided to resist moisture penetration and aid water run-off.

Air with a high moisture content will always tend to move to areas with lower moisture content (high to low vapour pressure) and will pass through partitions and internal walls. If the temperature within a wall at any point drops below the dew point temperature, interstitial condensation will occur. This form of condensation can cause rot, decay, corrosion of metal studding and fittings and staining, and reduces the effectiveness of insulation. The problem can be reduced or avoided by providing a vapour check or barrier on the warm side of insulation in the wall. Vapour barriers are only fully effective if completely sealed and unperforated (at service holes and joints for instance). When choosing

surface materials, the method of heating should be borne in mind, to ensure the comfort of the occupants. Materials with a low thermal capacity would be more appropriate than those with high thermal capacity in areas to be heated intermittently allowing a faster warm up (fast thermal response) so thermal comfort is achieved rapidly when the heating cycle starts. Internal walls may also have to resist high local surface temperatures from heating appliances, radiators or direct sunlight (adjacent to south-facing windows for example). Resulting thermal movement can lead to severe stress problems unless anticipated in the design. Consider the position, width, depth and filling of movement joints, edge restraints to wall panels and components, also the colour and composition of surface finishes likely to be heated.

See general references also:

BS 874:1973 (1980), Methods of determining thermal insulating properties with definitions of thermal insulating terms
BS 3837 Part 2: 1990, Specification for extruded boards
BS 3869:1965, Specification for rigid expanded polyvinyl chloride for thermal insulation purposes and building applications
BS 3927:1986, Specification for rigid phenolic foam (PF) for thermal insulation in the form of slabs and profiled sections
BS 4841 Rigid (PUR) polyurethane foam and polyisocyanurate (PIR) foam for building applications. Part 1: 1993, Laminated board for general purposes. Part 2: 1975, Laminated board for use as a wall and ceiling insulation
BS 5250:1975 (1995), Code of basic data for the design of buildings: the control of condensation in dwellings
BRE Digest 108: 1975 (rev. 1991), Standard U-values
BRE Digest 110: Condensation
BRE Digest 355: 1990, Efficiency in dwellings
CIBSE Guide: Vol. A, Building Energy Code (four parts), regular revisions by CIBS
Building Regulations 1991, Document L, Conservation of fuel and power

7 Noise barrier

Factors which determine the amount of sound transmitted through internal walls are:

(a) mass of wall;
(b) airtightness of construction;

(c) stiffness of wall;

(d) flanking construction and/or air paths.

The acoustic problems associated with partitions are fully set out in BS 5234 Part 1: 1992. See also relevant BRE publications such as Sound insulation of separating walls and floors, Part 1: Walls and *Noise Control in Buildings*, McMullan, BCB, 1991.

Statutory requirements for internal walls in the Building Regulations Document E only apply to walls between dwellings and walls between dwellings and other areas within the same building, e.g. machinery or tank rooms. Requirements are particularly stringent between dwellings and refuse chutes.

See references in **External walls Section 3**, item 8, and **Floors Section 7**, item 6.

Building Regulations 1991, Document E

8 Movement

For general comments which will also apply to movement in internal walls see **Foundations Section 1**, item 4; **External walls Section 3**, item 7; and **Floors Section 6**, item 4.

Wherever internal walls cross over movement joints in floors, the joint must be continued vertically for the full height of the wall. When walls cross beneath movement joints in roofs, the wall must also contain a vertical movement joint, *unless* a horizontal slip joint is provided at the head of the wall.

8.1 Thermal movement

Thermal movement in internal walls and partitions is generally quite small. Movement joints may be required, however, in long walls adjacent to, or enclosing, boiler rooms and cold stores. Junctions between internal walls and the external enclosing elements of a building may need to be designed to allow for thermal movement (expansion and contraction) in the external walls and roofs responding to external temperature changes. A roof slab will move considerably during a daily cycle of hot sunshine followed by cold nights. In this case, the roof may be designed to slide over the heads of internal walls.

8.2 Structural movement

Can be caused by:

(a) settlement of foundations;

(b) seasonal changes in ground conditions (e.g. on clay soils);

(c) deflection under loading which may be fully or partly reversed when loads (live and/or wind) are removed.

Loadbearing internal walls and structural members which are part of a wall should be designed to accommodate or resist structural movement in accordance with regulations and codes of practice. Non-loadbearing walls are also subject to stress induced by changes in the position of the adjacent structure. Consider:

(a) the deflection of floor slabs, floor and roof support beams above the wall and on which the wall is standing;

(b) racking of structural frames, columns and beams due to differential settlement or lateral forces.

These movements can cause severe distortion and/or overstressing in the wall. Deflection must be anticipated within limits set by British Standards codes of practice for different structural materials.

Isolation of the wall from surrounding structure may be necessary. Edges of walls need to be restrained for stability within chases or between metal/timber battens for example, but movement of the structure is permitted by providing an appropriate width of joint between the wall edges and the surrounding structure. The joint is filled by a suitable resilient material, which can compress to absorb movement but will return to its original width if the movement is reversed (without falling out or leaving a gap through the wall). Joints must continue through wall finishes to ensure that the wall is fully independent from the surrounding structure and to avoid surface cracking. Joints can be masked in a variety of ways, often with cover strips which conceal horizontal and vertical slippage.

8.3 Moisture movement

Moisture movement of internal walls will generally occur during:

(a) drying-out after construction;

(b) seasonal or climatic changes in atmospheric humidity.

Most materials expand when they absorb moisture (and many construction materials absorb moisture) and contract when they dry out or harden. After any construction or finishing operation which uses water, there will be some shrinkage. The extent of movement varies according to the type of material. Clay and certain concrete bricks will show a small amount of movement but more absorbent wood-cement products and timber will have a great deal.

Materials to be used internally and dry-fixed, which also have potentially large moisture movement characteristics, must be protected from contact with moisture at all stages during storage and construction. Moisture movement is generally reversible except that in concrete, mortars and plaster the initial shrinkage will exceed future reversible moisture movement as water is needed in chemical reactions in the hardening process. The amount of moisture movement for timber and timber composite materials is known and can be allowed for to some extent. The moisture content of timber can be specified to suit the likely internal temperature and humidity levels. Moisture content is adjusted by controlled seasoning or drying and can be maintained by protecting and sealing the timber during manufacturing processes and installation until the building is fully occupied. This can reduce the risk of shrinkage which would otherwise occur when damp site conditions are replaced by a centrally heated environment.

The need for special care and moisture control principally applies to joinery components and finishes. The seasonal movement of timber cannot be completely avoided except perhaps if the building has a totally controlled internal environment (full air-conditioning for example). Careful selection of timber species, choosing wood likely to show least movement, and detailing to allow for movement will minimize the problem.

Internal walls at ground level must be protected from rising damp by a suitable dpc. Particular attention must be paid to damp-proofing walls where a change in ground level occurs which may require tanking.

BRE Digest 245: 1984, Rising damp in walls: diagnosis and treatment
BRE Digest 163: 1974, Drying out buildings
BRE Digests 227, 228 and 229: 1979, Estimation of thermal and moisture movements and stress: Parts 1, 2 and 3.

9 Security

Internal walls and partitions generally do not have to provide the same degree of security as is required from the enclosing elements (external walls, roofs, windows and doors) of a building. Exceptions are walls separating different tenants or users and walls enclosing areas with a particular security risk.

Security requirements may include one or more of the following:

(a) To prevent entry from outside an area protected to avoid theft: this would include strong-rooms, warehouses and storage areas, the risk varying according to the value of the contents.
(b) To resist attack from outside an area (either as vandalism or malicious damage); this can range from damage to communal areas in housing schemes to attacks on vital equipment (such as security control/lighting/batteries/generators) as a prelude to theft in another area.
(c) To restrain people (or animals) within an area: cells within prisons, court buildings or police stations for example and walls within special hospitals or institutions.

The degree of risk and/or the value of contents to be protected will determine the extent of the security and protection required. Detailed advice should be obtained from specialist consultants, insurers, police authorities and manufacturers or other appropriate organizations at an early stage in the design.

Security is not always concerned with creating a barrier against the unauthorized passage of people or projectiles; it can also apply to walls which must resist potentially harmful radiation, for example X-rays, radioactive material and micro-wave emissions. These are highly specialized areas of design and must conform to stringent government safety standards. However, the use of various forms of radiation is increasing in many fields of medicine and industry so the problems are likely to be met in many building types.

BS 5051 Security glazing. Part 1: 1988 (1994), Specification for glazing for interior use (includes bullet-resistant glazing)
BS 5544:1978 (1994), Specification for anti-bandit glazing (resistant to manual attack)

Trade and research organizations

British Gypsum Ltd, Technical Service Deptartment, East Leake, Loughborough, Leics LE12 6JT (tel. 0115-945 6123).

Chartered Institution of Building Services Engineers (CIBSE), Delta House, 222 Balham High Road, London SW12 9BS (tel. 0181-675 5211, fax 0181-673 5880).

Health and Safety Executive, Broad Lane, Sheffield S3 7HQ (tel. 0114-289 2345, fax 0114-289 2333).

Partitioning and Interiors Association, 692 Warwick Road, Solihull, West Midlands B91 3DX (tel. 0121-705 9270, fax 0121-711 2982).

TRADA Technology Ltd (Timber Research and Development Association), Stocking Lane, Hughenden Valley, High Wycombe, Bucks HP14 4ND (tel. 01494-563091, fax 01494-565487).

Internal Walls in Detail Section 13

SMM7: F Masonry, G Structural carcassing – Timber, M Surface finishes,

K Linings/Dry partitioning

Notes and references

Items are cross-referenced from the diagrams and divided into sections with a general comment followed by technical references, Building Regulations and relevant trade and research organizations. British Standards and BRE Digests should be checked for current amendments.

This section contains specific items 10 to 15, and should be read in conjunction with **Internal Walls: General Section 12.**

10 Walls common to adjoining buildings

All party walls are common to two or more buildings and in separate occupation become compartment walls.

10.1 Structural fire precautions

Walls common to two or more buildings and in separate occupation must resist fire from both sides independently for minimum periods of time as specified in Table A2 in Building Regulations 1991, Document B. This will be for at least 1 hour and this period will increase according to the building use and size. These walls must give complete vertical separation between buildings, including roof spaces. Openings for people through compartments are controlled by Document B Section 8, and for services and junctions with roofs and external walls by Document B Section 10.

Walls common to two or more buildings are regarded as a special form of compartmentation that must restrict the spread and size of a fire. As fire engineering is now an accepted discipline these walls may not have to be entirely non-combustible if there are adequate precaution and firefighting measures, for example sprinkler systems. Only firefighting shafts and hospitals will have to have compartment walls of limited combustibility (e.g. two-hours' fire resistance). As surface finishes are a significant factor in spreading fire, care should be taken in the choice of materials used, especially in areas used for escape. Section 6 of Document B should be used for guidance, but generally ordinary rooms in dwellings can

have limited combustibility (class 3), circulation spaces should achieve class 1 and other circulation areas between dwellings used as means of escape should comply with class 0. Structural elements have to comply with the same requirements for fire resistance as compartments and reference should be made to Appendix A Table A1 of Document B.

Openings for pipes can be made if continuity of the fire resistance of the wall is not impaired. This means that services must be well-protected and sealed. Pipe materials should be specified so that they do not soften or distort causing a new pathway for fire and are likely to be cast iron or steel, complying with Table 15 in section 10. Other likely openings would be for use as a means of escape, which must be protected by fire resisting doors that comply with Table B1 of Appendix B in Document B. In a compartment wall separating buildings the requirement is for one hour.

Junctions with external walls must be constructed to maintain the integrity of fire resisting elements by either being bonded together or fire-stopped. Cavities at the wall perimeter should be sealed by a barrier in the same place as the wall to stop pathways for fire around walls. They should have fire integrity of at least 30 minutes fire resistance. Continuous boxed-in eaves fascia cavities must be provided with cavity barriers to maintain separation.

Compartment walls must not assist the spread of fire over a roof by radiation or fire penetration. They must retain the overall fire resistance needed by fire-stopping at the roof/wall junction, have zones of 1.5 m wide on either side of the wall finished with non-combustible material or (and traditionally) projecting at least 375 mm above a roof (see sections 8.23, 8.24, 8.25 in Document B). Compartment walls are regarded as elements of structure in respect of the fire resistance needed.

10.2 Structural stability

Walls common to buildings may require lateral restraint at floor and roof levels, see Building Regulations, Document A Diagram 13, and **Floors, detail Section 7.** Minimum thicknesses of compartment walls are given

8. Structural forces which may act on load bearing and non load bearing internal walls

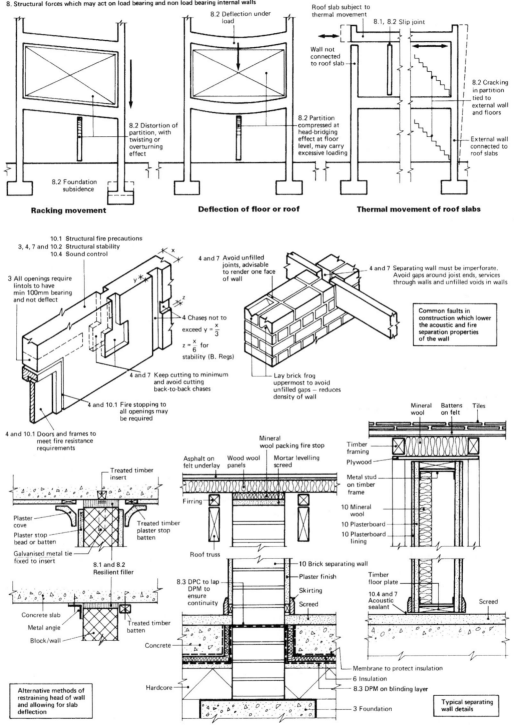

Racking movement

8.2 Distortion of partition, with twisting or overturning effect

8.2 Foundation subsidence

Deflection of floor or roof

8.2 Deflection under load

8.2 Partition compressed at head-bridging effect at floor level, may carry excessive loading

Thermal movement of roof slabs

Roof slab subject to thermal movement

8.1, 8.2 Slip joint

Wall not connected to roof slab

8.2 Cracking in partition tied to external wall and floors

External wall connected to roof slabs

10.1 Structural fire precautions
3, 4, 7 and 10.2 Structural stability
10.4 Sound control

3 All openings require lintols to have min 100mm bearing and not deflect

4 and 7 Avoid unfilled joints, advisable to render one face of wall

4 and 7 Separating wall must be imperforate. Avoid gaps around joist ends, services through walls and unfilled voids in walls

4 Chases not to exceed $y = \frac{x}{3}$

$z = \frac{x}{6}$ for stability (B. Regs)

4 and 7 Keep cutting to minimum and avoid cutting back-to-back chases

4 and 10.1 Fire stopping to all openings may be required

4 and 10.1 Doors and frames to meet fire resistance requirements

Lay brick frog uppermost to avoid unfilled gaps — reduces density of wall

Common faults in construction which lower the acoustic and fire separation properties of the wall

Treated timber insert

Plaster cove

Plaster stop bead or batten

Galvanised metal tie fixed to insert

Treated timber plaster stop batten

8.1 and 8.2 Resilient filler

Concrete slab

Metal angle

Block/wall

Treated timber batten

Alternative methods of restraining head of wall and allowing for slab deflection

Asphalt on felt underlay

Wood wool panels

Mineral wool packing fire stop

Mortar levelling screed

Firring

Roof truss

8.3 DPC to lap DPM to ensure continuity

Concrete

Hardcore

Mineral wool

Battens on felt

Tiles

Timber framing

Plywood

Metal stud on timber frame

10 Mineral wool

10 Plasterboard

10 Plasterboard lining

10 Brick separating wall

Plaster finish

Skirting

Screed

Timber floor plate

10.4 and 7 Acoustic sealant

Screed

Membrane to protect insulation

6 Insulation

8.3 DPM on blinding layer

3 Foundation

Typical separating wall details

in Table 5 of Document A, Structure, and are dependent on total wall height and length.

10.3 Condensation/insulation

Compartment walls at junctions with external walls must be insulated to avoid cold bridging and subsequent risk of local condensation, especially if in contact with external leaf of wall when acting as a cavity barrier, and still maintain the integrity of fire resistance in item 10.1 above. Insulate surface of separating wall for suitable length within building to maintain target U-values if an overlapping detail is unavoidable and provide a vapour barrier, possibly using a dry-lining form of wall finish.

10.4 Sound control

All brick or other block/masonry joints, especially perpends, must be fully filled with mortar to prevent a source for airborne sound, known as 'airpaths'. Walls not to be plastered, in roof spaces for example, may require rendering on at least one side to ensure complete sealing. This will also apply to areas of wall at floor level between floor/ceiling finish, especially if joists are built into the wall. At roof level gaps must be sealed particularly where trusses, ties or plates pass through walls. Note the fire requirements in these cases and avoid such details if possible.

Chases/cut-outs in the wall should be minimum depth compatible with requirements to provide sufficient mass to avoid the transmission of sound. Avoid placing these details back-to-back or breaking through, see Diagram 35 in Document E showing details for wrapping services to ensure discontinuity of sound paths.

See Section 1 of Document E (Resistance to the passage of sound) for different specifications for walls required to provide sound insulation. Obvious conflicts are using less dense materials for a high degree of thermal insulation when denser structures are more appropriate for sound control. For example, using lightweight thermal insulation blocks in cavities and at junctions with external walls to avoid cold bridging.

The sealing of gaps, perpends, joist ends, wall-plates and at top of wall to the underside of the roof construction (where wall does not rise above roof) is also essential to ensure fire resistance is maintained.

Note: work to party walls, previously only properly legislated for in London, is now governed by the Party Wall Act 1996 which applies to England and Wales. Briefly, notice must be given to adjoining owners of any

work to be done and the adjoining owner has the right to appoint their own surveyor. In the event of a dispute, an independent third surveyor is appointed to review the situation and make 'a party wall award' which settles the dispute and apportions cost. For details on administering the process refer to: *Architect's Guide to Job Administration: The Party Wall Act 1996*. RIBA Publications or, *Party Walls and What to do With Them*. RICS Books.

11 Compartment walls

These are used with compartment floors where necessary, to divide buildings into compartments and 'form a complete barrier to fire between the compartments they separate' (section 8.19 of Document B). They must resist fire from both sides, and have a fire resistance as specified in Appendix A, Tables A1 and A2 of Document B. In separating dwellings these are likely to be for one hour, and for separating a protected corridor or lobby within a dwelling, 30 minutes. There are maximum dimensions for buildings or compartments which are larger than individual dwellings and these vary according to purpose groups and are set out in Table 12 of Document B. All beams and columns, which form part of a compartment wall with a specific fire resistance, or any structure which carries a compartment wall with a specific fire resistance, must have the same fire resistance.

Surface finishes should comply with Section 6 of Document B, surface spread of flame requirements, and Section 7 where elements of structure form part of the compartmentation and may have to comply with higher levels of fire resistance.

Openings in compartment walls must be limited to:

(a) Door openings that have the appropriate fire resistance specified in Appendix B, Table B1.
(b) Openings for protected shafts that comply with Diagram 25 in Section 8 of Document B.
(c) Openings for ventilation ducts, pipes and chimneys that comply with Section 10 guidance.
(d) Refuse chute openings made from non-combustible construction.

Junctions between compartment walls and between compartment walls, floors, external or separating walls, must maintain the integrity of the fire resistance and be bonded together or fire-stopped. At junctions with roofs, see item 10.1 above. Combustible materials may be built into, carried through or across the ends of a compartment wall as long as the material or type of construction does not render ineffective the fire resistance of the wall.

12 Fixed partitions

These are non-demountable, and include loadbearing partitions. Generally constructed of materials and/or components that, if non-loadbearing, would still be uneconomic to dismantle and reassemble elsewhere and this includes most timber stud and masonry (brick/block) partitions.

Where fixed partitions contain windows this section should be read in conjunction with **Windows: General Section 16**.

BS 5234 Partitions. Part 1: 1992, Code of practice for design and installation

BS 5268 Structural Use of Timber. Part 2: 1991, Code of practice for permissible stress, design materials and workmanship

BS 5385 Wall and floor tiling. Part 1: 1995, Code of practice for the design and installation of internal ceramic wall tiling and natural stone wall tiling and mosaics in normal conditions

BS 1230: Gypsum plasterboard. Part 1: 1985 (1994), Specification of plasterboard excluding materials submitted to secondary operations

BS 5492:1990, Code of practice for Internal plastering

13 Demountable partitions

These are non-loadbearing partitions which can be dismantled and reassembled without substantial repair of components and redecoration/replacement of finishes. Most proprietary factory assembled systems come into this category. Traditional site assembled partitions are tailored to suit details and dimensions of a particular location so may not be reusable without repair/replacement of components or finishes. They are more appropriate for office or commercial use.

Consider how frequently relocation is likely to be required in the life of the partition. Compare costs of occasional relocation of site assembled partitions, such as plasterboard on timber stud framing, with initial cost of fairly sophisticated proprietary systems which may offer greater potential for changing wall layouts than is actually required. If fairly frequent change is anticipated, the higher initial cost of a system designed for

easy and fast dismantling and reassembly can be offset against extra labour costs involved in taking down and rebuilding a 'traditional' partition. Include the cost of repair/replacement of components and finishes together with length of time required to take down/move/reassemble the 'traditional' partition. Commercial buildings have a limited life in their internal configuration as the only known factor for most businesses is that they have to adapt to continual change. The decisions to use a particular partition may also be decided by tax advantages and not necessarily user requirement. Non-demountable partitions are more likely to be regarded as a capital cost that can be offset against tax, whereas demountable partitions may have to be accounted for as equipment and written off over a longer period.

Consider quality of finish, appearance of partition, the range of surface materials available. Most proprietary relocatable partition systems offer a wide range of choice in each of these areas related to cost and aesthetic requirements. For selection criteria, see BS 5234 Partitions, Part 1: 1992, Code of practice for design and installation.

14 Cubicles

These are usually fixed non-loadbearing partitions used to create compartments (for privacy) in toilets, showers and changing rooms. They may include doors but generally the main wall panels are made to a standard height (approx 2 m) and supported above the floor to allow for easy floor cleaning. The materials, construction and fixing details must:

(a) Resist vandalism and impact damage. Horizontal rails and ties, above doors, for example, must be avoided or be strong enough to withstand people swinging on them (especially in schools, etc.).

(b) Be strong enough to take door fittings, toilet roll holders, coat hooks etc. Vandal-resistant fixings are recommended.

(c) Have surfaces that resist abrasive or chemical cleaners and are hygienic and can be readily cleaned. Graffiti removal/prevention should be considered.

(d) Resist damp, humid atmospheric conditions and repeated washing. Surfaces must not delaminate from core materials and cores must not deteriorate. Metals must resist corrosion. Timber and timber composite materials should be used with care.

Suitable preservatives and waterproof adhesives must be used and surfaces must be sealed to resist moisture penetration.

Cubicles are principally for privacy and so do not need to meet other performance requirements. Panels are generally of a minimum thickness compatible with strength to allow the maximum utilization of restricted plan areas.

15 Mobile partitions

Main types are:

(a) Sliding or folding sliding, restrained at top and/or bottom by tracks or guides for linear movement. They may fold for easy and compact storage when not required, or may slide unfolded into a storage cavity, and are often used to sub-divide large rooms, especially in schools, lecture halls, canteens and social areas. They are frequently required to be sound barriers and fire resistant, so details at perimeter and meeting edges are critical. Similar in many respects to large sliding folding doors often using the same suspension and track fittings.

(b) Unrestrained at top and bottom, usually freestanding screens, not room height and not part of the building structure or fabric. Used especially in office layouts where work positions can be made and quickly altered in large open-plan areas. These screens are generally classed as furniture and supplied as part of furnishing/interior design scheme. As such, they do not need to comply with Building Regulations but as they are used to provide a degree of sound control and visual privacy they should be designed to give high performance.

BS 5234 Partitions. Part 1: 1992, Code of practice for design and installation

Trade and research organizations

Brick Development Association (BDA), Woodside House, Winkfield, Windsor, Berkshire SL4 2DX (tel. 013447-885651, fax 01344-890129).

British Ceramic Tile Council, Federation House, Station Road, Stoke-on-Trent, Staffs ST4 2RU (tel. 01782-747147, fax 01782-747161).

British Cubicle Manufacturers' Association, 17 Bridge Street, Evesham, Worcs WR11 4SQ (tel. 01386-6560, fax 0121-420 2246).

British Laminated Plastics Fabricators' Association, 6 Bath Place, Rivington Street, London EC2A 3JE (tel. 0171-457 5000, fax 0171-457 5045).

British Woodworking Federation, 82 New Cavendish Street, London W1M 8AD (tel. 0171-580 5588, fax 0171-436 5398).

Fibre Building Board Development Association, 1 Hanworth Road, Feltham, Middx TW13 5AF (tel. 0181-751 6107, fax 0181-890 2870).

Finnish Plywood International, PO Box 99, Welwyn Garden City, Herts AL6 OHS (tel. 01438-798746, fax 01438-798305).

Gypsum Products Development Association, c/o KPMG Peat Marwick, 165 Queen Victoria Street, London EC4V 4DD (tel. 0171-583 1886, fax 0171-583 1886).

TRADA Technology Ltd (Timber Research and Development Association), Stocking Lane, Hughenden Valley, High Wycombe, Bucks HP14 4ND (tel. 01494-563091, fax 01494-565487).

Stairways, Ramps, Handrails and Balustrades: General
Section 14
SMM7 L Stairs, M Surface finishes

Lizard (Moorish Gecko)
Other species have great mechanical advantages for climbing, spiders have a highly efficient system of hydraulics that rotates their hinged joints, lizards have highly developed ribbed pads, the increased surface area providing great friction and adhesion.

Stairs, Naxox Greece (Rich)

Notes and references
Items are cross-referenced from the diagrams and divided into sections with a general comment followed by technical references and the Building Regulations in context. Addresses of relevant trade and research organizations are given at the end of the section. British Standards and BRE Digests should be checked for current amendments.

Stairways are the one area where most sections of the Building Regulations apply, purely because these elements have to be considered as integral parts of the three dimensional space they occupy. Consequently there are environmental needs for lighting, ventilation and sound transference, precautions for fire and safety as well as a structural need for safe use and stability. Ironically, stairways are often areas given the least thought and yet can make a building more or less easy and joyful to use depending on their design. Thought should be given to the design of treads and risers to make ascending a stair as easy and effortless as possible; this adds to the enjoyment as much as the materials chosen for use. Stairs and ramps can be made out of a great range of materials. Unlike other elements in this book (which naturally suggest their materials – pitched roofs for example) reference should be made back to **Floors: general Section 6** and the reference section on materials at the end of this book. This is one area where it is often a false economy to use cheap materials; they have to take a punishing amount of wear and as an introduction to the rest of the building display an approach to detailing characteristic of the designer or constructor.

This section contains general factors, items 1 to 11; specific factors are contained in **Stairways and ramps: general Section 15**.

General references
Mitchell's Building Series: Structure and Fabric, Part 1: Jack Stroud Foster, Chapter 10; Part 2, Jack Stroud Foster and Raymond Harrington, Chapter 8. Longman, 1994.
BS 5395:1977 (1984), Code of practice for the design of straight stairs
BS 5578 Building Construction – Stairs. Part 2: 1978 (1995), Modular co-ordination: specification for co-ordinating dimensions for stairs and stair openings
BS 6100 Part 1: 1989, Section 1.3 sub-section 1.3.4

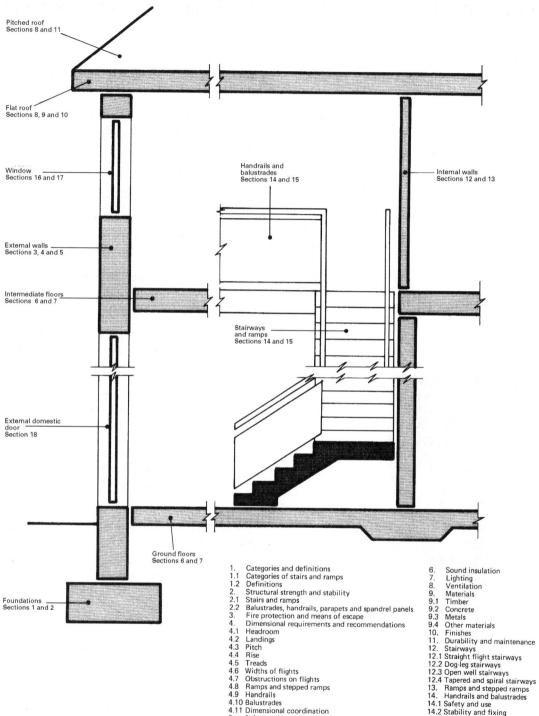

Pitched roof
Sections 8 and 11

Flat roof
Sections 8, 9 and 10

Window
Sections 16 and 17

External walls
Sections 3, 4 and 5

Intermediate floors
Sections 6 and 7

External domestic
door
Section 18

Foundations
Sections 1 and 2

Handrails and
balustrades
Sections 14 and 15

Internal walls
Sections 12 and 13

Stairways
and ramps
Sections 14 and 15

Ground floors
Sections 6 and 7

1.   Categories and definitions
1.1   Categories of stairs and ramps
1.2   Definitions
2.   Structural strength and stability
2.1   Stairs and ramps
2.2   Balustrades, handrails, parapets and spandrel panels
3.   Fire protection and means of escape
4.   Dimensional requirements and recommendations
4.1   Headroom
4.2   Landings
4.3   Pitch
4.4   Rise
4.5   Treads
4.6   Widths of flights
4.7   Obstructions on flights
4.8   Ramps and stepped ramps
4.9   Handrails
4.10 Balustrades
4.11 Dimensional coordination
5.   Safety and ease of use

6.   Sound insulation
7.   Lighting
8.   Ventilation
9.   Materials
9.1   Timber
9.2   Concrete
9.3   Metals
9.4   Other materials
10.   Finishes
11.   Durability and maintenance
12.   Stairways
12.1 Straight flight stairways
12.2 Dog-leg stairways
12.3 Open well stairways
12.4 Tapered and spiral stairways
13.   Ramps and stepped ramps
14.   Handrails and balustrades
14.1 Safety and use
14.2 Stability and fixing
14.3 Materials

Designing for the Disabled, Selwyn Goldsmith. RIBA,1976 (3rd edition). Sections 31, 32, 33.

Stairs, Steps and Ramps, Alan Blanc. Architectural Press, 1996.

The New Metric Handbook, Patricia Tutt and David Adler, eds. Architectural Press, 1979.

Specification Vols 1–5, David Martin, ed. Architectural Press, (latest edition).

Mechanical Services for Buildings, Eastop and Watson. Longman, 1992.

The Architecture of Building Services, Gordon Nelson. Batsford, 1995.

General research sources

National Building Studies Research Paper 32: The Forces applied to the floor by the foot in walking. (a) Walking on a slope. (b) Walking on stairs.

1 Categories and definitions

1.1 Categories of stairs and ramps

This section is about stairways, ramps and stepped ramps together with associated handrails and balustrades. Only those elements that are part of a building used by people on foot or in wheelchairs are considered here. Specific factors for vehicle ramps, stairs over 42° pitch, ladders and ramps over 1 in 12 slope are not covered. Special requirements for stairways and ramps outside buildings, forming external works, are also excluded but many of the principles covered here will apply.

Categories of stairways and ramps are defined in Document K of the Building Regulations 1991 for England and Wales. Table 1 gives specific requirements for stairways and ramps by reference to the main purpose groups and type of use, private, institutional and assembly and other buildings.

Ramp design is discussed under item 4.8 Ramps and stepped ramps, and 10 Finishes.

Stairs may also be classified according to their configuration. Four principal types of stair are given in BS 5395:

(a) Straight flight. Flights of parallel steps with or without landings but with no change of direction.
(b) Dog-leg. At least two flights, not necessarily of equal length, and a half landing. Generally refers to stair with a rectangular half landing (no tapered treads), no central well and with a central single newel post.

(c) Open well. Stair of two or more flights (with half or quarter landings) with generous horizontal space between flights.
(d) Geometrical. Includes helical spiral, circular or elliptical stairs. Generally all treads and landings are tapered. Flights which describe a helix round a vertical post common to all treads are commonly called spiral stairs. Helical flights can also rise around an open well. Other geometrical stairs form circles or ellipses on plan.

In addition the alternating tread stair can be used for access to one room, described as wide tread portions alternating on consecutive treads (see diagram 9 of Document K of the Building Regulations).

Stairways may often combine more than one configuration, for example open well or dog-leg stairs with tapered treads in place of the half landing forming a part circular stair.

Ramps and stepped ramps can be similarly classified according to their configuration.

1.2 Definitions

Definitions of terms used in relation to stairways and ramps are given in the introduction to Document K of the Building Regulations and BS 6100 Part 1: 1989, Section 1.3 sub-section 1.3.4. For other terms refer to BS 565 Part 1: 1989, and BS 5395. Terms associated with fire and means of escape are defined in BS 476 and BS 4422, Parts 1, 2 and 3, and reference should be made to BS 5588 Fire Precautions in the design construction and use of buildings, Part 6 Code of practice for places of assembly.

Main terms are outlined below.

* *Associated landing*. Part of a floor, balcony, platform, paving or ground at the top or bottom of a stairway, ramp or stepped ramp.
* *Baluster* (BS 5395). Infilling member of a balustrade.
* *Balustrade or guarding*. Element protecting the sides of a stairway, ramp or balcony, and including a wall, screen or railing.
* *Clearance* (BS 5395). Unobstructed height measured at right angles to the pitch line.
* *Length of tapered treads*. When consecutive tapered treads are of different lengths the length of the shortest tread should be considered the length of all the treads.
* *Flight*. The part of a stairway, stepped ramp or ramp with a continuous series of steps or continuous slope.

- *Going*. The distance on plan between a tread nosing and the nosing of the next tread, landing or ramp above. Also the distance on plan across a landing measured on the projected centre line of the flight or ramp adjacent to the landing.
- *Landing*. A platform between consecutive flights of a stairway, may also refer to associated landings.
- *Length of tread*. The shortest distance measured on plan between the sides of a tread.
- *Nosing*. The front edge of a tread; or of the landing or ramp at the top of a flight.
- *Pitch*. The angle between the horizontal and the notional line (called the pitch line) connecting the nosings of all the treads in a flight including the nosing of the landing or ramp at the top of the flight.
- *Protected stairway*. A staircase including any passageway linking to a final exit and place of safety which is enclosed with fire-resisting construction. The term protected shaft can include a stairway or ramp which enables people to pass between different compartments of a building enclosed by fire-resisting construction.
- *Ramp*. Any part of a building with an inclined surface steeper than 1:20 providing a route of travel for pedestrians or wheelchair users between levels.
- *Rise*. The height between two consecutive treads or between a tread and a landing or ramp immediately above. Also includes the distance from the top of any threshold on top of a tread or landing to the tread or landing at the bottom of the step. The minimum rise for domestic stairs is normally 140 mm and the maximum rise, 220 mm.
- *Spiral stairs*. A stair configured as a helix around a column occupying a cylindrical volume.
- *Stair*. Any part of a building linking levels by steps and landings.
- *Step*. Normally excludes an internal door threshold up to 40 mm high, and an external door threshold up to 75 mm high, although a minimum rise is no longer prescribed in the Building Regulations. (See rise)
- *Stepped ramp*. Route of travel formed by a combination of one or more flights and one or more ramps.
- *Tapered steps*. The preferred definition of steps with tapered treads – not 'winders'.
- *Tapered treads* do not have parallel nosings and will form a stair contained within a spiral volume.
- *Tread*. The upper horizontal surface of a step.

- *Width of stairway or ramp*. The unobstructed width from side to side clear of handrails or other projections, but may include strings to a total width of 30 mm and handrails up to 100 mm.
- *Width of tread*. The distance from the nosing to the face of the riser or back edge of the tread. In BS 5395 this distance is called the depth of the tread.

See general references.

BS 5395:1977 (1984), Code of practice for the design of straight stairs

BS 5578 Building Construction – Stairs. Part 2: 1978 (1995), Modular co-ordination: specification for co-ordinating dimensions for stairs and stair openings

BS 6100 Part 1: 1989, Section 1.3 sub-section 1.3.4

2 Structural strength and stability

2.1 Stairs and ramps

It is useful to think of stairs or ramps as cranked beams that have to span from one level to another carrying specific loads, so the main factors controlling the structural design of stairs and ramps will be the load to be carried and the length of span. The load will consist of dead load, live or imposed load and in some cases wind load. There will also be temporary loads from equipment, machinery or furniture being moved.

The stair or ramp construction may also contribute to the overall stability of the enclosing building or structure. In this case the connections between the stair or ramp components and the adjoining structure must be carefully considered.

With some designs, especially when using prefabricated components, there may be temporary instability, structural distortion or uneven distribution of load during erection. The designer should consider the construction sequence and ensure adequate ties are provided to prevent progressive failure of flights.

Accordingly, as stairs and ramps can be built out of the fullest range of materials, the British Standards and codes of practice for individual materials will have to be referred to, and the sequence of design will be the same as for any structure.

Dead loads include the weights of all materials and finishes used in the construction. Live (or imposed) loads are loads produced by the intended occupancy or use and include distributed, concentrated, impact, inertia and snow loads. Building Regulations Document A requires these loads to be calculated in accordance with BS 6399 Part 1: 1984, Code of practice for dead and imposed loads.

Wind loading should be calculated in accordance with BSCP 3 Chapter V, Part 2: 1972, which now overlaps with BS 6399 Loading for Buildings, Part 2: 1997, Code of practice for wind loads. See also *Windloading Handbook: Guide to the Use of BS 6399 Part 2*, Tom Lawson. Architectural Press, 1996.

Safety factors are added to the calculated loading to allow for unforeseen applied loads (accidental overloading) and variations in materials and workmanship.

2.2 Balustrades, handrails, parapets and spandrel panels (guarding generally)

These elements must be designed for the horizontal loading requirements of BSCP Chapter V, Part 1. A detailed and comprehensive guide to the design of railings and balustrades is given in BS 6180:1982 Code of practice for protective barriers in and about buildings.

BS 6399 Part 1: 1984, Code of practice for dead and imposed loads

BSCP 3 Chapter V, Part 2: 1972, which now overlaps with BS 6399 Loading for Buildings, Part 2: 1997

BS 8110 Structural use of concrete. Part 1: 1985, Code of practice for design and construction, Design materials and workmanship. Part 3: 1985, Design charts for singly reinforced beams, doubly reinforced beams and rectangular columns. Part 2: 1985 Code of practice for special circumstances

BS 5268 Structural use of timber. Part 2: 1991, Code of practice for permissible stress design, materials and workmanship

BSCP 8118 Structural use of aluminium. Part 1: 1991, Code of practice for design. Part 2: 1991, Code of practice for materials workmanship and protection

BS 449 Specification for the use of structural steel in building. Part 2: 1969, Amd to 1995

BS 585 Wood stairs Part 1: 1989, Specification for stairs with closed risers for domestic use, including straight and winder flights and quarter or half landings. Part 2: 1985 (1990), Specification for performance requirements for domestic stairs constructed of wood based materials

BS 6399 Part 1: 1984, Code of practice for dead and imposed loads

BS EN 485: 1994–5, Aluminium and aluminium alloys. Sheet strip and plate. Parts 1–4

BS 4169:1988, Specification for manufacture of glued-laminated timber structural members

BS 4357:1968, Specification for precast terrazzo units (including stair treads risers and landings)

BS 4592:1987–95, Industrial type flooring, walkways and stair treads. Parts 1–5 according to materials used and their configuration

BS 5628 Code of practice for use of masonry. Part 1: 1992, Structural use of unreinforced masonry

BRE Digest 12: 1961, Structural design in architecture

BRE Digest 346: 1990, Parts 1–8, The assessment of wind loads

The Way We Build Now, Andrew Orton. Van Nostrand Reinhold, 1988.

DG 13: Loadbearing Brickwork Crosswall Construction, Curtin Beck and Bray. Brick Development Association, 1983.

Publications from the Timber Research and Development Association including: STEP Volumes 1 & 2 for timber engineering, and Design Examples Series 'F' for flexural members, including sheets on joists and beams and Floor Joist Span Tables EDA1.

Architecture and Construction in Steel, Alan Blanc, Michael McEvoy and Roger Plank, eds. The Steel Construction Institute. Section 33 Staircases and Balustrades. This section contains some very useful case studies.

Building Regulations 1991, Document A: Structure. Generally the same sequence will apply to staircases as to any other structural element, establishing the loading conditions and then designing the structure in accordance with codes of practice for the materials chosen.

3 Fire protection and means of escape

Stairways are the main routes for escape from fire on the upper storeys of buildings. They must remain structurally sound and safe to use in fire for sufficient time to allow all occupants to escape. Ramps may also be used for escaping from fire especially in buildings occupied (permanently or only temporarily) by elderly or disabled people.

Stairways and ramps used as escape routes must be in fire-resisting enclosures and they must be constructed in materials to comply with the right degree of fire resistance which will vary according to their purpose group. The three main categories in the Building Regulations include protected stairways in dwelling houses (section 1), flats and maisonettes (section 2) and design for vertical escape in buildings other than dwellings (section 3). After checking requirements in these sections see Tables A1 and A2 of Appendix A of Document B (Fire safety) of the Building Regulations for fire resistance required linked to purpose groups. The enclosures must also be ventilated to ensure the rapid dispersal of smoke and hot gas which would otherwise make the escape route impassable. Minimum widths, numbers and locations of escape routes, including stairways and ramps, are given according to the type of building and its occupancy. Requirements are set out in Building Regulations which also make reference to relevant standards and codes of practice.

Stairways and ramps are not classed as elements of structure and are not required to be fire resistant unless they form part of the enclosure to a protected shaft. Table A1 of Appendix A requires protected stairways to have a minimum fire resistance of thirty minutes. All escape stairways and landings for buildings other than dwellings must be constructed of materials of limited combustibility. Means of escape routes are protected by fire-resisting enclosures, with the structure and construction meeting the requirements for protected shafts in the Building Regulations (see **Internal Walls Section 13**). Protected shafts consisting of a stairway have stringent requirements if they contain pipes for gas or oil (see paragraphs 8.3 onwards in Document B) and pipe work and ventilation ducts should meet the requirements of Section 10 in Document B. When designing stairways services should be contained in separate shafts if possible.

Ramps used for means of escape must not slope more than 1 in 12. Stepped ramps are not permitted but see means of escape for fixed seating in BS 5588 Part 6. Ramped corridors or passages leading to staircases must level out at the top or bottom of the staircase for a distance at least equal to the width of the corridor or passage.

BS 5588 Fire precautions in the design and construction and use of buildings. Part 1: 1990, Code of practice for residential buildings (Parts 2–10 deal with other building purpose groups and aspects of fire precautions)
BS 476 Fire tests on building materials and structures. Parts 6 and 7
BS 1635:1990, Recommendations for graphic symbols and abbreviations for fire protection drawings
BS 4422:1987–90, Glossary of terms associated with fire (Parts 1–5)
BS EN 2:1992, Classification of fires

BS 5268 Codes of practice for the structural use of timber. Part 4: Section 4.1, 1978 (1990), Recommendations for calculating the fire resistance of timber members
BS 5499 Fire safety signs, notices and graphic symbols. Part 1: 1990 (1995), Specification for fire safety signs
BRE Digest 208: rev. 1988, Increasing the fire resistance of existing timber floors
BRE Digest 225: 1986, Fire terminology
BRE Digest 230: 1981, Fire performance of walls and linings
BRE Digest 294: 1985, Fire risk from combustible cavity insulation
BRE BR 128: 1988, Guidelines for the construction of fire-resisting structural elements
BRE 367 1991: Fire modelling
BR 225: 1993, Aspects of fire precautions in buildings
Fire and the Design of Educational Buildings. Building Bulletin No. 7. HMSO, 1981.
Fire from first principles, Stollard and Abrahams, 1995.
Building Regulations 1991, Document B:
    Section 2: Flats and maisonettes. Common stairs and external escape stairs
    Section 4: Design for vertical escape in buildings other than dwellings
    Section 5: General provisions common to buildings other than dwelling houses

Structural fire precautions. There are no fire resistance requirements for stairways but requirements for limited combustibility and enclosure by protecting structure.

BS 5588 Fire precautions in the design and construction and use of buildings. Part 1: 1990, Code of practice for residential buildings (Parts 2–10 deal with other building purpose groups and aspects of fire precautions). Part 8: 1988, Code of practice for means of escape for disabled people.

4 Dimensional requirements and recommendations

General requirements common to all stairways and ramps given here are from Building Regulations 1991 Document K. Other recommendations are principally from BS 5395.

Specific requirements for stairways and ramps in England and Wales are given under three categories:

1 Private
2 Institutional and assembly stair
3 Other stair

Requirements are then given for these three categories of stairway or ramp according to the use or intended use of the building or compartment in which they are situated.

Category	Maximum rise (mm)	Minimum going (mm)
1 Private stair	220	220
2 Institutional or assembly stair	180	280
3 Other stair	190	250

Widths of escape routes and protected staircases are related to numbers of occupants and use.

4.1 Headroom
For the whole width of any stairway, ramp or stepped ramp the minimum headroom must be 2000 mm clear measured vertically from the pitch line or top surface of any ramp or landing, see Diagram 2 of Document K. BS 5395 recommends a clearance measured at right angles to the pitch line of 1500 mm. This is the critical dimension with pitches over 41.5°. Clearance and headroom should allow for movement of goods or furniture on the stair. On short flights, of three or four steps across a corridor for example, this should be increased to 1800 mm to allow for people jumping down the steps. It can be difficult to meet headroom requirements on some spiral stairs in which case a relaxation of the regulations will have to be sought.

4.2 Landings
Level unobstructed landings must be provided at the top and bottom of stairways, ramps and stepped ramps and between flights. Landings should be in width and length as long as the smallest width of the flight of steps. Doors swinging over landings at the bottoms of flights must leave an area of at least 400 mm in depth. A landing is not required between an external door opening inwards and the top of an external stairway or ramp rising not more than 600 mm. A landing of even ground at the top or bottom of an external flight or ramp may slope to a maximum of 1 in 20 but only if the ground is paved or made solid.

4.3 Pitch
BS 5395 suggests the range of pitches for stairs is between 15° and 55°. The maximum pitch for a private stair is 42°. Pitches flatter than 15° are treated as ramps and over 55° considered to be ladders. Generally the flatter the pitch the safer the stair is to use. A stairway must not have a flight nearer to the exit from the building with a steeper pitch than a flight further away.

4.4 Rise
The rise of any step must be uniform along the length of the step and the same as every other step in the flight. The maximum number of risers in any flight is 16 for shops or places of assembly, and for more than 36 rises in consecutive flights, there should be a change of direction of at least 30° or more. It is not good practice to have more than 6 m total rise if the stairway is exposed to the weather.

The minimum number of risers allowed in a flight is generally two or three depending on the category of stair. A single step is usually permitted at the bottom of a stairway if inside or used solely by one dwelling. The sum of the 'going' and 'twice the riser' must not be less than 550 mm or more than 700 mm (paragraph 1.5 of Document K). For tapered treads, the going should be measured at the centre of the tread for a stair width less than 1 m, and for stairs over 1 m width the 'going' dimension used should be measured 270 mm in from each side.

4.5 Treads
All treads must be level and the width of the tread (called depth of tread in BS 5395) must not be less than the going. The tread length must not be less than the width of the stairway, which is not specified in Document K but determined in Document B on Fire safety. Stair width can include up to 30 mm for a stringer and also 100 mm for a handrail. Each tread in a flight must be either parallel or tapered whether or not its nosing is straight or curved on plan. One or both sides of the two bottom treads in a flight may be rounded or splayed.

All parallel treads must have the same going. Consecutive tapered treads must each have the same going measured either at the centre of the length (or the deemed length) of each tread, or at a specified point on the tread 270 mm in from each end of the tread (diagram 8 of Document K). Tapered treads must each have the same rate of taper and all narrow ends must be at the same side of the flight.

The nosing of a tread above an open riser must overlap the back of the lower tread by at least 16 mm (Building Regulations). The relationship between rise, going and pitch is shown in Figure 11 in BS 5395.

Also see item 5, Safety and ease of use.

4.6 Widths of flights

There is no minimum requirement for the width of a flight or ramp in Document K and reference has to be made to Document B on Fire safety. It is good practice to try and achieve stair widths of at least 900 mm. Stairways that exceed 1800 mm in width, should be divided with a handrail provided between sections.

4.7 Obstructions on flights

No door, shutter or threshold may be placed across any flight or ramp, or between a landing and any flight or ramp without giving at least 400 mm clearance. A wicket gate may be allowed between any landing and any flight or ramp. A door or shutter may be placed in line with a single step giving access to a shop window or certain small rooms.

4.8 Ramps and stepped ramps

No ramp must exceed 1 in 12 although a 1 in 20 slope is preferred. Landings must be provided whenever doors occur alongside the ramp as well as at the top and bottom and should be equal to the width of the ramp.

Steps and ramps in stepped ramps must comply with the relevant requirements for either stairways or ramps respectively (Section 2 of Document K).

4.9 Handrails

Handrails are to assist people using a flight or ramp. As well as providing support and maintain helping to balance for everybody, handrails are used by elderly and disabled people to pull themselves up and must be securely fixed, enabling people to gain a good grip.

All flights and ramps rising over 600 mm must have at least one handrail. Flights or ramps 1000 mm or more in width must have handrails on both sides. The minimum fixing height is 900 mm, the maximum height 1000 mm when measured vertically above pitch line or ramp surface to the top of the handrail. Recommendations for loading requirements are given in BS 6399 Part 1: Table 4 (Horizontal loads on parapets and balustrades) and these can go up to 3.0 kN/m run for the worst case for staircases, ramps or landings in public places. Handrails above tapered treads to flights less than 1000 mm wide should be on the wider side of the tread. Handrails must be continuous for the length of a flight or ramp but can stop above the third riser at the foot of a stairway. Handrails should be continuous, especially around the half landing of a dog-leg stair, with no sudden change in level or pitch.

Handrail supports should not obstruct the hand, a clearance of 50 mm is recommended in BS 5619. A circular section between 45–50 mm in diameter is most comfortable to grip. Ends of handrails should be detailed to avoid catching at clothing, especially handrails dividing a flight or ramp. Scrolling, wreathing, ramping to the floor or fixing to newel posts are all methods used to overcome this problem.

BS 5619:1978, Code of practice for design of housing for the convenience of disabled people

4.10 Balustrades

Balustrades guard the sides of flights, ramps and landings to prevent people falling. Building Regulations Document K sets out requirements for balustrades. They are to be provided at each side of a flight or ramp, at edges of landings, floors or any adjacent ground or paving with a drop of more than 600 mm in dwellings; and a change in level of two or more risers in any other building (or 380 mm if not part of a stair). See BS 6399 Part 1: Table 4 (Horizontal loads on parapets and balustrades). Glazed parts must only be made of glass blocks, toughened or laminated safety glass.

Any buildings likely to contain children under 5 should have any openings in balustrades restricted so that no opening could permit a 100 mm sphere to pass through. Horizontal rails should be avoided to make it impossible for children to climb up.

The minimum heights and strengths of guard and barrier design are set out in Diagram 11 of Document K. See BS 6180:1995, Code of practice for barriers in and about buildings. The height should be measured vertically above the pitch line of a stairway or top surface of a ramp or landing to the top of a handrail. The minimum height of a balustrade to a landing at the top of a flight or ramp may be reduced to allow the top of the balustrade to the flight or ramp to run on at a continuous angle.

BS 6399 Part 1: Table 4, Horizontal loads on parapets and balustrades

4.11 Dimensional coordination

The basic principles of dimensional coordination and rationalization of buildings and components as they apply to stairways are set out in BS 5395 Stairs, ladders and walkways, Part 1: 1977 (1984), Code of practice for the design of straight stairs, which refers to dimensional co-ordination.

BS 6750:1986, Specification for modular co-ordination in building

BS 5578 Part 2: 1978 (1995), Modular co-ordination: Specification for co-ordinating dimensions for stairs and stair openings

BS 4467: 1991, Guide to dimensions in designing for elderly people

5 Safety and ease of use

The requirements of the Building Regulations are primarily aimed at making stairways and ramps safe both for everyday use and when used as a means of escape in the event of fire. Stairways are now considered to be the principal routes for escape from fire on the upper floors of buildings (rather than relying on fire brigade ladders and escape appliances). Most accidents in homes are caused by falling and a high proportion of these are associated with stairs. The elderly, disabled and very young are the groups most at risk.

Research shows that safety and ease of use of stairs relates more to tread width than height of riser. The tread should be wide enough to allow at least a part of the user's heel to rest on the tread in a normal position. This allows people to pause on the stair flight without loss of balance. Tread widths between 250–300 mm are suggested as this is easier on the spine, giving less of an impact shock than high risers. Risers less than 75 mm high are unsafe but over 230 mm high are uncomfortable to use easily and the maximum recommended riser for domestic use is 220 mm.

The recommended tread width (going) to riser relationship is based on the average length of stride for most people being between 550–700 mm. The optimum proportion is 2 × rise plus going = 600 mm. This is illustrated, together with an acceptable range of variation, in BS 5395. See item 4 for more dimensional information.

Rise and going must be uniform throughout a flight with exceptions made in Regulations for bottom steps of external stairways and tapered treads.

Open risers may create insecurity in elderly users. In no case can openings between treads exceed 100 mm. Nosings of treads above open risers must overlap lower treads by 16 mm.

Generally, single steps are not permitted as they cause falls. The minimum number of risers allowed is two or three depending on the category of stair. Where single steps exist and cannot be eliminated they should be clearly visible especially to elderly people or others with poor eyesight. This can be achieved to some extent by ensuring that there is a contrast between the tread and the riser, or between step and surrounding floor finish. The lighting level over the step should also be increased in relation to that over the surrounding floor areas.

On stairways used by elderly people choose contrasting colours for treads and risers or use contrasting nosings to treads. Handrails for elderly and disabled persons must be securely fixed and steady to give confidence. Handrails should be provided on each side of a flight so that both may be gripped at the same time. BS 5619 recommends that staircase handrails be continuous and if a second handrail is fitted it should project at least 300 mm horizontally beyond top and bottom nosings of flight. Handrails must be a shape and size which can be securely gripped by arthritic hands and spaced sufficiently from walls to avoid grazed knuckles. See item 4 in this section and **Stairs in detail Section 15**, item 14.

In buildings where large numbers of children are likely to use flights on stairways and ramps consider installation of a lower additional handrail which should be suitable for small hands to grip safely. Tapered treads are permitted but should be avoided in public stairways and only used at the foot of flights in private stairways to reduce the risk of falls. See sketch, 'hazards to avoid'.

Stairs within dwellings can be steeper in pitch, with narrower treads and higher risers, because users will be familiar with the stairway. Stairs in use by the general public must allow for unfamiliar users.

The step at the head of a flight should not be cut into landings or circulation spaces. Steps at the bottom of flights should not project into circulation areas when the step is hidden from view or likely to be tripped over.

On open well stairways (and ramps) users must be protected from falling objects; consider also the possibility of children climbing into the well.

All stairways and ramps rising more than 600 mm must be guarded by balustrades in dwellings, or where there are level changes in other buildings of at least 380 mm, and have at least one handrail. See also items 3, 4, 7, 10 and 11.

In additional to technical references listed under items 2, 3, 4 and 7:

BS 6262 Glazing for buildings. Part 4: 1994, Code of practice for safety. Human impact

BS 5619:1978, Code of practice for design of housing for the convenience of disabled people

BS 5776:1979, Specification for powered stairlifts

BS 5810:1979, Code of practice for access for the disabled to buildings

Building Regulations 1991, Document M, Access and facilities for disabled people

6 Sound insulation

Stairways and general circulation areas transfer airborne sound between floor levels within a building. Movement of people on the stairway creates impact sound which is transmitted directly through the structure to adjoining rooms. Airborne and impact sound from stairways can also bypass any intermediate structure and affect adjoining areas by flanking sound transmission through adjacent walls.

Hard durable surfaces are often chosen for heavily used circulation areas but increase the amount of sound generated, especially as impact sound transmission from footsteps, creating a particular problem on stairways. Document E sets out minimum sound insulation standards for dwellings, which apply to the walls or floors between dwellings and stairways or ramps. Sound resisting construction or sound insulation can be achieved by using the recommended diagrams in Document E showing typical situations, or by demonstrating that the required minimum performance standard can be met by testing with a method given in paragraph 3.5 of Document E and in accordance with BS 2750 Part 4: 1990.

Generally, insulation depends on minimizing the transfer of sound either by sheer mass of construction or by isolating the sound at source through using discontinuous construction. In lightweight structures (timber frame houses for example), insulation can be achieved by isolation and separation (BRE Digest 347: 1989). Insulation can be considerably reduced by windows, doors or areas of lower mass. Openings including cracks, gaps and ventilation grilles which have no insulation value and provide direct sound paths. Weak points must be avoided by careful detailing and workmanship.

Sound-sensitive areas, such as bedrooms, should be planned away from noisy circulation areas, buffered by intervening rooms in which higher noise levels can be tolerated such as kitchens or living rooms. Bedrooms should not be placed below circulation areas. Doors, ducts and service voids can also provide direct sound paths and must be thoughtfully sited and detailed.

BS 8233:1987, Code of practice for sound insulation and noise reduction for buildings

BS 2750:1980 (1993), Measurement of sound insulation in buildings and of building elements

BRE IP 6/88: 1988, The insulation of dwellings against external noise

BRE Digest 143, Sound insulation basic principles

BRE Digest 347: 1989, Sound insulation of lightweight dwellings

BRE Digest 238: 1993, Sound control for homes

BRE Digests 333 (1988) and 334 (1993), Sound insulation of separating walls and floors. Part 1: Walls, Part 2: Floors

Noise Control in Buildings, McMullan. BCB, 1991.

Acoustic & Noise Control, Smith, Peters and Owen. BCB, 1996.

Building Regulations 1991, Document E contains requirements for separating floors and walls in adjoining dwellings and between a dwelling and other communal areas such as stairs, passageways or refuse chutes in the same building

7 Lighting

Natural and artificial lighting – general requirements: Stairways and ramps should be well lit to ensure they can be used safely at all times. Ideally light should be directed onto stairways at right angles to the pitch line but with the source, whether a lamp, window or rooflight, positioned to avoid light shining into user's eyes and causing glare. Strongly directional light from the top of a stairway or ramp flight will place people descending into their own shadow, increasing the risk of wrong-footing or falling.

Lights and windows must be easily accessible from the stairway or ramp for cleaning or changing fittings. It is dangerous to rely on people climbing a ladder in stairways to carry out basic maintenance. Also see comments in item 5. Always anticipate that disabled, elderly or young children may use the stairway or ramp, and need high levels of illumination.

Contrasting surface finishes will help to differentiate treads or tread nosings and risers. The first and last steps in each flight and any changes in direction should be clearly visible. Ramps can be difficult for users to see if they are a continuation of the normal floor finish.

All parts of stairways, ramps, stepped ramps and associated landings must be artificially lit if used as a means of escape (Building Regulations, Document B, Section 5.33 Table 9). External stairways or ramps serving only one dwelling are excluded from this requirement. The lighting must be controllable by any users or must operate when required by users. Two-way switching at the top and bottom of flights is essential. See BS 5266 for emergency lighting of premises. BS 5395 recommends a minimum illuminance of 100 lux for stairs in dwellings and 150 lux elsewhere in general building areas. Exit signs should be in accordance with BS 5499 Part 1: 1984. Lighting specifications also have to comply with requirements in Document L Conservation of fuel and power, Section 2. Time switches using photoelectric systems are encouraged. See also the CIBSE publication: *Code for Interior Lighting*, 1994.

Safety or emergency lighting is required in nearly all building types, and some residential buildings; but the fire authority may request emergency lighting in residential buildings where, for example, old people are living or when there is no natural light to the escape route (BS 5266).

Emergency lighting should be powered from a source independent of the main lighting supply. It can operate either automatically on failure of the main power supply (non-maintained system) or at all times when natural light is not sufficient for means of escape purposes (maintained system). The independent power source can be a central battery, batteries to each light fitting, or a generator.

BS 5925:1989, Code of practice for ventilation principles and designing for natural ventilation

BS 8206 Lighting for buildings. Part 1: 1985 (1992), Code of practice for artificial lighting. Part 2: 1992, Code of practice for day lighting

BS 5266 Emergency lighting. Part 1: 1988, Code of practice for the emergency lighting of premises other than cinemas and certain other specified premises used for entertainment

BRE Digest 232, Energy conservation in artificial lighting. Recommendations for emergency power, heating and lighting

Code for Interior Lighting, CIBSE, 1994.

Lighting guides on various building types from CIBSE

See also technical recommendations for disabled and elderly in item 5, Safety and ease of use

See requirements in item 3, Fire protection and means of escape

Building Regulations 1991, Document B Section 1 Means of escape

8 Ventilation

All stairways should be adequately ventilated as part of the main building and to comply with the requirements of Document F of the Building Regulations. There are no specific guidelines given in the Regulations as to some extent air change rates will interact with the requirements of Document L, Conservation of fuel and power. Where possible passive stack ventilation systems should be used. As windows or rooflights will be able to provide ventilation as well as light they should be accessible for easy control or incorporate methods of permanent trickle ventilation.

Common escape routes in flats and maisonettes should have at least 1.5 m² free area to ventilate stairways and can be permanently open (grilles or louvres) or triggered through automatic smoke detection. Basement areas should escape straight out to the ground as smoke from a basement fire will rise to ground floor level internally. See diagrams 10, 11 and 12 for specific situations in Document B Fire safety. Opening windows must be provided at each storey height and stairways without an external wall must have a permanent vent at the top. Natural ventilation for smoke dispersal should be by cross ventilation with two or more openings preferably at different levels and/or on different faces of the building. Any electrically-operated ventilator must be on a separate circuit to normal lighting circuits, preferably operating on an emergency battery supply.

Smoke may be controlled by maintaining a higher air pressure on the escape route using mechanical ventilation. This pressurization will force air and the smoke with it out of the building by the shortest route away from the escape route.

BS 5925:1991 (1995), Code of practice for ventilation principles and designing for natural ventilation

BS 493:1995, Specification for air bricks and gratings for wall ventilation

BS 3456 Part 202: Section 202.4 1990, Specifications for safety of household and similar electrical appliances. Particular requirements: Spin extractors

BS 5720:1979, Code of practice for mechanical ventilation and air conditioning in buildings

BRE BR 162: 1989, Background ventilation of dwellings: a review, Christine E. Uglow

BRE 260 1982: Smoke control in buildings, design principles

CIBSE Guide: Volume B, Installation and Equipment Data (1986)

CIBSE Technical Memoranda: TM19, Relationships for smoke control calculations

Building Regulations 1991, Document F (F1) Means of ventilation

9 Materials

As staircases can be made out of the complete range of materials used for constructing whole buildings, it is better to refer to individual codes of practice and textbooks for references on individual materials. Staircases can be frame-like with structures of timber or steel, or more monolithic and made from concrete or brickwork. The staircase can be designed as a series of independent elements, with steps that are cantilevered from walls in precast concrete or part cantilevered and part corbelled in stone. The underlying structure of the stair can be a completely separate material from the treads, but care then has to be taken with fixings to secure all of the different elements. Light tensile structures can use combinations of materials with tensioned elements made from cable and treads from glass. Unusual combinations of materials need joint design with the staircase fabricators and manufacturers of different materials. Whatever the choice or combination of materials, they will have to comply with standards for fire and safety (see Document B of the Buildings Regulations and, in this section, item 3, Fire protection and means of escape), have adequate structural integrity (item 2, Structural strength and stability) and be safe to use (see item 5, Safety and ease of use, and the following item, 10 Finishes).

10 Finishes

Finishes to tread, landing and ramp surfaces must not come loose and cause people to trip or fall, more likely on stairs where people are shifting their balance at the same time as moving vertically. The Building Regulations (5.25 Document B) require that all escape routes including all surfaces of steps and ramps should be as non-slip as possible when wet. Building Regulation K (1.8) requires all steps to be level. Slatted or perforated surfaces to ramps, treads and landings may give special problems and may only be permitted in certain building types. There are people with a phobia of heights who are quite unable to manage stairs if they can see the ground at a distance below and through the stairs. Consequently patterned open grilles for stairs are often restricted to external escape stairs and industrial use. Openings in the upper surface of a step should not usually exceed 20 mm in width.

Communal stairways and landings must have finishes with a high slip resistance, especially nosings of treads, surfaces likely to get wet and stairways or ramps used by disabled or elderly people. A minimum coefficient of friction of 0.4 is required to avoid slipping. In the areas of greater risk noted above, the coefficient of friction should be at least 0.75 and not less than 0.6. Carpet or textured clay tiles will meet this recommendation but granolithic or terrazzo may not be suitable when wet or polished. Non-slip nosings are necessary on terrazzo stair treads and landings. Most materials have a better slip resistance when dry, and are usually more slippery when wet, worn or polished. Tables in BS 5395 give the slip resistance for various commonly used floor and tread finishes tested both when wet and dry.

Outside ramps, especially if used by the disabled, may require electric heating to prevent icing even when non-slip finishes are used. This may also apply to some exposed stairways.

Every escape stair should be of limited combustibility in situations outlined in paragraph 5.19 of Document B of the Building Regulations. See Appendices A6, A7 and A8 on guidance to the use of materials for fire and safety. See also items 5 and 11 in this section.

BS 4357:1968, Precast terrazzo units (including treads, risers and landings)

BS 5325:1983, Code of practice for installation of textile floor coverings

BS 5442 Part 1: 1989, Adhesives for use with flooring materials

BRE Digest 33: 1971, Sheet and tile flooring made from thermoplastic binders

BRE DAS 51: 1984, Floors: cement based screeds – specification (design)

Building Regulations 1991, Document B Fire safety

BS 8204: Parts 1, 2, 4 (1993) & 5 (1994). In situ floor finishes includes concrete bases and screeds, terrazzo and mastic asphalt

BS 776:1972, Materials for magnesium oxychloride (magnesite) flooring

BS 1711:1975, Solid rubber flooring

BS 6826:1987, Specification for linoleum and cork carpet sheet and tiles

BS 3187:1978, Electrically conducting rubber flooring

BS 3260:1969 (1991), Specification for semi flexible PVC floor tiles

BS 3261 Unbacked flexible PVC flooring. Part 1: 1973 (1991), Homogeneous flooring

BS 6341 Ceramic wall and floor tiles (note 23 parts.) Part t deals with sizes

BS 7263 Part 1: 1994, Precast concrete flags

BS 1297:1987, Specification for tongued and grooved softwood flooring

BS 1187:1959, Specification for wood blocks for floors

BS 4050 Specification for mosaic parquet panels. Part 1: 1977, General characteristics. Part 2: 1966, Classification and quality requirements

BS 3655:1974, (1991) Recommendations for informative labelling of textile floor coverings

BS 1006:1978, Methods for colour fastness of textiles and leather

BS 4051:1987, Method of determination of thickness of textile floor covering

BS 4098:1975 (1988), Method for the determination of thickness compression and recovery characteristics of textile floor coverings

BS 4131:1973, Specification for terrazzo tiles

BS 4682 Part 2: 1988, Determination of dimensional changes due to changes in ambient humidity. Part 3: 1987, Determination of dimensional changes after exposure to heat. Part 4: 1987, Determination of dimensional changes after immersion in water

BS 4790:1987, Method for determination of the effects of a small source of ignition on textile floor coverings

BS 5442 Classification of Adhesives for construction. Part 1: 1989, Classification of adhesives for use with flooring materials

BS 5669 Part 2: 1989, Specification for wood chipboard

BRE Digest 33, Sheet and tile flooring made from thermoplastic binders

BRE DAS 103: 1987, Reducing risk of recurrent dry rot (design)

BRE DAS 73: 1986, Suspended timber ground floors: remedying dampness due to inadequate ventilation

Rigid Paving with Clay Pavers, Mammett and Smith. Brick Development Association, 1988.

11 Durability and maintenance

Stairways and ramps should have the same life expectancy as the other structural elements of a building, are subject to surface wear, and need regular cleaning. Stairways and ramps forming part of a means of escape route must be available for safe use at all times during the life of the building.

Materials used in construction and finishes should resist decay and deterioration by natural weathering, ageing, biodegradation or insect attack as well as normal usage. External stairways and ramps are especially vulnerable to corrosive atmospheric environments. Metal components such as balustrade and handrail fixings are potentially weak points which will require regular maintenance unless corrosion-resistant materials are used. Loss of strength at these fixings can be a serious safety hazard.

Public stairways and ramps are subject to misuse, abuse and vandalism along with normal wear and tear. These factors must be borne in mind when selecting materials and fittings and handrails and balustrades are especially vulnerable. Normal paint finishes are rarely adequate unless for light or domestic use. Other equipment, such as light fittings, should resist corrosion and vandalism, and be easy to replace when damaged.

Potential movement from deflection in the underlying structure of the stairway or ramp, after dynamic loading from people, can cause cracking in rigid finishes that cannot take bending. Materials have to be chosen and detailed in such a way that cracking is avoided.

For safety in use, the surfaces of treads, ramps and landings must be well maintained. Worn finishes may cause slipping or tripping, and finishes should be easy to replace when damaged or worn. Incorrect maintenance can increase the hazards facing the user. After polishing surfaces, or if polish is transferred from other floor areas, smooth materials such as terrazzo can become very slippery. Some cleaning methods and materials (solvents, harsh chemicals and abrasives) can attack surfaces causing rapid wear and/or corrosion of fittings and fixings.

Durability of materials also depends on good workmanship during construction. If materials are used incorrectly (for example when finishes susceptible to damp are laid on ground floors where adequate dampproofing measures have not been taken) failures are inevitable.

Premature breakdown of finishes can reduce safety by increasing the risk of slipping and tripping. Thin screeds laid on concrete ramps, stair treads and landing surfaces are potential problem areas, careful attention must be paid to detailing and workmanship. The choice of materials must be compatible with the thickness of finish required and the type of substrate. Loss of adhesion between substrate and screed will cause breakdown of the finish.

BSCP 3 Chapter IX: 1950, Durability

BSCP 209 Care and maintenance of floor finishes. Part 1: 1963, Wooden flooring

BSCP 231:1966, Painting of buildings

BS 3842:1965, Treatment of plywood with preservatives

BS 5268 Code of practice for structural use of timber. Part 5: 1977, Preservative treatments for constructional timber

BS 5493:1977, Code of practice for protective coating of iron and steel structures against corrosion

BRE Digest 45, Design and appearance: 1

BRE Digest 46, Design and appearance: 2

BRE Digest 75, Cracking in buildings

BRE Digest 113, Cleaning external surfaces of buildings

BRE Digest 126, Changes in the appearance of concrete on exposure

BRE Digest 139, Control of lichens, moulds and similar growths

BRE Digest 152, Repair and renovation of flood-damaged buildings

BRE Digest 177, Decay and conservation of stone masonry

BRE Digest 200, Repairing brickwork

BRE Current Papers: CP 55/74, Maintenance standards and costs. CP 59/74, The use of adhesives in maintenance. CP 3/78, Collection and use of building maintenance cost data.

Trade and research organizations

Aluminium Federation, Broadway House, Calthorpe Road, Five Ways, Birmingham B15 1TN (tel. 0121-456 1103, fax 0121-456 2274).

Association of Structural Fire Protection Contractors and Manufacturers, 45 Sheen Lane, London SW14 (tel. 0181-876 4415).

Brick Development Association (BDA), Woodside House, Winkfield, Windsor, Berks SL4 2DX (tel. 01344-885651, fax 01344-890129).

British Carpet Manufacturers' Association Ltd, 5 Portland Place, London W1N 3AA (tel. 0171-580 7155, fax 0171-580 4854).

British Cement Association (BCA), Century House, Telford Avenue, Crowthorne, Berks RG11 6YS (tel. 01344-762676, fax 01344-761214).

British Ceramic Tile Council, Federation House, Station Road, Stoke-on-Trent, Staffs ST4 2RU (tel. 01782-747147, fax 01782-747161).

British Constructional Steel Association (BSCA), 4 Whitehall Court, Westminster, London SW14 2ES (tel. 0171-839 8566, fax 0171-976 1634).

British Floor Covering Manufacturers' Association, 5 Queen's Square, Brighton, East Sussex BN1 3FD (tel. 01273-727906).

British Plastics Federation, 6 Bath Place, Rivington Street, London EC2A 3JE (tel. 0171-457 5000, fax 0171-457 5038).

British Wood Preserving and Damp-proofing Association, 6 Office Village, 4 Romford Road, Stratford, London E15 4EA (tel. 0181-519 2588, fax 0181-519 3444).

British Woodworking Federation, 82 New Cavendish Street, London W1M 8AD (tel. 0171-580 5588, fax 0171-436 5398).

Building Maintenance Information, 85–87 Clarence Street, Kingston upon Thames, Surrey KT1 1RB (tel. 0181-546 7555, fax 0181-547 1238).

Building Research Advisory Service, Fire Research Station, Bucknalls Lane, Garston, Watford, Herts WD2 7JR (tel. 01923-894040).

Building Research Advisory Service, Building Research Establishment, Bucknalls Lane, Garston, Watford, Herts WD2 7JR (tel. 01923-664664, fax 01923-664010).

Building Research Establishment (BRE), Bucknalls Lane, Garston, Watford, Herts WD2 7JR (tel. 01923-894040, fax 01923-664010).

Chartered Institution of Building Services Engineers (CIBSE), Delta House, 222 Balham High Road, London SW12 9BS (tel. 0181-675 5211, fax 0181-673 5880).

Cleaning and Support Services Organisation, 73–74 The Hop Exchange, 24 Southwark Street, London SE1 1TY.

Contract Flooring Association, 4c St Mary's Place, The Lace Market, Nottingham NG1 1PH (tel. 0115-941126, fax 0115-942238).

Disabled Living Foundation, 380–384 Harrow Road, London W9 2HU (tel. 0171-289 6111).

Fire Insurers' Research and Testing Organisation (FIRTO), Melrose Avenue, Borehamwood, Herts WD6 2BJ (tel. 0181-207 2345).

Fire Offices Committee, Aldermary House, Queen Street, London EC4N 1TT (tel. 0181-207 2345).

Fire Protection Association, 140 Aldersgate Street, London EC1A 4HX (tel. 0171-606 3757, fax 0171-600 1487).

Glass and Glazing Federation, 44–48 Borough High Street, London SE1 1XB (tel. 0171-403 7177, fax 0171-357 7458).

Health and Safety Executive, Broad Lane, Sheffield S3 7HQ (tel. 0114-289 2345, fax 0114-289 2333).

Heating Ventilation and Air Conditioning Manufacturers' Association (HEVAC), Sterling House, 6 Furlong Road, Bourne End, Bucks SL8 5DG (tel. 01628-531186).

Lighting Industry Federation Ltd (LIF), Swan House, 207 Balham High Road, London SW17 7BQ (tel. 0181-675 5432, fax 0181-673 5880).

Mastic Asphalt Council and Employers' Federation (MACEF), Lesley House, 6–8 Broadway, Bexley Heath, Kent DA6 7LE (tel. 0181-298 0414, fax 0181-298 0381).

National Federation of Terrazzo/Mosaic Specialists, PO Box 50, Banstead, Surrey SM7 2RD (tel. 01737-360673).

Precast Concrete Frame Association Ltd, 60 Charles Street, Leicester LE1 1FB (tel. 0116-2536161).

Royal Association for Disability and Rehabilitation, 25 Mortimer Street, London W1N 8AB (tel. 0171-637 5400).

Spiral Stair Manufacturers' Association, 18 Ellington Street, London, N7.

Steel Construction Institute, Silwood Park, Ascot, Berks SL5 7QN (tel. 01344-23345, fax 01344-22944).

TRADA Technology Ltd (Timber Research and Development Association), Stocking Lane, Hughenden Valley, High Wycombe, Bucks HP14 4ND (tel. 01494-563091, fax 01494-565487).

Stairways, Ramps, Handrails and Balustrades in Detail
Section 15
SMM7 L Windows, M Surface finishes

Notes and references
Items are cross-referenced from the diagrams and divided into sections with a general comment followed by technical references and the Building Regulations in context. Addresses of relevant trade and research organizations are given at the end of the section. British Standards and BRE Digests should be checked for current amendments

This section contains specific items 12 to 14, and should be read in conjunction with the general items in **Stairways, ramps generally, Section 14**.

12 Stairways

12.1 Straight flight stairways
This is the most basic form of stairway, a series of parallel treads with or without risers, with no change of direction.

Structurally this type of stair may be formed in a number of ways:

- from individual treads or the entire flight slab spanning between loadbearing side walls;
- from an inclined slab spanning between floor levels;
- from inclined strings or spine beam, carrying treads and/or risers, spanning between levels.

All of these may be constructed of concrete, metal, timber and, less commonly, stone. Principal forms of construction are:

1 *Concrete.* Inclined slab in situ or precast, spanning between beams or trimmers at landing levels. Cranked slab continuous with floor or landing slab, spanning to main structural frame or walls. This may not require side support so the stairway can be adjacent to non-structural (even glazed) side walls. Inclined upstand or downstand strings or downstand spine beam spanning between floor levels or as cranked beams to more remote structural frame. With beam or side strings the waist (the

thickness of the slab excluding the step profile) of the stairway can be thinner than with a cranked or inclined slab. Strings or beam can be in situ or precast elements with precast treads, treads and risers or step units, or metal, timber or stone step/tread/riser elements can be combined with concrete string or spine beams. Strings may also be supported on or within side walls, on one or both sides. Simple precast treads or step units can span between side walls.

2 *Metal, timber and laminated timber.* Used in the form of inclined or cranked strings or spine beams. Treads and risers may be in a similar or alternative material, perhaps metal strings supporting timber treads. A straight flight stairway with adequate landing areas is recommended in two-storey housing to be used by the disabled (BS 5619). This will enable powered stairlifts to be installed (BS 5776). See **Stairways, ramps generally, Section 14**.

12.2 Dog-leg stairways
Two parallel straight flights with a half landing between floor levels at right angles to the line of flights. Flights are usually of equal length with no open central well between them. This is a very compact plan form with inner strings of both flights housed in a single newel post at half-landing level in the case of a timber stair, or with a central spine wall. The total width of stairway enclosure is reduced to the minimum possible by accommodating the widths of two stair flights and the width of the centre string or spine wall and outer strings. It is generally used where space is very limited.

With timber dog-leg stairways the newel post is usually carried to the lower floor level and fixed for greater rigidity and support.

The principal disadvantage of this form of stairway is that the handrail and balustrade to the inner edge of the lower flight stop at the underside of the string to the upper flight. Apart from the unsightly detail of a raking joint at the string, a handrail which does not continue to the top of a flight is hazardous to users (see **Stairways, ramps generally, Section 14**).

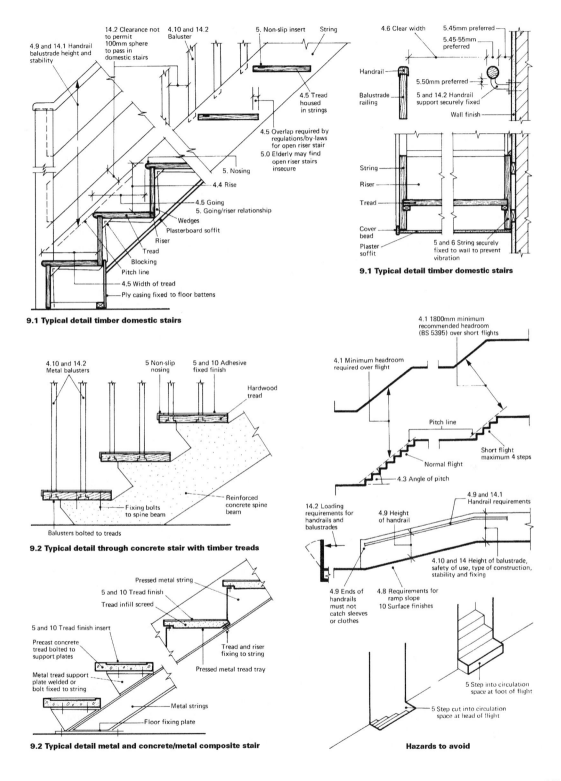

9.1 Typical detail timber domestic stairs

9.1 Typical detail timber domestic stairs

9.2 Typical detail through concrete stair with timber treads

9.2 Typical detail metal and concrete/metal composite stair

Hazards to avoid

145

If the handrail is positioned inside the flight to avoid this collision, the problem of continuity still occurs at half-landing level unless one flight is well offset in plan from the other. This not only increases the total length of the stairway enclosure, but creates problems with the landing soffit appearance.

Where safety and ease of use are of great importance, (e.g. in elderly persons' accommodation or where young children are using the stairway), the dog-leg arrangement should be avoided unless alternative provision is made for a continuous handrail (on the outer side of the flight and half-landing for example). See **Stairways, ramps general, Section 14**, items 4.9, 4.10 and 5.

A concrete spine wall may be used to support fully cantilevered flights and half-landing, avoiding the need for side wall support. The stair, being self-supporting, can be isolated from adjoining enclosing structure on at least three sides. This can reduce impact sound transmission to surrounding areas.

12.3 Open well stairways

This is a plan arrangement of at least two flights parallel to each other between main floor levels with an open space, or well, between them, intermediate landing or landings with going at right angles to line of flights. This is similar to a dog-leg stairway in that the introduction of intermediate landings allows for compact layout on plan. The open well increases total width of stairway enclosure but has advantages over the dog-leg stair:

(a) Handrails and balustrades can be continuous around inner edges of flights and landings. It is especially important for disabled or elderly users that handrails to lower flight are not interrupted by string of upper flight.

(b) Depending on width, the open well stair allows a third flight to be incorporated at right angles to main flights running between quarter landings. This gives greater flexibility of stairway layout to suit planning requirements.

(c) Open well stairs may be used to house a lift either in an enclosed shaft or within an open structural framework (the stair-user is protected by infill material such as metal mesh, metal sheet or glass).

12.4 Tapered and spiral stairways

Tapered treads can be used in conjunction with straight flights to reduce the length of space taken up by the stairway on plan. Frequently used on stairways within dwellings. Must meet building regulation requirements and safety recommendations; should only be used at the bottom of flights in domestic stairways and should be avoided on public stairways (see **Stairways, ramps general, Section 14**).

Tapered treads may also replace half or quarter landings in dog-leg or open well stairways, so creating a part circular stairway. If no intermediate landing is provided, the straight flights and tapered treads are still a single flight which limits the total number of risers permitted to 16. Tapered treads combined with straight flights introduce construction and detailing problems, especially with timber strings. On traditional timber stairways with treads housed into side strings, it is necessary to build up the string to maintain a margin over the nosings of tapered treads which is equal to the margin over the nosings to normal parallel treads. The increased width of the tapered treads adjacent to the outer string creates a lower angle of pitch which the string must follow.

An additional support member may be required under each tapered tread because of the increased span of the tread from the outer string to the newel post or central well. The junction at the inner end of tapered treads (which in domestic stairways is traditionally around a timber newel post), is a complicated piece of joinery requiring careful detailing and skilled workmanship.

Tapered treads may be used around an open well forming a helical or elliptical stair (circular or elliptical on plan). This can form a generous and visually impressive stairway flowing between floor levels, especially if formed without intermediate landings and supporting structure (such as walls, columns or piers). It requires a suitable self-supporting material either to form the complete flight as a monolithic whole, or to support treads and risers as strings or spine beam. Reinforced concrete, structural steel and laminated timber are the most suitable materials. Poured in situ reinforced concrete requires complex reinforcement which is difficult to design and construct and needs elaborate shuttering.

Laminated timber and metal prefabricated sections can be used either as side strings or spine beams. Risers may be omitted, the treads spanning between strings or cantilevering on either side of a spine beam.

Tapered treads formed around a central newel post are generally referred to as spiral stairways or circular stairs. The Building Regulations refer to spiral stairs in

Paragraph 1.21 of Document K and then to BS 5395 Stairs, ladders and walkways. Part 2: 1984, Code of practice for the design of helical and spiral stairs. Spiral stairs may meet the requirements for small stairways within dwellings, but the tapered treads requirements for other stairways tend to prohibit simple, compact and economical spiral stair design. In most cases a relaxation of the Regulations must be sought if spiral stairs are to be used.

Spiral stairs are generally constructed in precast concrete, metals such as cast iron, steel or aluminium, stone or a combination of timber treads on metal support brackets. The individual tapered step elements are prefabricated and assembled on site by threading onto a newel post (normally metal) or by bolting or site welding to a metal newel post. Steps are usually formed without risers for lightness, ease of transport and assembly. Lightness of weight is a very important consideration in conversion and rehabilitation work within existing buildings, where the compact plan form of this type of stairway may be a deciding factor in its use.

With standardized components and simplified assembly methods spiral stairs may be tailored to suit a wide range of individual requirements and be readily erected inside or outside new or existing buildings. The stair can be self-supporting except for lateral restraint at landing (floor) levels, and only requires a suitable floor or foundation pad capable of carrying concentrated loads transmitted to the base by the newel post. Apart from requirements for balustrade and handrail continuity and landing connections, the stair can be free-standing. This permits greater freedom of design and the separation from any enclosing or loadbearing structure reduces the problem of impact sound transmission.

13 Ramps and stepped ramps

Similar configurations as for stairways are possible, but because of longer spans of flights, timber is not generally used for structural purposes except in the form of laminated strings or spine beams.

Ramps are often used by disabled persons, and BS 5619, and *Designing for the Disabled* by S. Goldsmith (RIBA, 3rd edition 1976), should be referred to.

(a) Approach ramps to dwelling entrances should be 1 in 12 (approximately 5° slope) and 1000 mm wide.

(b) For ramps between 1 in 15 and 1 in 12 (between 4° and 5° slope) the unbroken length of a ramp flight should not be more than 10 m.

(c) For ramps between 1 in 20 and 1 in 12 (between 3° and 5° slope) a level platform with 1000 mm minimum width and 1200 mm minimum going should be provided at the head of the ramp. This should be inclined slightly (less than 1 in 20 slope is regarded as level) to allow surface water to run off, if outside building or uncovered.

(d) All ramps must have slip-resistant surfaces. *Design for the Disabled* recommends ramps 1500 mm wide to allow wheelchairs to pass. Long ramps should have resting places with 1800 mm going at not more than 10 m centres. Ambulant disabled persons may find steps easier to negotiate than a ramp.

Non-slip surfaces can be formed by using an in situ topping or aggregate surface finish integral with concrete or screed. Alternatively, a non-slip pattern may be formed in the surface of the concrete. This applies equally to in situ or precast concrete ramps. Perforated or slatted materials must not be used in buildings of purpose group II, unless used only by staff, or purpose group VII, if serving an area over 100 m² and used for assembly purposes. This rules out metal industrial-type flooring which has better non-slip characteristics than sheet metal. Even with surface patterning, sheet metal soon becomes slippery, especially if wet. Ramps that may be exposed to rain, snow and ice should be covered or electrically heated.

BSCP 1018:1971 (1993), Electric floor-warming systems for use with off-peak and similar supplies of electricity

14 Handrails and balustrades

14.1 Safety and use

See **Stairways, ramps general, Section 14**, items 4.9, 4.10 and 5. Handrails must be smooth and special care must be taken with timber to provide a finish without roughness or splinters. Metal handrails and handrail support brackets should not have sharp projections or edges. Metal castings must have all excess metal and roughness removed and this also applies to site-welded joints. Inspect samples of metal fittings when choosing, rather than relying on trade descriptions or catalogue illustrations, to ensure finish and shape are suitable.

Proprietary plastic handrails, formed around a metal core for rigidity and strength, can provide a smooth continuous rail. This type of handrail may be tailored

147

to suit a wide range of flight configurations and flight to landing junction conditions, either as part of a balustrade or as an independent rail fixed to the enclosing walls.

Where it is likely that young children will attempt to climb balustrades avoid:

(a) horizontal railings, which create a ladder;
(b) open patterns in metal (meshes) or masonry (e.g. hollow blockwork) which give footholds for climbing.

Simple vertical railings or solid, smooth-surfaced balustrades give the best protection in these circumstances.

14.2 Stability and fixing
See **Stairways, ramps general, Section 14**, items 2, 4.9, 4.10 and 5.

Handrails to the open sides of timber straight flight, dog-leg or open well stairs are traditionally tenoned into newel posts at the top and bottom of each flight. Balusters are housed into the underside of the handrail and top of side strings. For economy and simplicity, balusters are often replaced with one or more intermediate rails either of solid wood, plywood or other composite board. The choice depends on depth of rail required and fixing details to be used. The depth and number of rails may be determined by the need to comply with paragraph 1.29 of Document K of the Building Regulations for dwellings or buildings (e.g. hospitals or hostels) where young children live, restricting openings in balustrades so that a 100 mm spherical ball cannot pass through. Long-span handrails and balustrade rails may require intermediate support in the form of a newel post or structural baluster to meet lateral loading requirements of BS 6180:1995.

Any additional support must be securely fixed to the stair string, or in the case of landings to floor edge, floor joists or joist trimmer.

The code gives the following values for the horizontal loading to be assumed from BS 6399 Part 1: 1996:

(a) 0.22 kN/m for stairways up to 600 mm wide;
(b) 0.36 kN/m for domestic stairways, landings and balconies over 600 mm wide;
(c) 0.74 kN/m for other stairways, landings and balconies, parapets and handrails to roofs. Where large numbers of people may surge against balustrades, loads as high as 3.0 kN/m need to be

allowed for. See *Guide to Safety at Sports Grounds*, HMSO, 1973.

The infill panels of balustrades will have to withstand uniformly distributed loads and point loads of 0.5 kN/m² for single dwellings and 1.0 kN/m² elsewhere except for places of public assembly.

See **Stairways, ramps general, Section 14**, item 2.

BS 7818:1995, Specification for pedestrian restraint systems in metal
BS 4125:1991, Specification for safety requirements for child safety barriers for domestic use

14.3 Materials
See **Stairways, ramps general, Section 14**, item 19.

Handrails are generally made of wood, metal or a combination of either wood or plastic reinforced by metal. If using wood, short runs using natural poles or thinnings should be considered to save cutting timber and then producing waste by turning it into round sections. They can also be part of the balustrade, where a cast panelled material is profiled in such a way that it develops into a section of a baluster. See Peckham Health Centre 1936 (building by Owen Williams).

Balustrades can be constructed in many ways but are usually in one or in a combination of one or more of the following forms:

(a) Vertical balusters at close centres with horizontal connecting rails for stability and support. Individual balusters housed into the surface of the stairway or ramp flight (treads, landings and/or strings), or housed into or mechanically connected to side faces of flights and landings. To avoid multiplicity of fixings, balusters may be fixed to a horizontal rail at low level which in turn is fixed to stairway or ramp at wider internals (either directly or through stub posts).
(b) Thin rigid sheet material either self-supporting or, more usually, in a supporting structural frame, which is fixed between intermediate posts, newels or piers.
(c) Thick material such as masonry or concrete, often as an extension of enclosing walls or stair support structure. Some masonry (e.g. lightweight blocks) may require reinforcement to withstand lateral pressures. See manufacturers' literature on the design of parapets, retaining and free-standing walls.

Balusters are usually timber or metal although reinforced concrete (in situ or precast) may be used. Sheet material can be any suitable wood-based product, such as plywood, block board or laminated board. Alternatively, metal sheet or metal mesh can be used either structurally or as in filling between structural elements (e.g. balusters, newel posts, handrails). Non-structural material such as laminated or toughened safety glass can be used. Other materials used for balustrade construction are concrete, brick or block masonry suitably reinforced if needed.

See **Stairways, ramps general, Section 14**, items 9, 10 and 11.

BS 5493:1984, Code of practice for the protective coating of iron and steel structures against corrosion

Trade and research organizations

Spiral Stair Manufacturers' Association, c/o Albion Design Group, 18 Ellington Street, London N7.

Windows: General Section 16

SMM7 L Windows

(See Section 17 for Windows in detail)

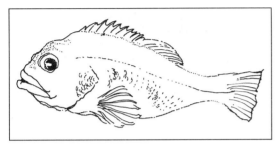

Fish (Honey comb rockfish, California)
Eyes are windows of the mind and some animals have a great range, viewing in near darkness. This fish has to see at depths between 15–263 fathoms.

Thai window (Dean)   Windows, Amsterdam (Rich)

Notes and references

Items are cross-referenced from the diagrams and divided into sections with a general comment followed by technical references and the Building Regulations in context. Addresses of relevant trade and research organizations are given at the end of the section. British Standards and BRE Digests should be checked for current amendments.

General references

Document N of the Building Regulations 'Glazing – materials and protection' gives guidance for ensuring that glazed parts of a building are safe. Section N1 applies to dwellings and gives area limits for glazing in relation to glass thickness (Diagram 2).

The Agrément Board MOAT No 1, UEAtc Directive for the Assessment of Windows, 1974

Fenestration 2000, D. Button and R. Dunning. Pilkington Brothers Ltd, 1989.

BS 8213 Windows, doors and roof lights. Part 1: 1991, Code of practice for safety in use and during cleaning of windows and doors

BS 8000 Part 7: 1990, Code of practice for glazing

BRE AM2 1987: Window design

BRE 377 1992: Selecting windows by performance

BRE 304 1985: Preventing decay in external joinery

The New Metric Handbook, P. Tutt and D. Adler (eds.). Architectural Press Ltd, 1996.

Collins Complete Woodworker's Manual, Jackson and Day. Collins, 1989.

Wood windows – Design selection and installation, TRADA, 1993.

1 General purpose of window

Windows have many functions, admitting light, energy, fresh air and sunshine, and can change the feel and quality of a space in a building by their proportions, framing materials and position. They have to serve particular spaces or rooms linked with very different activities and occupants whether children, workers who have different tasks to carry out or the elderly or people with limited mobility who need a window as an amenity to frame a view. Use the following criteria in relation to possible room activities and likely categories of occupants.

2 Daylight and passive solar energy

Consider area, shape and location of window in the room in relation to the lighting levels needed in the

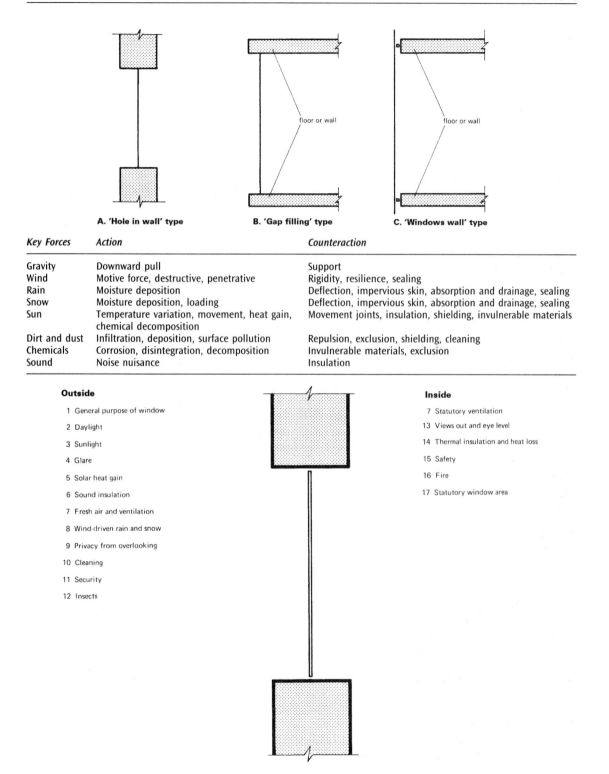

| A. 'Hole in wall' type | B. 'Gap filling' type | C. 'Windows wall' type |

Key Forces	Action	Counteraction
Gravity	Downward pull	Support
Wind	Motive force, destructive, penetrative	Rigidity, resilience, sealing
Rain	Moisture deposition	Deflection, impervious skin, absorption and drainage, sealing
Snow	Moisture deposition, loading	Deflection, impervious skin, absorption and drainage, sealing
Sun	Temperature variation, movement, heat gain, chemical decomposition	Movement joints, insulation, shielding, invulnerable materials
Dirt and dust	Infiltration, deposition, surface pollution	Repulsion, exclusion, shielding, cleaning
Chemicals	Corrosion, disintegration, decomposition	Invulnerable materials, exclusion
Sound	Noise nuisance	Insulation

Outside

1 General purpose of window

2 Daylight

3 Sunlight

4 Glare

5 Solar heat gain

6 Sound insulation

7 Fresh air and ventilation

8 Wind-driven rain and snow

9 Privacy from overlooking

10 Cleaning

11 Security

12 Insects

Inside

7 Statutory ventilation

13 Views out and eye level

14 Thermal insulation and heat loss

15 Safety

16 Fire

17 Statutory window area

room for different tasks, or display and size with respect to environmental comfort and passive solar energy input to the building.

BRE Digests 309 and 310: 1986, Estimating daylight in buildings. Parts 1 and 2
BRE IP 15/88: Average daylight factor: a simple basis for daylight design
BS 5925:1991 (1995), Code of practice for ventilation principles and designing for natural ventilation
BS 8206 Part 2: 1992, Code of practice for daylighting
BRE IP/93: 1993, Heat losses through windows
BRE AP 68: 1993, Daylight Protractors
Building Regulations 1991, Part F Ventilation
Building Regulations 1991, Part L Conservation of fuel and power
Building Regulations 1991, Part N Glazing

3 Sunlight

Direct sunlight may give unwanted glare due to the contrast between highly lit and shadowy areas if the daylighting design is uneven. If the building has been designed to optimize passive solar gain in winter, autumn and spring there could be considerable overheating in summer. Both conditions mean that incoming light and energy needs control that can be varied throughout the day as the sun path moves round, as the intensity of light varies through the day and seasonally. People should be able actively to control all of these changing conditions by filtering, blocking or varying daylight penetration by using roller or venetian blinds, screens, fixed or adjustable louvres or brise soleil.

BS 8206 Part 2: 1992, Code of practice for daylighting
Lighting in Buildings: Environmental Aspects (Environmental Action guide Advisory Notes 6), DOE 1993.

5 Solar heat gain

As well as the devices mentioned in 4 above, solar heat control glass can be specified which will also reduce glare; tinted films can also be used.

Window Design 1987 by CIBSE for BRE

6 Sound Insulation

There are situations where windows need to be a protective element against sound penetration. This can

be due to local traffic or proximity to busy streets or in order to isolate quiet industrial areas from noisy areas where visual links are still needed. Every situation should evaluate the external sound sources and internal activity in space served by window. Investigate using thicker than normal glass, windows with vacuum filled separating spaces, and gaskets that can help isolate parts of the construction and eliminate the transfer of sound.

BRE 238 1993: Sound control for homes
BRE IP 21/93: The noise climate around our homes
BRE 338 1988: Insulation against external noise
BRE IP 6/94: The sound insulation provided by windows
BS 8233: 1987, Code of practice for sound insulation and noise reduction for buildings

7 Fresh air and ventilation

Windows often incorporate a means of ventilation. To comply with the requirement to provide background ventilation, windows have to be designed to incorporate trickle ventilators or adjustable locking positions. The amount of ventilation needed should satisfy statutory requirements and the environmental design requirements for the number of air changes needed per hour. If windows are to be used actively for ventilation they should be accessible and catches and stays easily operated. Conversely they should not present a security problem and invite burglars, and window locks or permanent ventilators should be part of the window accessories, often with lockable fasteners that allow for different opening positions. Opening portions of windows should be located and designed to minimize draughts, and not to open onto curtains, blinds, internal or external projections, fittings or people walking along line of windows (see item 10, Cleaning). Continental window details often open inwards making it easier and safer for cleaning but take up internal space. They are also set further into the construction making weathering details far easier. It is always worth thinking whether these kinds of details could be used instead of repeating the status quo.

BS 5925:1991 (1995), Code of practice for ventilation principles and designing for natural ventilation
BS 5720:1979, Code for mechanical ventilation and air conditioning in buildings
BRE BR 162: 1989, Background ventilation of dwellings: a review

BRE Digest 338: 1988, Insulation against external noise

BRE Digest 162: 1979, Traffic noise and overheating in offices

BRE BR 162: 1989, Background ventilation of dwellings: a review

Building Ventilation: Theory and Measurement, Etheridge and Sandberg. Wiley 1996 (Note: US origin).

Naturally Ventilated Buildings, Clements Croome. CIBSE (input by Natural Ventilation Group) 1996.

Building Regulations, Document F Section 1: Domestic Buildings, shows that habitable rooms should have ventilation openings equal to not less than 1/20 of floor area of room, some part of such area must be not less than 1.75 metres above floor level, with background ventilation of 8000 mm². Kitchens and utility rooms or bathrooms should have an opening window, but the size is not specified, with background ventilation of 4000 mm². Sanitary accommodation should have 1/20 the floor area or mechanical extract at 6 litres/sec and 4000 mm² of background ventilation. See Table 1 of Document F for ventilation requirements and diagram 1 which gives details showing ventilation through windows.

8 Wind-driven rain and snow

Rain and snow can be driven in any direction depending on the wind, horizontally and even upwards on high buildings. Details should be designed so that water cannot lie on windows and cills. Check exposure grading and state standard required before specifying tests to BS 4315.

BS 6399 Part 2: 1997, Code of practice for wind loads

BS 4315 Methods of test for resistance to air and water penetration. Part 2: 1970, Permeable walling constructions (water penetration)

BRE Digest 127, Index of exposure to driving rain

BRE DAS 98 Windows: resisting rain penetration at perimeter joints (design)

BRE 377 1992: Selecting windows by performance

BRE 350 1990: Climate and site development. Part 1: General climate of the UK

BS 8104:1992, Code of practice for assessing exposure of walls to wind driven rain

9 Privacy from overlooking

Good views out imply good views in, especially at night. Twenty metres is an approximate distance at which facial features and expressions can be recognized. Thoughtful location of windows as well as various screening devices at or adjacent to the window can minimize overlooking problems. Consider obscured glass, blinds, louvres and curtains at window and/or screens, projections (blinkers), planting boxes, etc., adjacent to windows.

10 Cleaning

Consider the practicalities of cleaning from inside only by use of extending hinges (allowing a minimum arm clearance of 150 mm), reversible windows, partially or completely inward opening portions. Check that catches and ironmongery provide safety during reversing, opening and cleaning operations. If cleaning is required from outside, consider permanent access methods, safety and working conditions of operatives, and cater for the smallest person who might be cleaning windows with limited arm length. Although there is a vogue for cleaning high-level atriums and difficult areas by using mountaineers, these active techniques increase risk to people carrying out the cleaning, however skilled, and also risks to people who might have cleaning tools or equipment fall on them from above.

BS 8213 Windows, doors and roof lights. Part 1: 1991, Code of practice for safety in use and during cleaning of windows and doors

11 Security

Prevention of burglars and vandals – consider locking devices, catches, grilles, bars and roller blinds that are also child-proof. Police crime prevention officers will visit a property and give free advice. Insurance companies also have a great deal of expertize and often impose their own conditions with regard to security. Normally most buildings are expected to have lockable windows at least up to first floor level. A client will not thank you if substantial ironmongery accessories have to be installed after completion before a building can be insured.

BS 8220 Guide for security of buildings against crime. Part 1: 1986, Dwellings

BRE DAS 88: 1986, Windows: discouraging illegal entry

BRE IP/94: The role of windows in domestic burglary

12 Insects

Check the size of mesh required before specifying internal or external insect screens. Also check accessibility of ventilating or opening portions.

13 Views out and eye level

Consider the quality of the surroundings outside the window and the degree of view needed or thought appropriate. Views can be limited or obscured by the choice of glass (quality, texture and colour), blinds, curtains, louvres, horizontal and vertical subdividing members, cill and head height. Various parts of a window can be designed to suit different criteria, e.g. the small clear viewing panel in the centre of the obscured glass panel in the lavatory of a railway carriage, or large opening that is subdivided to give areas of clear and obscured glass to control light transmission. Consider eye level:

Eye level	Dimension
average male adult standing	1600 mm
average male adult sitting	1200 mm
average female adult standing	1510 mm
average female adult sitting	1110 mm
average child standing 3 yr old	500 mm
average child standing 6 yr old	750 mm
average child standing 9 yr old	1000 mm
average bedridden person domestic	700–1000 mm
average bedridden person hospitalized	900–1400 mm

BS 952 Glass for glazing. Part 1: 1995, Classification, Part 2: 1980 Terminology for work on glass

14 Thermal insulation and heat loss

Consider this in conjunction with items 2 and 3 as it will decide the glass area and economics of various forms of double glazing. Some forms of solar control will also help to minimize heat loss at the same time as minimizing heat gain. Check cleaning and maintenance methods.

See Document L of the Building Regulations (1995 edition) for the basis of calculating the energy rating of dwellings and the U-value requirements for elements. Windows, doors and rooflights will comply if they have a U-value of 3.3 W/m² for a SAP energy rating over 60, or a U-value of 3.0 W/m² for a SAP energy rating of 60 or below. A U-value of 3.3 W/m² will be met by a double glazed window in wood with a 6 mm air gap, and a U-value of 3.0 W/m² will be met by a double glazed timber window with a 12 mm air gap or 6 mm air gap but with low E glass. See Table 2 of Document L for indicative U-values for windows, doors and rooflights and how they can be achieved.

BS 8211 Energy efficiency in housing. Part 1: 1988 (1995), Code of practice for energy efficient refurbishment of housing

15 Safety

Decide upon the cill height, opening section and height of catches and stays, cleaning operations and childproof locking devices. Consider a form of safety glass or wire mesh for internally or externally vulnerable areas of glazing (where at risk from chairs, children's toys, cycles, etc.).

BS 8213 Windows, doors and roof lights. Part 1: 1991, Code of practice for safety in use and during cleaning of windows and doors
BS 952 Glass for glazing. Part 1: 1995, Classification, Part 2: 1980, Terminology for work on glass

16 Fire

Check building and room category for requirements of statutory authorities. Openings in fire-resistant doors will have to offer the same degree of protection.

BS 476 Part 22: 1987, Methods for determination of the fire resistance of non-loadbearing elements of construction
PD 6512-3 Part 3: 1987, Guide to the fire performance of glass
See Building Regulations, Document B: Section 13 for the calculation of permitted limits of unprotected areas and generally for guidance.

17 Statutory window area

For certain windows, area, ventilation area and ventilation height are laid down in Building Regulations (see items 2, 7 and 14).

Trade and research organizations

Fire Research Station (BRE), Bucknalls Lane, Garston, Watford, Herts WD2 7JR (tel. 01923 894090).
Glass and Glazing Federation, 44–48 Borough High Street, London SE1 1XB (tel. 0171-403 7177, fax 0171-357 7458).

Windows in Detail Section 17

SMM7 L: Windows

(See Section 16, Windows: General)

Notes and references

Items are cross-referenced from the diagrams and divided into sections with a general comment followed by technical references and the Building Regulations in context. Addresses of relevant trade and research organizations are given at the end of the section. British Standards and BRE Digests should be checked for current amendments

18 Rain and dirt

BS 4315 Methods of test for resistance to air and water penetration

The Changing Appearance of Buildings, R. B. White. HMSO, 1967.

19 Absorbent wall can be saturated

Brickwork can be saturated for certain periods of the year. Water can then run down the internal face of the external leaves of cavity walls. Non-absorbent walls place a greater rainwater load on all joints. See detail 1.

20 Path of damp and heat loss if no barrier

Provide a suitable dpc at window head. Cavity dpcs in this position should run at least 115 mm past the jamb. Consider an internal insulation lining to prevent condensation. See detail 1.

BS 743:1970 (1991), Specification for materials for damp-proof courses
BS 5390:1976 (1990), Code of practice for stone masonry
BS 5628 Code of practice for use of masonry. Part 1: Structural use of unreinforced masonry. Part 3: 1985, Materials and components, design and workmanship
BS 3837 Expanded polystyrene boards. Part 2: 1990, Specification for extruded boards
BS 6093:1993, Code of practice for design of joints and jointing in building construction

21 Moisture in cavities

Cavities in all forms of construction should be drained. In brick cavity walls, provide weep-holes at 900 mm centres. On exposed sites, high buildings might require special plastic drainage tubes to prevent rain penetration. See detail 1.

22 Water can run back on soffit

Provide a check or drip to limit the amount of rainwater blown onto pointing material. See detail 1.

BS 5628 Code of practice for use of masonry, Part 1: Structural use of unreinforced masonry. Part 3: 1985, Materials and components, design and workmanship

23 Water must not get behind frame

Use of mastics and sealants is now common practice in this location, but they must be correctly specified and applied as they vary considerably in their properties of adhesion, elasticity and durability (mastics are not elastic whereas sealants are). Consider size of gap to be filled and nature of materials and likely regularity of surrounding surfaces to be joined. Specify correct gap-filling materials to be placed behind mastic. Make sure site operatives follow manufacturer's requirements. Consider rebate in wood frames to allow correct sealant dimension. See detail 1.

'A Guide to the Use of Sealants and Mastics', R. G. Groeger, *Architects' Journal*, **5**, June 1968.
Light Cladding of Buildings, Chapter 15, Jointing and sealing.
Mitchell's Building Series: Materials, Y. Dean, Chapter 10 Polymers for plastic materials, gaskets, sealants generally and *Mitchell's Building Series: Finishes*, Y. Dean, Chapter 2 for principles of adhesion. Longman, 1996.

24 Set-back

Windows (finishes and sealants) that are recessed or protected by overhangs receive considerably less wear

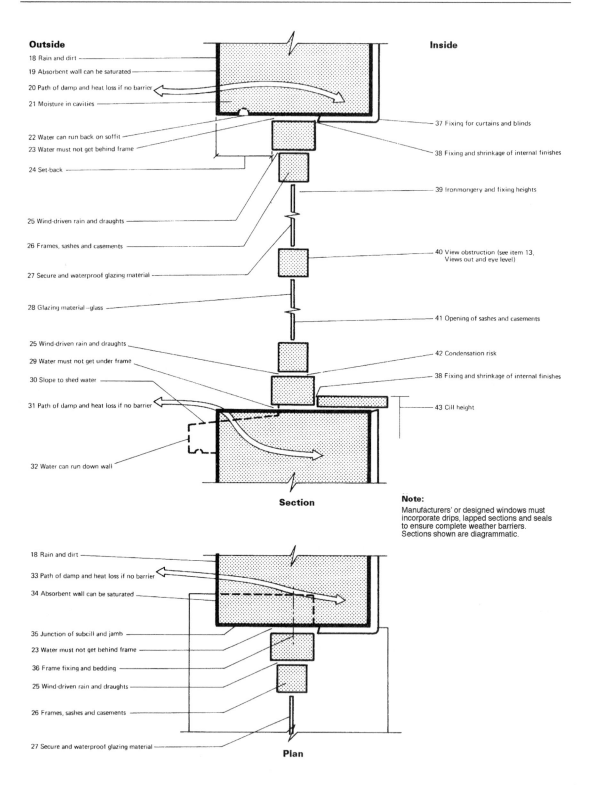

Outside

18 Rain and dirt

19 Absorbent wall can be saturated

20 Path of damp and heat loss if no barrier

21 Moisture in cavities

22 Water can run back on soffit

23 Water must not get behind frame

24 Set-back

25 Wind-driven rain and draughts

26 Frames, sashes and casements

27 Secure and waterproof glazing material

28 Glazing material—glass

25 Wind-driven rain and draughts

29 Water must not get under frame

30 Slope to shed water

31 Path of damp and heat loss if no barrier

32 Water can run down wall

Inside

37 Fixing for curtains and blinds

38 Fixing and shrinkage of internal finishes

39 Ironmongery and fixing heights

40 View obstruction (see item 13, Views out and eye level)

41 Opening of sashes and casements

42 Condensation risk

38 Fixing and shrinkage of internal finishes

43 Cill height

Section

Note:
Manufacturers' or designed windows must incorporate drips, lapped sections and seals to ensure complete weather barriers. Sections shown are diagrammatic.

18 Rain and dirt

33 Path of damp and heat loss if no barrier

34 Absorbent wall can be saturated

35 Junction of subcill and jamb

23 Water must not get behind frame

36 Frame fixing and bedding

25 Wind-driven rain and draughts

26 Frames, sashes and casements

27 Secure and waterproof glazing material

Plan

than windows placed flush with the external wall surface. Setting back windows often implies a larger cill or subcill to shed rainwater clear of the wall. In cavity brick walls, window frames are best located to cover vertical dpcs at jambs.

See Architects Working Details published by the *Architects Journal* 1993
External walls, Watersports Centre (Kit Allsopp Architects) and Meeting Hall Edward Cullinan Architects pp 61–67

25 Wind-driven rain and draughts

See **Windows generally, Section 16**, item 8, for general comments and references. Timber window frames are normally rebated (single, double or treble) while metal frames are shaped to provide weatherproof and draught-proof sections. Weather-stripping can be incorporated in all forms of windows. See standard EJMA double rebated sections. Also note checks or drips on timber sashes and frames.

Architects' Standard Catalogue, see Windows pp. 76–78, 1997 edition.

26 Frames, sashes and casements

The criteria for choosing window frame materials are complex variables and considered outside the scope of this checklist. Sizes of frame and casement members should be checked for strength and stiffness against wind load and span, especially where hollow aluminium or plastics frames are used. See detail 1.

Wood windows:

BS 644 Wood windows. Part 1: 1989, Specification for factory assembled windows of various types
BS 7359:1991, Nomenclature of commercial timbers, including sources of supply
BS 1186 Timber for and workmanship in joinery. Part 1: 1991, Specification of timber, Part 2: 1988, Specification for workmanship
BS 1282:1975, Guide to the choice, use and application of wood preservatives
BS 1336:1971 (1996), Knotting
BS 4756:1971 (1991), Aluminium wood primers
BS 5358:1993, Specification for solvent-borne wood priming paints for woodwork
BS 5082:1993, Specification for water-borne priming paints for woodwork

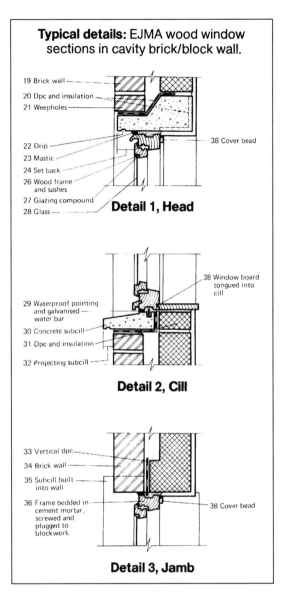

Typical details: EJMA wood window sections in cavity brick/block wall.

19 Brick wall
20 Dpc and insulation
21 Weepholes
22 Drip
23 Mastic
24 Set-back
26 Wood frame and sashes
27 Glazing compound
28 Glass
38 Cover bead

Detail 1, Head

29 Waterproof pointing and galvanised water bar
30 Concrete subcill
31 Dpc and insulation
32 Projecting subcill
38 Window board tongued into cill

Detail 2, Cill

33 Vertical dpc
34 Brick wall
35 Subcill built into wall
36 Frame bedded in cement mortar, screwed and plugged to blockwork
38 Cover bead

Detail 3, Jamb

BS 7543:1992, Guide to the durability of buildings and building elements, products and components
BRE IP 5/91: Exterior wood stains
BRE BR 229: Wood preservatives in Europe: development of standards for preservatives and treated wood
BRE 304 1985: Preventing decay in external joinery

BRE IP 16/87: Maintaining paintwork on exterior timber

BRE 321 1987: Timber for joinery

Steel windows:

BS 6510:1984, Specification for steel windows, sills, window boards and doors

BS 1706:1960 (1996), Method for specifying electro-plated coatings of zinc and cadmium on iron and steel

BS 7079 Preparation of steel substrates before application of paints and related products. Part O: 1990, Introduction

Aluminium windows:

BS 4873:1986, Specification for aluminium windows

BS 1615:1987 (1994), Method for specifying anodic oxidation coatings on aluminium and its alloys

BS 3987:1991, Specification for anodic oxidation coatings on wrought aluminium for external architectural applications

BS 6496:1984 (1991), Specifiation for powder coatings to aluminium

Plastics windows:

Mitchell's Building Series: Finishes, Y. Dean, Chapters 2 and 3 for the theory and the application of coatings. Longman, 1996.

27 Secure and waterproof glazing material

Wood sashes are best 'rebated out of the solid' to receive glazing material. Single glazing is held in place by glaziers' sprigs at approximately 450 mm centres. In metal frames, spring clips or metal pegs are used. Externally planted wood beads have a tendency to move and can cause leaks. CP 152 gives details of various glazing systems. See detail 1.

BS 6262:1982 (1994), Code of practice for glazing for buildings

28 Glazing materials – glass

For single glazing, check glass area against thickness specified (document N, Section 1 of the Building Regulations gives guidelines). Consider glass type – solar control, anti-glare, obscured, etc. (see **Windows generally, Section 16**, items 2, 3, 4, 5, 9, 13, 15 and 16), sound reduction (see **Windows generally, Section 16**,

item 6) and thermal insulation (see **Windows generally, Section 16**, item 14).

BS 952, Glass for glazing. Part 1: 1995, Classification. Part 2: 1980, Terminology for work on glass

BS 6262:1982 (1994), Code of practice for glazing for buildings

Mitchell's Building Series: Components, Section 5.

Glass in Building, D. Button and B. Pye. Architectural Press, 1994 (both authors are Pilkington Glass consultants).

29 Water must not get under frame

Mastics and sealants as for item 23, but cills and frames should be bedded on cement mortar. A good detail will also incorporate a rustproof metal water bar (25 mm × 6 mm bedded in mastic) between a timber cill and subcill. See detail 2.

30 Slope to shed water

Rainwater or melting snow must not be allowed to 'puddle' against pointing and timber frame. The slope should be sufficient to drain off water and, where subcills are used, start behind the front line of the timber cill (which in turn should have a check or drip on its underside). See detail 2.

BS 5642 Cills and Copings. Part 1: 1978, Specification for window cills of precast concrete, cast stone, clay ware, slate and natural stone

31 Path of damp and heat loss if no barrier

Provide a suitable dpc under or around permeable cills (or under impervious cills if jointed). Comments as for item 20. A rigid dpc (slate) is sometimes used to both close a cavity brick wall and support a subcill. See detail 2.

BS 5628 Code of practice for use of masonry. Part 1: Structural use of unreinforced masonry

BS 743:1970 (1991), Specification for materials for damp-proof courses

32 Water can run down wall

Staining around window openings can destroy much of a designer's work. Unless considerable thought and extra careful detailing has been undertaken, it is advisable to project cills or subcills to throw rain and melting snow clear of wall surfaces. See detail 2.

33 Path of damp and heat loss if no barrier

Provide a suitable dpc at jamb. Comments as for items 20 and 31. Dpcs around openings must all be in a similar plane in order that the vertical and horizontal dpcs can be properly overlapped so as to direct water from inside to outside. See detail 3.

References as for item 31.

34 Absorbent wall can be saturated

Comment as for item 19. Jambs (especially the lower portions next to cills and thresholds) are sometimes subjected to more severe wind and rain conditions than many other parts of a building. Unless vertical dpcs are correctly detailed and installed, dampness can penetrate to internal finishes. Concrete jambs without dpcs can sometimes allow the penetration of dampness. See detail 3.

35 Junction of subcill and jamb

This is a vulnerable area as it often receives a considerable rain and wind load. Subcills (other than softwood) should be built into jambs and pointed. See detail 3.

36 Frame fixing and bedding

Frames are usually bedded in cement mortar and fixed to brick walls with rustproof metal (galvanized mild steel) fishtailed cramps (or lugs), screwed to the backs of frames and built into place, or by fixing direct to plastic or wood plugs in surrounding structure or framework. Timber cills are not normally fixed down nor are timber head members fixed to soffits unless deflection or movement of head members is possible due to long spans between jambs or mullions. See detail 3.

BS 729:1971 (1994), Specification for hot dip galvanised coatings on iron and steel articles
BS 6093:1993, Code of practice for design of joints and jointing in building construction

37 Fixing for curtains and blinds

Consider how occupiers will fix curtains, thermal screens, or blinds, and method of locating fixing blocks if hidden by internal finishes.

38 Fixing and shrinkage of internal finishes

Allow for fixing internal finishes around window opening. Wet finishes (plaster) will shrink away from window frames, cills, boards, etc. Frames will also shrink and expand. Provide a cover mould or groove or overlap frames to cover shrinkage cracks. See details 1, 2 and 3.

39 Ironmongery and fixing heights

Many partners in practices make sure that the ironmongery is chosen by them and fully approved by the client, who often sees a complete door 'mocked up' with the ironmongery. It is one of the few areas in the building where people have immediate contact with materials and their quality. The choice is analogous to car manufacturers spending time on making sure the car door handles and 'click' feel positive and solid as a direct reflection of car quality.

Consider type of occupants and check on accessibility, fixing heights, safety (see **Windows generally, Section 16**, item 15) and security (see **Windows generally, Section 16**, item 11).

BS 7352:1990, Specification for strength and durability of hinges
BS 6100 Part 1: 1991, Section 1.3 subsection 1.3.6, Glossary of terms relating to builders' hardware

40 View obstruction

Check height and depth of horizontal rails and transom against various critical eye levels (see **Windows generally, Section 16**, item 13).

41 Opening of sashes and casements

Consider advantages and disadvantages of various opening methods. Check against requirements of cleaning, getting in the way of curtains and blinds, night as well as day ventilation, draught-proofing, security, maintenance etc. For noise control see **Windows generally, Section 16**, item 6.

BRE Digest 338: 1988, Insulation against external noise

BRE Digest 406: Wind actions on buildings and structures

Mitchell's Building Series: Components provides a comprehensive range of possible openings

BS 8213 Windows, doors and rooflights. Part 1: 1991, Code of practice for safety in use and during cleaning

42 Condensation risk

If there is a possibility of severe condensation (e.g. by tenant's non-use of heating or ventilation facilities) consider use of condensation grooves or channels properly drained to the outside. Patent aluminium condensation channels are available.

BRE 304 1985: Preventing decay in external joinery

BRE IP 12/94: Assessing condensation risk and heat loss at thermal bridges around openings

BRE BR 162: Background ventilation of dwellings: a review

BS 5250:1989 (1995), Code of basic data for control of condensation in buildings

43 Cill height

Consider eye level (see **Windows generally, Section 16**, item 13 and for safety, item 15), work top height (900 mm) or fittings and cupboards under cills. Also consider height of window from ground level (for safety, to avoid vertigo, etc.).

Trade and research organizations

Aluminium Window Association, 26 Store Street, London WC1E 7EL (tel. 0171-636 3578).

British Glass Manufacturers' Confederation, Northumberland Road, Sheffield S10 2UA (tel. 0114-268 6201, fax 0114-268 1073).

British Wood Preserving and Damp-proofing Association, 6 Office Village, 4 Romford Road, Stratford, London E15 4EA (tel. 0181-519 2588, fax 0181-519 3444).

British Woodworking Federation, 82 New Cavendish Street, London W1M 8AD (tel. 0171-580 5588, fax 0171-436 5398).

Building Research Advisory Service, Bucknalls Lane, Garston, Watford, Herts WD2 7JR (tel. 01923-894040, fax 01923-664010).

Glass and Glazing Federation, 44–48 Borough High Street, London SE1 1XB (tel. 0171-403 7177, fax 0171-357 7458).

Guild of Architectural Ironmongers, 8 Stepney Green, London E1 3JU (tel. 0171-790 3431, fax 0171-790 8517).

Paint Research Association, 8 Waldegrave Road, Teddington, Middx TW11 8LD (tel. 0181-977 4427, fax 0181-943 4705).

RAPRA Technology Ltd (Rubber and Plastics Research Association of Great Britain), Shawbury, Shrewsbury, Shropshire SY4 4NR (tel. 01939-250383, fax 01939-251118).

Steel Window Association, The Building Centre, 26 Store Street, London WC1E 7BT (tel. 0171-637 3571).

TRADA Technology Ltd (Timber Research and Development Association), Stocking Lane, Hughenden Valley, High Wycombe, Bucks HP14 4ND (tel. 01494-563091, fax 01494-565487).

External Domestic Doors Section 18

SMM7 L: Doors

Trapdoor spider
Pieces of bark or leaves conceal entrances to a protected tunnel.

Church door, Wiltshire (Dean)

Door, window Tuscany Italy (Rich)

Notes and references

Items are cross-referenced from the diagrams and divided into sections with a general comment followed by technical references and the Building Regulations in context. Addresses of relevant trade and research organizations are given at the end of the section. British Standards and BRE Digests should be checked for current amendments

Most domestic doors are factory-made and manufacturers' catalogues should be referred to for full details. To design doors requires a wealth of knowledge which should be comparable to that of a joiner. As most doors are often composite materials it is normal to specify the door panel to be supplied which is usually delivered with door frames as a 'door set'.

Architectural Woodwork, Stephen Major. Spon.
The Agrément Board, MOAT No 7, Internal and External Door sets; MOAT No 11 UEAtc Directive for the assessment of doors, 1969
Timber in Joinery. Introduction to BS 1186, TRADA, rev. 1992 (WIS 4)
Mitchell's Building Series: Components, A. Blanc. Longman, 1994.

1 Function

As these doors are the main openings to domestic buildings, consider the likely users, which may be children, people with a disability, elderly people, tradesmen or workmen, and the kinds of objects or equipment that need easy access including wheelchairs, prams, furniture, household white goods, replacement tanks and equipment.

2 Weather barrier – rain, wind, snow, air and dirt

Unlike windows, definitive standards do not yet exist for rain and wind penetration. BRE suggest that the BSI draft DD4 1971 (relating to windows) should be adapted for use with external doors. Tests can be specified to BS 4315 Part 1 but as this standard only describes test methods, performance criteria must also be specified. BSI DD4 gives a method of assessing a building's exposure and, depending on severity, recommends one of three grades of airtightness. Similarly three performance levels of air pressures are given before rain will penetrate windows. BRE suggest that the performance levels for doors could be 5, 10 and 15 mm water gauge for low, medium and high building exposure.

Key Factors	Action	Counteraction
Wind	Motive force, destructive, penetrative	Rigidity, resilience, sealing
Rain and snow	Moisture deposition	Deflection, impervious skin, absorption and drainage, sealing
Sun	Temperature variation, movement, heat gain, chemical decomposition	Movement joints, insulation, shielding, invulnerable materials
Dirt and dust	Infiltration, deposition, surface pollution	Repulsion, exclusion, shielding, cleaning
Chemicals	Corrosion, disintegration, decomposition	Invulnerable materials, exclusion
Sound	Noise nuisance	Insulation

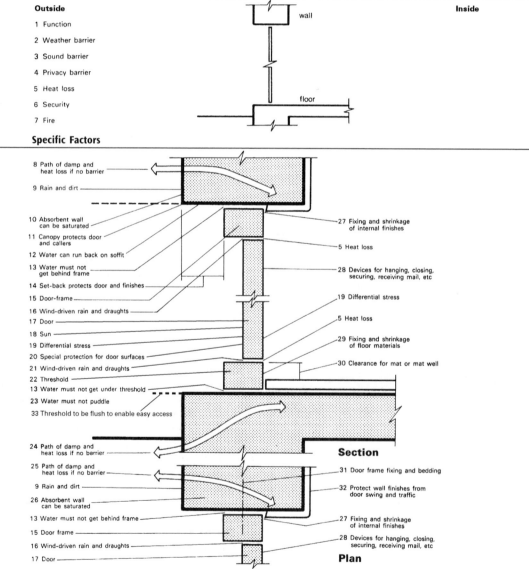

General Factors

Outside

1 Function

2 Weather barrier

3 Sound barrier

4 Privacy barrier

5 Heat loss

6 Security

7 Fire

wall

floor

Inside

Specific Factors

8 Path of damp and heat loss if no barrier

9 Rain and dirt

10 Absorbent wall can be saturated

11 Canopy protects door and callers

12 Water can run back on soffit

13 Water must not get behind frame

14 Set-back protects door and finishes

15 Door-frame

16 Wind-driven rain and draughts

17 Door

18 Sun

19 Differential stress

20 Special protection for door surfaces

21 Wind-driven rain and draughts

22 Threshold

13 Water must not get under threshold

23 Water must not puddle

33 Threshold to be flush to enable easy access

24 Path of damp and heat loss if no barrier

27 Fixing and shrinkage of internal finishes

5 Heat loss

28 Devices for hanging, closing, securing, receiving mail, etc

19 Differential stress

5 Heat loss

29 Fixing and shrinkage of floor materials

30 Clearance for mat or mat well

Section

25 Path of damp and heat loss if no barrier

9 Rain and dirt

26 Absorbent wall can be saturated

13 Water must not get behind frame

15 Door frame

16 Wind-driven rain and draughts

17 Door

31 Door frame fixing and bedding

32 Protect wall finishes from door swing and traffic

27 Fixing and shrinkage of internal finishes

28 Devices for hanging, closing, securing, receiving mail, etc

Plan

BS 4315 Methods of test for resistance to air and water penetration. Part 2: 1983, Permeable walling constructions (water penetration)

BS 4787 Internal and external wood doorsets, doorleaves and frames. Part 1: 1980 (1995), Specification for dimensional requirements

BS 6100 Parts 1, 3 and 5 for glossary

BRE Digest 406, Wind actions on buildings and structures

BS 6399 Part 2: 1997, Code of practice for wind loads

3 Sound barrier

Consider external noise sources and decide if special precautions are necessary. A standard wood flush door and frame of medium weight will give an approximate insulation value of 20 to 21 dB, depending on how well the door fits into the frame. Heavier fire doors to BS 459 Part 3 are sometimes specified in order to give slightly higher insulation values (around 26 dB) but care must be taken to have only minimum gaps between door and frame and properly sealed construction between frame and surrounding wall. An extra three or four dB can be obtained by fitting seals at all edges (including threshold) of door. Double wood doors of medium weight could be expected to provide an insulation value of about 35 to 40 dB.

BRE Digest 338: 1988, Insulation against external noise

4 Privacy barrier

Locate door and arrange door swing to minimize loss of privacy by direct views from passers-by or callers.

5 Heat loss

Provided air and wind infiltration have been allowed for, heat loss is not normally considered a problem – especially as doors usually provide a better thermal insulation than windows.

6 Security

This is an important aspect of external door design and advice on choice of locks is available from police security officers. Check the location and fastening of adjacent opening windows, sidelights and fanlights to ensure that they will not allow access to door lock(s). At least two locks are thought to be the minimum for

security with one as a five-lever deadlock. Most insurers will now set standards that householders have to attain before any policy is valid. It is important that adequate security is installed at the outset. Also check that locks cannot be reached from letter flaps. Consider use of 'inspection eye' or panel to view callers. Some forms of 'overnight bolt' allow the door to be partially opened to view callers. The police have crime prevention officers in every area who will give free advice on security aspects generally.

BS 3621:1980, Specification for thief resistant locks

BS 2911:1974 (1980), Specification for letter plates

7 Fire

Check building category for requirements of the Building Regulations and statutory authorities. Doors between dwellings and internal communal areas will require a stipulated fire resistance; glazed areas in and around doors will also be controlled. Check local fire officer's requirements for self-closing devices, means of escape and smoke control.

BS 476 Fire tests on building materials and structures. Part 22: 1987, Methods for determination of the fire resistance of loadbearing elements of construction (includes doors and doorsets)

BS 459:1988 (1995), Specification for matchboarded wooden door leaves for external use

Technology of fire resisting door sets, TRADA, rev. 1991 (WIS 1–13)

Timber building elements of proven fire resistance, TRADA, 1991 (WIS 1–11/ 5–12)

BRE Digest 320: 1988, Fire doors

Building Regulations 1991, Document B, see Fire Resistance of doors section 5.6 and Appendix B Table B1, section 10.4 with regard to fire doors which also refers back to Appendix B

8 Path of damp and heat loss if no barrier

Provide a suitable dpc at door head. Cavity dpcs in this position should run at least 115 mm past the jamb. Consider an internal insulation lining to prevent a cold bridge.

BS 743:1970 (1991), Specification for materials for damp-proof courses

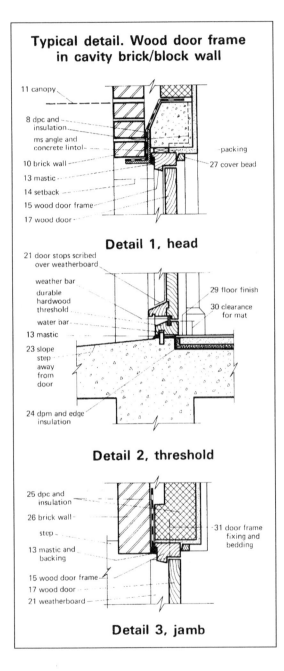

Typical detail. Wood door frame in cavity brick/block wall

11 canopy

8 dpc and insulation

ms angle and concrete lintol

10 brick wall

13 mastic

14 setback

15 wood door frame

17 wood door

packing

27 cover bead

Detail 1, head

21 door stops scribed over weatherboard

weather bar

durable hardwood threshold

water bar

13 mastic

23 slope step away from door

24 dpm and edge insulation

29 floor finish

30 clearance for mat

Detail 2, threshold

25 dpc and insulation

26 brick wall

step

13 mastic and backing

15 wood door frame

17 wood door

21 weatherboard

31 door frame fixing and bedding

Detail 3, jamb

BS 5390: 1976 (1990), Code of practice for stone masonry

BS 5628 Code of practice for use of masonry. Part 1: Structural use of unreinforced masonry. Part 3: 1985, Materials and components, design and workmanship

BS 3837 Expanded polystyrene boards. Part 2: 1990, Specification for extruded boards

9 Rain and dirt

BRE Digest 127, Index of exposure to driving rain

The Changing Appearance of Buildings, R. B. White. HMSO, 1967.

10 Absorbent wall can be saturated

Brickwork can be saturated for certain periods of the year. Water can then run down the internal face of external leaves of cavity walls. Non-absorbent walls place a greater rainwater load on all joints.

11 Canopy/porch

Consider using some external construction to protect callers and doors. On exposed elevations or where wind eddies can be expected any protection will help in preventing rain penetration between door and frame.

12 Water can run back on soffit

Provide a check or drip to limit the amount of rainwater blown onto waterproof pointing material.

BS 5628 Code of practice for use of masonry. Part 1: Structural use of unreinforced masonry. Part 3: 1985, Materials and components, design and workmanship

13 Water must not get behind frame

Mastics and sealants (mastics are not elastic whereas sealants are) are now common in this location but they vary considerably in their qualities of adhesion, elasticity and durability and must be chosen and applied with care. Consider size of gap to be filled, nature of materials to be joined and actual regularity or irregularity of surrounding surfaces. Make sure site operatives follow manufacturer's instructions especially regarding the surface quality of the materials to be joined. For maximum adhesion surfaces must be uncontaminated and correctly primed if specified. Otherwise sealants will be adhering to intermediate layers of dust or particles and be ineffective. Consider rebate in wood frames to allow correct sealant dimension. Specify correct backing or separating material.

'A guide to the use of sealants and mastics', R. G. Groeger. *Architects' Journal*, **5** June 1968.

Light cladding of buildings, Chapter 15, jointing and sealing.

Mitchell's Building Series: Materials, Y. Dean, Chapter 10 Polymers for plastic materials, gaskets, sealants generally and *Mitchell's Building Series: Finishes*, Y. Dean, Chapter 2 for principles of adhesion. Longman, 1996.

14 Set-back protects door and finishes

Doors (including finishes and sealants) which are set back in walls or protected by other overhangs are less exposed to the weather than doors placed flush with the external wall finish. In cavity brick walls, door frames are best located in relation to vertical dpcs at jamb (see detail 3).

15 Door frame

Door frames can be of durable wood or non-durable wood treated with preservative. Unprotected softwood should not be used. Planted door stops are now common but good quality frames are rebated out of the solid. Planted stops should be screwed to the frame at 600 mm centres commencing 75 mm from each end. Frames should be factory-primed before delivery to site. Steel and pvc door frames are also available.

Timber:

BS 7359:1991, Nomenclature of commercial timbers, including sources of supply

BS 1186 Timber for and workmanship in joinery. Part 1: 1991, Specification of timber. Part 2: 1988, Specification for workmanship

BS 4787 Internal and external wood doorsets, doorleaves and frames. Part 1: 1980 (1995), Specification for dimensional requirements

BS 1282:1975, Guide to the choice, use and application of wood preservatives

BS 1336:1971 (1996), Knotting

BS 4756:1971 (1991), Aluminium wood primers

BS 5358:1993, Specification for solvent-borne wood priming paints for woodwork

BS 5082:1993, Specification for water-borne priming paints for woodwork

BS 7543:1992, Guide to the durability of buildings and building elements, products and components

BRE IP 5/91: Exterior wood stains

BRE BR 229: Wood preservatives in Europe: development of standards for preservatives and treated wood

BRE 304 1985: Preventing decay in external joinery

BRE IP 16/87: Maintaining paintwork on exterior timber

BRE 321 1987: Timber for joinery

BS 1186 Part 3: 1990, Specification for wood trim and its fixing

Architect's Standard Catalogue, Volume 1, see technical section on doors pp. 81–83

Steel:

BS 1706:1960 (1996), Method for specifying electroplated coatings of zinc and cadmium on iron and steel

BS 7079 Preparation of steel substrates before application of paints and related products. Part 0: 1990, Introduction

BS 729:1971 (1994), Specification for hot dip galvanised coatings on iron and steel articles

Aluminium:

BS 1615:1987 (1994), Method for specifying anodic oxidation coatings on aluminium and its alloys

BS 3987:1991, Specification for anodic oxidation coatings on wrought aluminium for external architectural applications

BS 6496:1984 (1991), Specifiation for powder coatings to aluminium

Mitchell's Building Series: Finishes, Y. Dean, Chapters 2 and 3 for the theory and the application of coatings. Longman, 1996.

Joints:

BS 6093:1993, Code of practice for design of joints and jointing in building construction

Mitchell's Building Series: Components provides a comprehensive range of possible openings.

16 Wind-driven rain and draughts

See item 2 for general comments and references. Door frames are rebated, shaped or have planted beads in order to cut down air and water penetration. Weather-stripping can be incorporated on all forms of doors but care must be taken in both choosing and fixing weather-stripping. External doors liable to distortion due to differential stresses (see item 19) should not be fitted with complex weather-strips which for their continued effectiveness require repeated adjustments.

BS 7386:1990, Specification for draughtstrips for the draught control of existing doors and windows in housing (including test methods)

17 Door

Because doors – especially external doors – are subjected to continuous hard wear it is often a false economy to use the cheapest available. The moisture content of wood doors is an important factor in their performance so factory-priming and undercoating is recommended. Good site supervision in off-loading and storage is also essential. See section 15 for references on preparation for finishes and preservation of all materials relating to doors.

BS 6150:1991, Code of practice for painting of buildings

Wood doors:
BS 459:1988 (1995), Specification for matchboarded wooden door leaves for external use
BS 4787 Internal and external wood doorsets, doorleaves and frames. Part 1: 1980 (1995), Specification for dimensional requirements
BS 1186 Timber for and workmanship in joinery. Part 1: 1991, Specification of timber. Part 2: 1988, Specification for workmanship

Steel doors:
BS 6510:1984, Specification for steel windows, sills, window boards and doors

Aluminium doors:
BS 5286:1978, Specification for aluminium framed sliding glass doors

Glass:
Glass in Building, D. Button and B. Pye. Architectural Press, 1994 (both authors are Pilkington Glass consultants).
BS 952 Glass for glazing. Part 1: 1995, Classification. Part 2: 1980, Terminology for work on glass
BS 6262:1982 (1994), Code of practice for glazing for buildings
Mitchell's Building Series: Components, Section 5

18 Sun

See item 19. Solar heat and radiation also affects paint, mastic and sealant systems; see technical references under items 13, 15 and 17.

19 Differential stress and distortion

External doors form a division between outside and inside climates. In wood doors the temperature gradient across the thickness of the door and the resulting change in moisture content makes one face contract or expand relative to the other. In winter the cold side will tend to contract whilst the warm side will tend to expand and produce a bow towards the outside. In summer the reverse action can take place. This movement should be borne in mind when choosing the quality of external doors and associated fittings including weather-strips, bolts and locks. Metal and especially plastic doors can also suffer from a high degree of thermal movement. Tolerances should be allowed in fitting as seasonal moving can cause misalignment of bolts and locks.

20 Special protection for door surfaces

Consider type of traffic and user and specify kick-plates, finger-plates, and whether or not to use painted surfaces which can show wear in public areas with constant use.

21 and 22 Wind-driven rain and draughts at threshold

Comments as for item 16, but special care must be taken at thresholds where air pressure can carry water under the door. On exposed sites or where the doorway is likely to be subjected to strong wind eddies the most efficient threshold will be one that incorporates a water collection trough on the inside and adequate drainage through the threshold to the outside. Proprietary water stops and thresholds should be as simple as possible. Weatherboards should be tongued into wood doors. Door stops or rebated frames must be scribed around weatherboards. See detail 2.

Thresholds must be designed to throw off rainwater and to prevent rain penetration between substructure and underside of threshold. Wood thresholds should be of a durable hardwood bedded on cement mortar. A good detail will also incorporate a rustproof metal water bar (6 mm × 25 mm) bedded in mastic between threshold and substructure. See detail 2. Where a metal bar is used as a doorstop, it should be stout enough not to be bent by ordinary traffic (brass or aluminium bars are usually 6 mm × 25 mm and protrude 12 mm).

23 Water must not puddle against pointing and threshold

Wherever possible surfaces should fall away from the door. This is not always practicable on certain forms of access decks and in this case a minimum upstand of 150 mm is advisable – especially if the waterproof membrane is asphalt. See detail 2.

24 Path of damp and heat loss if no barrier

Provide a suitable damp-proof course or membrane to stop rising damp. Consider provision of edge insulation in solid floors to prevent a cold bridge while ensuring that the construction detail will carry expected traffic.

BS 743:1970 (1991), Specification for materials for damp-proof courses

BS 3837 Expanded polystyrene boards. Part 2: Specification for extruded boards

BRE Digest 110: 1972, Condensation

BRE DAS 77: 1986, Cavity external walls: cold bridges around windows and doors

Dampness in Buildings: The Professional's and Home Owner's Guide, T. A. Oxley, E. G. Gosbert. Architectural Press

25 Path of damp and heat loss if no barrier

Dpcs around openings in cavity walls must all be in a similar plane in order that vertical and horizontal dpcs can be properly overlapped so as to direct water from inside to outside. They must also be installed as specified and not damaged by frame fixings. Concrete or solid masonry jambs should incorporate thermal insulation to avoid cold bridges. See references in previous item 24.

26 Absorbent wall can be saturated

Comments as for item 10. Jambs (especially the lower portions next to cills and thresholds) are often subjected to more severe wind and rain conditions than many other parts of a building. Unless vertical dpcs are correctly detailed and installed, damp can penetrate to internal finishes, as well as cause woodwork to decay. Concrete jambs without dpcs can sometimes allow damp penetration. See detail 3.

27 Fixing and shrinkage of internal finishes

Allow for fixing internal finishes around door opening. Wet finishes (plaster) will shrink away from door frames and may also be subjected to vibration from door slamming. Timber frames will also shrink and expand. If architraves are not used, a cover mould should be provided to hide cracks or metal plaster beads used to control the line of any cracks. See detail 1.

28 Accessories for hanging, closing, securing, receiving mail, and ironmongery generally

Consider type of occupants, likely objects being carried or wheeled through door, security (see item 6), fixing heights and accessibility of bolts and locks, etc. In terms of cost, the quality of ironmongery should be in keeping with the general cost bracket and quality of the building as a whole. Cheap fittings are a false economy. Consider choosing from a 'related range'. This has the advantage of obtaining an aesthetic relationship between all fittings plus ordering from a single source. Letterboxes can be elaborate if they need to be two-sided deep boxes for secure delivery and collection. Letterboxes should be large enough to accommodate Sunday newspaper deliveries and large packets.

Make sure that the door construction is compatible with fixing requirements and that ironmongery is fixed to special rails and blocks and not fixed at joints where screws or leverage can weaken the door.

Doorbells should be considered at design stage as they can prove awkward or unsightly if added as an afterthought.

BS 7352:1990, Specification for strength and durability of metal hinges

BS 5872:1980 (1995), Specification for locks and latches for doors in buildings

BS 2911:1974 (1980), Specification for letter plates

BS 3621:1980, Specification for thief-resistant locks for hinged doors

BS 6100 Part 1: 1991, Section 1.3 subsection 1.3.6, Glossary of terms relating to builders' hardware

29 Fixing and shrinkage of floor materials

Allow for fixing floor finishes at threshold and for shrinkage of threshold and finishes. Provide a cover mould or groove or overlap frame to cover shrinkage cracks. See detail 2.

30 Mat or mat well

Allow for door to clear doormat, or provide a mat well to suit a standard size of mat. These are made from a variety of materials from the standard coir door mat to tufted and linked grids often combining fibre materials with metal strips.

31 Door frame fixing and bedding

Door frames must be securely fixed to the surrounding structure. Most frames are now built in as the work proceeds. The head usually projects about 70–90 mm beyond the posts and these projections, the 'horns' are built into the brick or blockwork walls to make the frame secure. Frames are usually fixed to brick walls with rustproof metal (galvanized mild steel) fishtailed cramps (or lugs) at approximately 600 mm centres screwed to the backs of frame and built into the surrounding joints. Frames can also be fixed direct to plastic or wood plugs in the surrounding structure or framework. Frames should be bedded in cement mortar as the work proceeds. Fixings should be in accordance with BS 4787. Dpcs must not be damaged or misaligned during frame fixing. Alternatively, door frames can be part of a glazed or panelled unit and surrounded by combinations of fanlight and sidelight. In this case, the frames must be securely jointed together and be of sufficient strength and stiffness to resist slamming and misuse. Steel and PVC-clad door frames are available, manufacturers' fixing instructions must be followed. See item 15 for references.

BS 6093:1993, Code of practice for design of joints and jointing in building construction

32 Protect wall finishes from door swing and traffic

Consider the use of protective casing beads on all corners around doorway. Position door stops to protect walls from damage by door knobs, letter boxes, etc.

Trade and research organizations

Aluminium Window Association, 26 Store Street, London WC1E 7EL (tel. 0171-636 3578).

APA The Engineered Wood Association, 65 London Wall, London EC2M 5TU (tel. 0171-287 2625, fax 0171-638 4545).

Association of British Plywood and Veneer Manufacturers Ltd, Riverside Industrial Estate, Morson Road, Ponders End, Enfield EN3 4TS (tel. 0181-804 2424).

British Glass Manufacturers' Confederation, Northumberland Road, Sheffield S10 2UA (tel. 0114-268 6201, fax 0114-268 1073).

British Wood Preserving and Damp-proofing Association, 6 Office Village, 4 Romford Road, Stratford, London E15 4EA (tel. 0181-519 2588, fax 0181-519 3444).

British Woodworking Federation, 82 New Cavendish Street, London W1M 8AD (tel. 0171-580 5588, fax 0171-436 5398).

Building Research Advisory Service, Bucknalls Lane, Garston, Watford WD2 7JR (tel. 01923-894040, fax 01923-664010).

Finnish Plywood International, PO Box 99, Welwyn Garden City, Herts AL6 OHS (tel. 01438-798746, fax 01438-798305).

Glass and Glazing Federation, 44–48 Borough High Street, London SE1 1XB (tel. 0171-403 7177, fax 0171-357 7458).

Guild of Architectural Ironmongers, 8 Stepney Green, London E1 3JU (tel. 0171-790 3431, fax 0171-790 8517).

Loss Prevention Council, Melrose Avenue, Borehamwood, Herts WD6 2BJ (0181-207 2345, fax 0181-236 9698).

Paint Research Association, 8 Waldegrave Road, Teddington, Middx TW11 8LD (tel. 0181-977 4427, fax 0181-943 4705).

RAPRA Technology Ltd (Rubber and Plastics Research Association of Great Britain), Shawbury, Shrewsbury, Shropshire SY4 4NR (tel. 01939-250383, fax 01939-251118).

Steel Window Association, The Building Centre, 26 Store Street, London WC1E 7BT (tel. 0171-637 3571).

TRADA Technology Ltd (Timber Research and Development Association), Stocking Lane, Hughenden Valley, High Wycombe, Bucks HP14 4ND (tel. 01494 563091, fax 01494-565487).

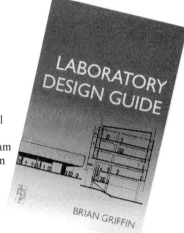

Also from
Architectural Press

Tony Hunt's Structures Notebook
Tony Hunt

This book is divided into seven main sections, in a logical sequence, and is written in easily understandable language. Each section has a comprehensive set of hand-drawn illustrations related to its text which show as simply as possible what the text is about.

0 7506 3519 3, 96 pp, 40 pp sketches, paperback, £9.99

Architecture: Design Notebook
Peter Fawcett

This is a handbook which focuses on the process of design as pragmatic and non-theoretical, where the skills required for designing at undergraduate level are clearly demonstrated.

This vital design companion will be the cornerstone of an architectural undergraduate's studies – studio design projects.

0 7506 3984 9, 112 pp, paperback, 1998, £12.99

EASY ORDERING
Fax: 01865 314091
Credit card hot line tel: 01865 314627
E-mail: bhuk.orders@repp.co.uk

Add £3.00 p&p for the UK, £6 for Europe and £10 for the rest of the world.

Please supply full delivery address and phone number with your order.

Prices are correct at time of going to press but may be subject to change, so please call before ordering to confirm current price.

Related titles from

![BUTTERWORTH HEINEMANN]

Building Construction Handbook
Third edition

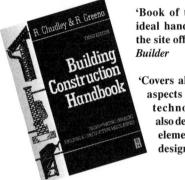

'Book of the Year ... the ideal handy reference for the site office.' *Professional Builder*

'Covers all the important aspects of construction technology ... While also detailing important elements of structural design.' *RIBA Journal*

'The student who memorizes the 'Building Construction Handbook' will be well informed indeed.' *New Civil Engineer/New Builder*

Building Construction Handbook summarizes concisely, in diagrams and brief explanations, all elements of the building process. Practice, techniques and procedures are clearly defined with supplementary references to regulations and relevant standards.

This third edition has been amended and updated to acknowledge current building and construction regulations. Where appropriate, it includes reference to the wider ranging European standards.

0 7506 3753 6, 624 pp, highly illustrated, paperback, £16.99

Estimating and Tendering for Construction Work
Second edition

Estimating and Tendering for Construction Work takes a practical approach to estimating from a contractor's point of view. It explains the estimator's function within the construction team, the techniques and procedures used in building up an estimate, and how to convert an estimate into a tender.

This new edition has been written to reflect recent changes in procurement. These include the recommendations of Sir Michael Latham in his 1994 report 'Constructing the Team', and new terminology introduction by the 6th edition of the CIOB Code of Estimating Practice 1997. The role of the estimator is covered in detail, from early cost studies through to the preparation of an estimate, and the handover of construction budgets for successful tenders.

The book includes copious examples of an estimator's data sheets and pricing notes and deals with co-ordinated project information. The chapter dealing with computer-aided estimating has been completely rewritten to reflect the advantages of electronic exchange of information.

0 7506 3404 7, 288 pp, paperback, 1998, £19.99